RIDING
THROUGH MY
LIFE

RIDING THROUGH MY LIFE

~ Her Royal Highness ~
THE PRINCESS ROYAL

WITH IVOR HERBERT

PELHAM BOOKS

PELHAM BOOKS

Published by the Penguin Group
27 Wrights Lane, London W8 5TZ, England
Viking Penguin, a division of Penguin Books USA Inc
375 Hudson Street, New York, NY 10014, USA
Penguin Books Australia Ltd, Ringwood, Victoria, Australia
Penguin Books Canada Ltd, 10 Alcorn Avenue, Suite 300, Toronto, Ontario, Canada M4V 35Z
Penguin Books (NZ) Ltd, 182–190 Wairau Road, Auckland 10, New Zealand

Penguin Books Ltd, Registered Offices: Harmondsworth, Middlesex, England

First Published 1991
1 3 5 7 9 10 8 6 4 2
Copyright © Her Royal Highness The Princess Royal, 1991

Designed by The Design Revolution, Brighton

Made and printed in Great Britain by William Clowes Ltd. Beccles, Suffolk

Typeset by Wyvern Typesetting Ltd, Bristol

A CIP catalogue record for this book is available from the British Library.

ISBN 0 7207 1961 5

CONTENTS

~

Preface and Acknowledgements

This book started with many days of recorded interviews between The Princess Royal and Ivor Herbert at Gatcombe Park, Windsor Castle and Buckingham Palace. The book was then entirely written by The Princess Royal over the period of a year while at Gatcombe and in spare moments during her travels overseas.

The Princess Royal would like to thank Apple Computers UK Limited for providing the technology which enabled her to write the book both at home and abroad, and Margaret Hammond for her general support and assistance especially in times of difficulty.

The Princess Royal, Ivor Herbert and Pelham Books would also like to thank: Lieutenant Colonel Sir John Miller, G.C.V.O., D.S.O., M.C., David and Dinah Nicholson, Major Malcolm Wallace, Director General of The British Equestrian Federation, and Mrs Carolyn Simm of The British Horse Society, for their help in providing photographs and statistics.

Pelham Books would like to thank Marian Eason for her help with picture research, and the following photographers and individuals for giving permission for the photographs listed below to be used in this book. Every effort has been made to trace the copyright owners but if there have been any omissions in this respect we apologize and will be pleased to make appropriate acknowledgement in any further editions.

The photograph on the front of the jacket of this book is from an original painting by the artist Susan Crawford and is used by gracious permission of Her Majesty The Queen. The photographs on pages 1 and 3 (top) are also from Her Majesty The Queen's collection and are used with kind permission. The photographs on pages 15, 16, 26, 45, 53, 55, 56, 57, 68, 117, 124, 136, 137, 142, 160, 165, 166, 167, 168, 170, 175, 247 are from Her Royal Highness The Princess Royal's collection. The photographs on pages 20, 21, 50, 51 are from Lieutenant Colonel Sir John Miller's collection.

The following photographs on the pages listed were taken by professional photographers, photographic agencies, and individuals as named: Srda Djukanovic: 31, 54, 61, 62, 63 (both photographs), 67, 72, 74 (all three photographs), 82, 84, 96, 99, 101, 108, 120, 178, 179, 192,

197, 198, 203, 204, 217, 229, 232; Tim Graham: back of jacket, vii; Camera Press: ii, 80, 165 (both photographs), 169, 172; Hulton-Deutsch Collection: 3 (bottom), 2, 8, 19, 42, 49, 144, 149, 152; Barry Gomer, *Daily Express*: 32; Riding for the Disabled, Bradbourne, Kent: 36, 37; Mrs R. C. Middleton: 39; Studio Lisa: 4, 6; Reed Photography: 10; Godfrey Argent: 11, 23, 29; W. S. Pearson: 17, Clive Hiles: 48, 65 (top), 68 (bottom); Montague Lewis: 52; Central Press Photos Ltd: 64; Sport and General: 66, 70; J. Findlay Davidson: 65; Peter Sweetman: 64 (top five photographs), 69 (both photographs), 76; Leslie Lane: 75 (top right), 77; Thompson Newspapers Ltd: 75 (top left); Werner Ernst: 121, 123, 125; Cappy Jackson: 126, 134, 135; Hugo M. Czerny: 140, 141; Marston Photographic: 128; Dinah Nicholson: 208; David Nicholson: 188; Kenneth Bright: 205; John Croft Photography: 215; Ed Byrne: 227; Alan Johnson: 206, 212, 225; Colin Turner: 216; Bernard Parkin: 199; Charles B. Parkin: 221; Kit Houghton: 228, 234, 240, 252; Bob Langrish: 239, 248; the photograph on page 93 is by an unknown Russian amateur photographer and was presented to Her Royal Highness by J. S. G. Simmons.

CHAPTER 1

Beginnings:

'Never the pony's fault'

ONCE upon a time there was a small girl of two-ish, who was placed on an almost equally small bundle of cream hair called Fum. What followed was a direct result of that apparently successful encounter and of being born into a family of talented equestrians (horse riders) and brought up in a lifestyle in which the horse played an integral part. My earliest memories of ponies, horses and riding are seriously confused by photographs, so that I can no longer differentiate between memories of events or photographs of the same events. Everywhere there were animals, horses, dogs, cows, sheep, pigs, and life was very country- and farm-orientated. The countryside was Berkshire, Norfolk and Aberdeenshire, a wonderful variety of farming and wildlife observed largely from the back of a pony or horse. Only later did I fully appreciate the luxury of growing up in those surroundings. Only later did I realise that all I had subconsciously learnt – and had assumed that everyone else knew – was in fact unknown to, or not appreciated by, a very large number of people. Things like where your daily pint of milk originally came from, that peas came out of a pod and not a tin, and the responsibility of looking after another living thing.

In the early fifties, when I was growing up, there were still lots of people working and living in the countryside. Information was passed down from parents to children; knowledge was absorbed rather than taught. My 'knowledge' of ponies, horses and riding was largely acquired that way, by absorption, and I know I was very fortunate. What I have learnt and am still learning through my equestrian experiences seems to relate to so many other interests that I now have. I will

On Fum at Sandringham.

With William.

With the Queen Mother and Prince Charles in Norfolk, 1956, talking to Major Bob Hoare,
Master of the West Norfolk Foxhounds.

try to explain why I feel there is more to enjoying horse riding than pure hippo-mania or the desire to be an Olympic gold medallist.

Fum (as in 'Fe, fi, fo, etc.') was no doubt a pretty unremarkable Shetland pony whom, I have to say, I don't really remember. Of the succession of quadrupeds that I have ridden since, some are infinitely more memorable than others and not always with any degree of fondness.

The pattern of my life from birth until I went to boarding school, at the age of thirteen, was living in London during the week and at Windsor at the weekends. The holidays were divided between Christmas and the New Year at Sandringham, Easter at Windsor and most of the summer holidays at Balmoral. We, my older brother and I, mostly accompanied by The Queen, rode at each of those venues and they were all different. The ponies lived at Windsor and we rode most Saturdays, but not on Sundays, because that was the grooms' day off. The Home Park and the Great Park at Windsor were wonderful places to ride: plenty of space and with logs and fallen branches to jump. In those days, hay was baled in small round bales, so the middle of June was an especially good time for the likes of me to do lots of jumping.

The best riding country was the wide open spaces of Norfolk. The miles of stubble fields around Sandringham were pure luxury by today's standards of relatively restricted hacking. There were, and still are, 'rides', which had been

On William at Balmoral.

planted or cleared for Queen Alexandra to be able to ride through the woods and all over the estate without getting her hat knocked off.

The best 'fun' riding was at Balmoral: riverside paths, woodland paths, hill paths and the golf course. It was all right if you rode on the rough, but you were definitely not popular if you got 'carted' and got run away with across the fairways.

But it was at Windsor where we did most of our riding and from where we started our modest competitive careers. The stables there, or Mews as they are known, are extensive, with stabling for a hundred or more horses and garages for a fleet of cars where there used to be carriages. There are four yards that spread down the hill towards the town, the top and middle yards separated by a purpose-built riding school. The stabling is a mixture of loose boxes and stalls, but most of the stalls now have doors on them so that they can be used as boxes as well. The lower yard must have been for the coaches and their horses and is where the Guards' Polo Club has been allowed to keep its polo ponies since I can remember. The bottom yard is smaller, but contains the biggest loose boxes, has its own tack room and backs on to the farrier's shop, where, I suspect, I spent a fair amount of time.

There was a great deal to watch and learn from our own ponies, The Queen's riding horses, Prince Philip's polo ponies, who lived in the bottom yard, and the carriage horses. The carriage horses spent most of their time in London, but they came down to Windsor every year for the Royal Windsor Horse Show and for Ascot Week. We would see the carriages

I don't remember this! But it was in 1954 and a procession was taking the royal party back from Westminster to the Palace.

every day in London from the windows of our rooms at the front of Buckingham Palace, either going out or coming back off exercise or transporting Ambassadors, who were presenting their credentials, or practising for State Visits, the State Opening of Parliament or any other special occasions. However, it was only while the carriages were at Windsor that we had the opportunity to get close to them and marvel at the harness and paintwork, and the sheer size of the horses.

The special treat for my brother and me was to be invited to join our grandmother when she drove in a carriage to watch the Trooping the Colour on Horse Guards Parade. Needless to say, I can't remember when that first happened. I can remember, one rather wet year, singing a fairly rousing chorus of 'I'm Singing in the Rain'. I also remember the dignified rush after the final Royal Salute in order to get back in the carriage, drive at a smart trot (sometimes a few canter strides were encouraged) up Whitehall and round into the Mall, before the troops, led by The Queen, also arrived in the Mall. The memory is of the wind in your face, the clip-clop of the hooves, the gentle sway of the carriage, the creak of the leather and the grey hairs from the horses that always seemed to get everywhere over your clothes and up your nose. Well, they did in my case, although I must admit that the hairs did not appear to cause my grandmother any problems.

Putting William back in the field.

Our carriage experience was limited, but I do have a vague memory of driving round the Home Park in a governess cart drawn, I think, by a fell pony. The main occupation, however, was the ponies, and after Fum there was a little blue roan named William and a slightly bigger, fat Welsh pony called Kirby Cane Greensleeves. I can't imagine why I can remember all that, but she was known as Greensleeves for short. I think I called her a few other things when she trod on my big toe in the field one day and nearly took it off. She may have been small but she was solidly built and, in that endearing way that ponies have, the more I shouted, the more I pushed and the more desperate I became, the harder she leaned on my toe. Perhaps that's why I remember her name so well – it's printed on my foot. I can also remember that it was a very long, uncomfortable walk back up the hill afterwards.

The ponies lived in a field at the bottom of the hill, quite a long way from the Mews, so often we would take the tack down in the car, tack them up in the field and take them out from there, having brushed the mud off them. These were pretty rough, scruffy little objects. They didn't have New Zealand rugs because we didn't do anything in the way of shows, so there was no need for them to be really tidy, and a lot of our riding was done straight out of the field. I don't remember any of our ponies being all that difficult to catch, but I dare say we learnt to be reasonably subtle in our approaches.

There was always information and advice available, whether it was my mother or the groom who used to come with us. We were very lucky because there was always someone to answer questions – for example, about how tight the girth should be, or about what ponies should eat. Perhaps the most important thing that was drummed into us was that whatever went wrong it was never the ponies' fault.

We were always expected to do a certain amount with the ponies before getting on and after getting off. That usually meant putting on the saddle and bridle and cleaning the same afterwards. I suppose, like the average girl, I was much keener on 'doing' them than my brother and would always spend time in the stables even if not riding. It's a sweeping generalisation, but an awful lot of girls seem to enjoy the 'looking after' as much as they do the riding, which is almost incidental. Boys, on the other hand, seem to prefer just to get on, ride, compete, enjoy themselves and get off – end of story.

To some degree that attitude is compounded by mothers and fathers who like their children to ride and so are prepared to do a certain degree of the donkey-work in order to keep the whole process going. I can quite see why in some respects, but I happen to think that if you're going to be involved with horses, you jolly well ought to learn that they're not bicycles, and if you can't be bothered to do the tacking up and preparation yourself, you shouldn't be involved with them. Because life's not like that; it's not that simple.

My brother and I were greatly helped by one of the grooms who spent the most amount of time with us, called Frank Hatcher – Frank to us. He was the person who helped us catch the ponies and made sure we brushed them, or rather got the worst of the mud off. He reminded us to pick their feet out, to ensure that there were no stones in them. He made certain that the bridle was put on correctly and the saddle was in the correct position and he used to accompany us – on foot, on a bicycle or mounted – to try to stop us doing anything too daft and to pick up the pieces. From leading rein to Pony Club, he was our source of information and friend.

All the stable staff were very tolerant of our comings and goings, especially the stud groom, Bert Wiles, whose responsibility The Queen's riding horses were. He was a great one for talking to the horse he was riding, but in a series of

Riding Greensleeves outside Windsor Castle – her official name was Kirby Cane Greensleeves.

stock phrases. For instance, when the horse stumbled, he would mildly remonstrate, saying, 'If you don't pick your feet up, I'll cut off your leg'; 'What, foot and all?'; 'Yes, foot and all' and other such phrases. I fear it was a habit that I must have picked up, although I believe there is more variety in my observations.

Our other source of information was The Queen, who certainly came with us when she could. To begin with, that would have been on foot or on a bicycle, but later, as we became more competent, we would all have gone for rides together. I really don't know how she put up with the noise and aggravation that almost always seemed to be unavoidable whenever my brother and I did anything together. The classic problem was created by the fact that William and Greensleeves did not go at the same speed. William was, as I have already mentioned, a small 12hh blue roan and Greensleeves was a chunky 13.2hh strawberry roan – the colours were irrelevant, but the size was critical. It always seemed to me that, whenever we started to canter, William would rush off and I would follow willy-nilly on Greensleeves, not quite in control. Needless to say, because Greensleeves was bigger, she invariably overtook William, which made William go faster, which encouraged Greensleeves to go faster and I invariably got to the end first.

Normally this was not a problem, because Greensleeves always stopped when she got to a road or a fence. However, there was a notorious occasion at Sandringham one year when this scenario was being repeated down a track which crossed open farmland but ended by going round some old cattle sheds that had recently been in use to winter some of the cattle. The cattle had been kept in with an electric fence and had made a real mess. Electric fences are not easy to see at the best of times and I was going quite quickly by the time Greensleeves and I reached the corner, which we failed to negotiate but got to the electric fence first. Greensleeves reacted instantly and, in hindsight, rather violently. She went quite high, but I went even higher, and when I came down Greensleeves was no longer there. What I landed in was soft, wet and very smelly. My companions roared past me, by now positively shrieking with mirth. If you asked my brother about this story, you would undoubtedly get a different version.

In complete contrast to the wide open spaces of Norfolk and our rather casual form of riding, it must have been about this time that my brother and I were sent to Miss Sybil Smith at Holyport to learn to ride. Well, I imagine that that was the intention, but I have to say that I don't remember the experience as being a particularly edifying one. Being put on a small, fat, white cob, on the end of a leading rein, one each side of a large, fat, white cob, ridden by Miss Smith, and being led, very sedately, around a cinder circle was not our idea of riding! I'm afraid I wasn't very impressed, but I did learn how to hold the reins of a double bridle, with which the ponies were equipped. I probably should have learnt a lot more, but I fear I was already used to a greater degree of independence.

Part of my problem was that I was spending a lot of time riding on my own in the Home Park at Windsor, playing I don't know what, jumping on and off, having bases under some of the big trees whose branches came right down to the ground and provided excellent cover and ambush potential. I must have frightened or annoyed a lot of people at that stage in my career.

Helping The Queen and being helped by the Duke of Beaufort, known as 'Master', at the Royal Windsor Horse Show in May 1959.

My first visit to Badminton to watch the three-day event must have occurred at about this time. We used to stay at Badminton, the Duke of Beaufort's home, which was a most delightful experience. When you're quite young you have impressions of places and mine of Badminton is that I always enjoyed going there, yet it was the house I enjoyed the most. I don't remember being particularly interested in the horse trials, but I enjoyed staying in the house; it was one of those big houses with lots of interesting places. Along the front there are some round windows as you look at it from the park. One of the rooms in which we stayed now and again was behind those round windows. I was absolutely fascinated by this because there was a sort of stair well where the round window was and a couple of small windows on each side. You were completely out of the way – it was like being in a different world. The rooms didn't relate to any of the other rooms along the front of the house. How somebody had managed to get the rooms in there was a mystery, but that was a lovely position to be in.

Then sometimes we'd be put at the back of the house, right up at the top, three storeys up, right amongst the chimney pots. From there you didn't see any of the crowds or tents or anything else, and again you could have been somewhere completely different.

There were always a lot of people staying, and it was a sort of mad house with comings and goings, rushed meals, huge teas and things like that. Lots of people say how good the old Duke of Beaufort was with young people, and the atmosphere in the house made it a lovely place to stay; children loved it. It was a big house, but it never felt unfriendly, which a lot of big houses do. The Duke was never somebody I found in the least bit frightening, which you might have expected of a senior duke. Certainly he was not somebody that you ever worried about, from the point of view of a child. The Duchess was a delight; she was great fun.

But I never ever remember thinking, as I sat watching other people competing – and I was quite small when I first went – that one day that's what I would be doing. It never crossed my mind. I wasn't conscious, seeing the size of the obstacles there, comparing them with what I'd jumped, of thinking I could ever jump them myself. I just thought it was something that somebody else did. That was the end of the story.

It would be different asking my own children now what they think about going to Badminton. The difference would be that *they* know what a three-day event is all about, for they have been brought up with horse trials. I had no idea

Riding Bandit at a Pony Club Hunter Trial. He was unusually charming and reliable.

what they were, but enjoyed the atmosphere.

I suspect that my so-called 'competitive' career must have started about then with my introduction to the Pony Club. Pony Club life was largely confined to the Easter holidays when we were at Windsor and our 'local' was the Garth. I think you could count the number of rallies I went to on the fingers of one hand. They were memorable for persuading me that gymkhana games were not my *forte*.

The pony I had at the time was a grey 13.2hh called Bandit, who was charming and reliable in every way except that he refused to repeat himself. By that I mean that he would take part in one bending race (racing in and out down a line of poles) but tried very hard not to take part in the next. Equally, he would jump one round, usually clear, but would then indulge in his well-known imitation of a horse rampant if asked to face up to round 2. The answer proved to be the reverse – that is, to approach backwards. This seemed to confuse him sufficiently to allow you into the ring, if not actually to start. I don't remember having the same problems with him at hunter trials, which might explain why I seem to enjoy riding cross country more than showjumping or dressage.

The hunter trials were good fun and I can remember several courses comparatively clearly. They involved a variety of types of fences, often of three different sizes. If you went on your own, you could jump any size for your class. In the pairs or teams of three, I think you had to say before starting which of you was going to jump which fence. I always seemed then to be going round the biggest, which I certainly didn't on my own.

After Bandit there was a succession of borrowed ponies of all colours and sizes, among which a roan and a coloured pony (skewbald, I think) were more memorable. I'm sure the experience that I gained during that period was invaluable to me later when faced with all sorts of horses to ride. Riding over different terrain must have been a help too in my later riding life.

The next important landmark in my equestrian career was the arrival of one bay 14.2hh pony called Watersmeet High Jinks. I must have been about twelve years old when Jinks arrived as a four-year-old and we grew up together. He was my 'motivation', if that's the right word, until I left school in 1968. He was not the 'perfect pony' – he would not jump a ditch on his own – but he was otherwise honest (brave and true) and polite, strong but not uncontrollable, and we had a lot of fun together wherever we were: competing from Windsor, doing paper chases at Sandringham or just messing about at Balmoral.

I must just try to explain some of the magic that existed for me at Sandringham and Balmoral that made hacking fun for me. Sandringham is steeped in equine history, from the days when it was bought by the then Prince of Wales, later King Edward VII. The statue of his 1896 Derby and St Leger winner Persimmon outside the Sandringham stud buildings is one of my earliest memories, although for years I'm not sure I knew what he had done to have been turned into a statue. That's not altogether too surprising, considering I first saw it from my pram!

The stud boxes were built of local stone and consisted of two yards, side by side and completely enclosed. They contained lovely big boxes designed for mares and foals, with a foaling box in each yard, but sharing feed store and tack room. The statue of Persimmon stood on a lawn in front of the buildings and out the back were the vehicle sheds and a stud groom's cottage, all built in the same style. Further back and up the hill was another complex of buildings that housed the stallion boxes, for the resident stallion and the 'teaser' (the undistinguished stallion used to 'try' the mares). These led out directly to two large paddocks. There was enough of a slope so that, when you were riding past, you could see the stallions in their respective paddocks. The ponies and The Queen's riding horses were stabled just across the road from those paddocks and up the

High Jinks at Windsor. This 14.2hh pony was an important landmark in my riding career. He arrived as a four-year-old and we grew up together.

road from the stud, so that often, when going out or returning from a ride, the resident stallion would come over to examine these newcomers. Sometimes he rather overdid his curiosity, which was fun to watch if you didn't happen to own the stallion. Over the years we have been treated to galloping, bucking and leaping displays from Doutelle and Shirley Heights.

Also on the estate is the Wolferton Stud, situated towards the Wash and built as a stud, but quite different from the Sandringham Stud. It was here that The Queen's good horse Aureole stood, with his own high-walled yard and personal covered exercise yard. His paddock was across the road with quite the grandest field barn I've ever seen, with a thatched roof, if you please. Bustino is presently taking advantage of those facilities. Now *there* is a horse that I would not have minded owning, but not as a racehorse. He has such good conformation and temperament, I'm convinced he could have done anything, including jump.

Being there in January, if we were lucky one or two of the mares might have foaled before we had to leave and that was a real treat. My children aren't so fortunate, because they have to be back at school much earlier than I did. In fact, before I went to boarding school, I used to have lessons at Sandringham, which meant I could stay until the end of January. Gone are the days.

The stables from which we rode were a row of big loose boxes facing a paddock with another one adjacent to it. The ponies lived out, but were very much more convenient than at Windsor or Balmoral and so were easier to feed and get in. You could ride anywhere, there was very little traffic and there were none of the problems of the ever-present press photographers that we get today. In fact, The Queen can no longer use those boxes because they back on to the road and there is no way of keeping them private. Recently the riding horses have been kept in a specially adapted yard that was part of the game department of the estate and cannot be seen from the road. I think it is a sad reflection of our times that The Queen and members of her family whom she may invite to share the relaxing qualities of the Norfolk countryside, and who spend so much of their time in the public eye, are subjected to continuing scrutiny from the media and a curious public. The intensity of public life is so much greater now than it was twenty years ago that the need for real privacy is much greater too.

Quite apart from any other considerations, I'm concerned for the safety of the various children who are now trying to enjoy the opportunities for riding at Sandringham that I enjoyed when I was their age. On more than one occasion I have had cause to remonstrate with photographers, who have been running about in front of and around the childrens' ponies. Not surprisingly, when this happens, the ponies often react by turning round or rushing past out of fear, thereby frightening the children. I don't believe I'm being unreasonable in asking the photographers to stand still, because they are creating potentially dangerous situations.

That was not a problem we had when I was young. We rode freely all over the estate without having to worry about being followed or photographed. Now that may seem an unnecessary whinge from somebody who is considered public property, but it is meant more as an observation on an unfortunate aspect of the passage of time. Although I personally find it less than relaxing to be faced with even one photographer on what is one of the few occasions in the year when I'm not officially 'on show'!

I digress. My memories of riding at Sandringham are very fresh, partly, I expect, because surprisingly little has changed there since my childhood. Well, that's if you don't count the fact that Suffolk Punches no longer work in the fields and all that stubble replaced by plough is now going back to grass for sheep. Yes, the tractors have grown, as have the sugar-beet lorries. We no longer enjoy threshing the straw and laughing at the corgis' inefficient attempts to kill rats that ran out from the shrinking stacks. This used to amuse us almost as much as watching the adults leaping over the low wire fence that was there to stop the rats escaping into the hedgerows where they might destroy the nests of the English partridge in the late spring.

There are still golden pheasants in the rhododendron bushes on the way down to Wolferton, although you don't see them so much now because the number of cars driving round those roads and parking in the bushes has driven these colourful but solitary birds further into the undergrowth. The number of rabbits varies with the weather and there are still foxes, deer and lots of hares, and the geese are back in vast numbers. The hare is a particularly important indicator species, because it is so susceptible to the effects of chemical sprays and loss of habitat. The wildfowl are still present in large quantities and many varieties, and the tiny snipe and visiting woodcock still create their own special excitement when you catch a glimpse of them. All this could be observed from our rides. It is there for my children as well, although, like me, they may well not always regard the hare or the pheasant with much affection when they wait until your mount is almost on top of them before moving – fast! So very little has really changed.

If the openness and accessibility of Norfolk has its problems, this is not true at Balmoral. The estate is bordered by roads, but no public roads run across it, so it is much more private, but it is Scotland, which means that it is hilly. This makes the riding quite different. The stables at Balmoral, again, were built as a block with two long sides, one containing the stalls for the hill ponies and the other the coach houses, now garages. At one end is a separate block which was where the riding horses lived and which had two big loose boxes and three stalls. Overhead was the food store that contained hay, straw, oats, bran and nuts and was reached by a narrow wooden spiral staircase. I can remember spending a lot of time up there, sometimes helping to throw bales down through the trap door as opposed to just playing amongst them (something I don't encourage my children to do after the hours I have spent stacking bales at Gatcombe). The buildings were completed by a central block which was built to house the carriage horses, but was then transformed into a big wooden-floored hall where the staff would have dances and play games such as table tennis.

I spent a great deal of time in and around the stables with my own ponies and the hill ponies. Our ponies lived out in one of the fields bordering the golf course. There were several fields, because at that time there was still a dairy herd on the estate, and our ponies couldn't always go in the nearest field if the cows were in there. I may say that the nearest field was half a mile from the stables and the furthest nearly a mile. This meant learning the art of leading one or more ponies from a bicycle and riding bareback with a headcollar and leading sometimes three, or very occasionally four if there was a crisis. Somehow it seemed easier than walking to and fro, a piece of logic that my children seem to share already.

So my brother's and my day would consist of going down to the stables to tack up the ponies, either riding with The Queen or being left very much to our own devices, chasing each other round the woods, climbing the hill paths or galloping down the side of the golf course – if you were in control. After the ride we (usually I) would take the ponies back to the field on foot, until I mastered the art of riding my bicycle and being towed by the pony. By then it was lunchtime and lunch was usually a picnic somewhere, after which there was often a bonfire to be fuelled with the debris from the severe gales of 1954. There were burns to be undammed. Then it was back for tea, after which I would go and get the ponies in for the night. That meant walking up to the field, catching the ponies and climbing on mine (I never could vault on) while keeping hold of others. Needless to record, this did not always work, but I didn't lose many. Back to the stables I would go to put them to bed and by then it was nearly my bedtime, but I seem to remember search parties being sent out for me and a degree of disapproval being communicated when I was found doing something which was apparently considered unladylike and 'after hours'.

Two incidents involving High Jinks are particularly clear in my memory. They are both examples of my own incompetence, but even I laughed at the vision they must have created. The first incident occurred at the end of my first day's experience of the art of stalking red deer in what felt to me like the vast expanses of the Highlands. I was following my brother – never again. I very nearly didn't make it back to the car as my legs seemed to have gone on strike. After a very welcome and refreshing cup of tea and the journey back, I set off as normal to collect the ponies. After putting on their headcollars, I decided, for some inexplicable reason, to attempt to vault on to Jinks, a feat never previously accomplished, so why try that night? I still can't answer this question, but the result was completely unexpected. Jinks was standing, waiting with a resigned expression on his face, for what he no doubt assumed would be the inevitable

High Jinks in the stables at Balmoral. This is the bicycle
on which I used to lead the ponies in.

thump against his side. I approached the problem in my usual way, more in hope than expectation, taking a run at Jinks' nearside. When I picked myself up from his offside, Jinks was staring at me in open disbelief and I was not conscious of having touched any part of him in my trajectory from one side to the other. I did have a quick look round to see if there was anybody on the golf course who might have witnessed this episode of pure comedy, before laughing weakly at my own unexpected achievement and at the thought of how funny it would have looked from a distance. I got to my feet and rather sheepishly had another go, and this time succeeded in ending up astride the pony. I have to record that it was a unique achievement: it was the only time I ever managed to vault on to Jinks.

That incident was unrelated to the next one, which again involved High Jinks, and again it was not his fault. I was riding Jinks, bareback, back from the field, leading another horse. As I approached the door into the stable block, the led horse decided to shy at my bicycle, which was in its normal place, leaning against the wall beside the door. This reaction was unexpected and my reaction was right in theory but wrong in execution. As we were so close to the door, I decided to let go of the led horse and put Jinks in his box first, before making sure that the other horse went into his box. Unfortunately my own wires got crossed and, as Jinks walked on, I let go of his headcollar rope and kept a firm grip on the led horse's lead rope, which resulted in my being pulled backwards over Jinks' bottom and executing a very hard landing on the cobbles. Meanwhile Jinks walked unconcernedly into the stables, into his own loose box, and turned round to find me sitting on the ground in the doorway. Not for the first time he looked genuinely surprised at the antics of his erstwhile rider, and his erstwhile rider was debating her sanity, also not for the first time. Again, I found myself

Jumping High Jinks at Balmoral.

looking round to see if this example of how not to do it had been witnessed, before once more laughing at the real-life comedy sketch I had perpetrated. I'm not sure that the tears were related to the laughter.

But my memories of Balmoral are also of the magic of the views of Lochnagar and the Dee valley, the beautiful autumn colours of the rowans and silver birches, the majesty of the old Scots pines of the Caledonian Forest and the animals and birds that live in these relatively unspoilt wild places. Riding through the woods and over the hills, we would come across red squirrels, roe deer, red deer, black game, capercaillie, buzzards and any number of small birds and wild flowers. One of the pleasures of returning is that, apart from the now mature trees that were planted to replace the ones lost in the gales, nothing has changed.

High Jinks shared all sorts of adventures with me at Balmoral, at Sandringham, at Windsor and at the Moat House riding school in Kent, where he

This was an 'activity ride' at the Moat House's open day, when I was at school. I was riding Jester.

lived during my last year at Benenden School. He took part in the school pageant, when I was given the role of an Elizabethan messenger, galloping up the park to announce the arrival of some important personage. He thoroughly enjoyed his part and each trip up the park got quicker and quicker and the gate we had to go through seemed to get smaller and smaller.

I had been riding regularly at the Moat House, every Thursday afternoon, during my school career. The owner and chief instructor was a lady called Cherry Hatton-Hall and I was fortunate to have been able to take advantage of her sound teaching and that of her very good staff. They were very patient, I know, because I must have been a menace, never having ridden in a 'ride' before. I wasn't very good at being one of a ride of twelve: 'Leading file trot on to the rear of the ride,' etc. (That meant that the one at the front trotted away from the rest until it caught up with the back marker.) I think I found the terminology and the instructions difficult to follow and, no doubt, wanted to discuss the comments made on my performance by the instructress.

In retrospect, the horses we rode there were remarkably good, given the variety of riders inflicted on them. Apart from the fact that they were civilised, they were well-schooled, and you could make a difference to them if you tried hard enough to follow your instructions. Some teaching was in the indoor school and some of the lessons were outdoors.

There was usually a competition in each of the terms. And there was a summer show, which was a sort of inter-school competition. There were several other schools in the area with pupils who rode at the Moat House. You drew straws and jumped the same horses – mostly showjumping and activity rides. We did things like riding and jumping bareback or without girths. Riding on a saddle, but without a girth, is in a funny sort of way much more difficult to do than just riding bareback.

One of the more amusing moments in my life then occurred during my last year there. I was riding High Jinks in the field adjacent to the indoor school, doing a bit of work before the show. There were some workmen in, putting chairs out. But they had stopped doing that and were leaning over the fence, looking at me riding about. They had also spotted my policeman, who was leaning against the end of the school, smoking a pipe and, I'm sorry to say, looking just like a policeman.

Eventually they called out, 'Oi! You!'

There was nobody else in the field so I answered, 'Yes?'

And they said, 'Are you royalty or something? Why's that man watching you?'

I looked at my policeman and he looked at them. At the age of sixteen or seventeen you're not terribly ready with instant repartee to queries like that, so I replied, 'Well, yes, I am.'

'*Nah*, you never are!' came the retort. Then followed this perfectly absurd conversation – 'You asked me if I was royalty,' 'No, you never are!' and so on. This went on for an amazingly long time before they finally gave up and I decided to go off and do my own thing. I don't think they believed me. Having come up with the suggestion, which was the most absurd thing they could think of, they weren't prepared to believe it.

I found quite often when I was riding that I was not recognised, because riding-hats always make people look different. Later I went through a phase where the only time I was ever seen in a picture was with a riding-hat on, and so people thought I only rode. They didn't think I did anything else. They

This is a gymkhana in the coach park of Ascot racecourse, and I am riding High Jinks in the Easter holidays of 1963.

wouldn't have recognised me *without* a hat on. Now it's gone full circle, and they ask me if I *still* ride. So I've gone back to square the first, as if I'd never started.

Cherry Hatton-Hall taught us a lot about competing and the manners and discipline required to do yourself and your horse justice. Certainly the discipline of riding in a group was very good for me. So was being responsible for my own and my horse's turn-out and my behaviour in the ring. There is no doubt that the level of involvement required in equestrian sport teaches young people a great deal about life, especially that 'life' is not fair. There are very few short cuts, you don't always go as well as you think you ought to and there are any number of disappointments caused by apparently unimportant things.

I enjoyed my time at school, and no doubt my riding experiences helped, but I was still not set on a competitive equestrian career. Everybody assumes I'm competitive, but I think it was simply that I *wanted to do things well*. If I was winning, that was a bonus. But if the horse or the pony went wrong – by which I mean if I got things wrong – it was extremely annoying. And I was brought up to believe that it was *always* my fault, not the pony's – which was true, usually. That was constantly drummed into me: it's never the pony's fault, it's always yours.

It is a very important idea to accept, because then you have to sit down and think about what you did that was wrong. There might have been any number of combinations of circumstances which made it wrong and it might not have been wrong by much, but it probably wasn't the pony's fault – more that you got the instructions wrong in the wrong place at the wrong time. I suppose I did get upset about not winning, but I used to be more upset with myself for getting it wrong than I did for not winning.

High Jinks won the Working Hunter Pony at Badminton –
the then Duchess of Beaufort is giving us our rosette.

One occasion when Jinks and I did manage to win was at Badminton of all places. That was in the days when there was a huge variety of other equestrian activities going on there, like hunter classes and showjumping. I was entered, unbeknownst to me, in a working hunter pony class. I don't remember knowing the first thing about it when I arrived, and I didn't know much more when I got in the ring. All the other ponies looked so smart and their riders were even smarter. I looked like a real country cousin, but fortunately there were more marks for the pony and the jumping than there were for the rider. We did manage to jump a clear round, which meant we stood second before the showing bit which was a complete mystery to me. Unlike everybody else, I had no idea what the judges were looking for, and I had never even heard of 'ringcraft' then. (Now I know it exists, but I still don't know what it means.) The pony standing above me was being ridden by a young lady called Jane Bullen, and even I knew that she was the best. Anyway, after the initial judging we were sent away to return at some later stage for the final judging in the main arena, if you please.

Well, I was so bemused by all this that I don't remember being any more appalled at the prospect of appearing in the main arena than taking part in an unknown competition. We walked, trotted, cantered and galloped round the arena and then we were called into our final placing. To my total astonishment, High Jinks was called in first with Jane Bullen in second. I now know that the judges thought that Jane's pony was not quite sound, which I was certainly not qualified to comment upon. I thought Jane and her pony were so smart that they couldn't help winning. I also now know that Jinks' conformation was good, he had plenty of bone, had good paces and jumped really well, so he was good enough to win in spite of me. For the record, Jane, now Mrs Holderness Roddam, is one of my hard-working and highly valued ladies-in-waiting and a much better and more successful equestrienne than me. She has won twice at Badminton and once at Burghley and was a team Olympic Gold Medallist in Mexico.

The value of ponies in my life was probably more apparent to those around me. My interest in them kept me out of all sorts of potential trouble, helped me learn to be considerate and consistent with animals, to learn to try to control my temper (that was probably less successful!) and to learn that good manners never hurt anybody.

That was April 1965. In the Easter holidays before I left school in 1968, I had my first contact with Alison Oliver and took part in a couple of Pony Club one-day events on a horse called Purple Star. Whatever happened in the competitions, Alison and I got on very well and Purple and I got on pretty well and thereby hangs a tale.

With Lieutenant Colonel Sir John Miller out with the Oxford Drag in 1965.

CHAPTER 2

Starting Eventing:

'Alison was the key'

WHEN I made my decision to try to make a success of riding, I was warned that I ran the risk of forever being labelled as horsy. It was a risk that I took, and I have indeed had to live with that label. But, thanks to people like Alison Oliver and the many others who shared their knowledge with me, it became apparent very early on that liking horses was just the beginning. There was so much to get to know about them in terms of nutrition, health care and preventive medicine, as well as all the other aspects of care and training that are essential to produce a horse ready to compete in any discipline.

I was also brought up to regard sport as a type of hobby and therefore horses were never the only interest in my life. Because they are animals, they do need to be looked after rather more conscientiously than a bicycle, boat or tennis racket and consequently do not leave a lot of time for any other activities. Having made the decision to compete, I knew that it would be only a part of my life, but a part to which I would apply the best of my ability.

In order to do that, I needed a lot of help. As you will have discovered by now, I knew startlingly little about any sort of competition, never mind the intricacies of a horse trial. Alison Oliver lived in Winkfield Row, the Windsor side of Bracknell, about twenty minutes from Windsor and an hour from London, if you were lucky with the traffic, and it was there that I went to get help.

Alison worked from stables owned by Mrs Joan Gold, one of Britain's few successful international dressage riders, who was still competing when I first went there. Her last Grand Prix standard horse, Roman Holiday, was stabled there and Mrs Gold was extremely generous in allowing novice riders to experience the sensation of what dressage – at its highest level – was all about. There is no doubt that the occasion when I was allowed that honour changed my attitude. It changed my understanding of all those hours spent riding in circles. To be able to achieve extended trot, collected canter, flying changes, canter half-pass and even passâge with apparently so little effort was a revelation of what proper training could produce. More importantly, it gave me an idea of what

Pride, given to The Queen by the King of Jordan.
He used to let his tongue hang out when he wanted a lump of sugar.

correct balance and impulsion should feel like. That experience had a very pro-
found effect on me, but it didn't turn me into a dressage rider.

Mrs Gold was also District Commissioner of the Pony Club, a job whose
difficulties I have come to appreciate and would not like to have. By the time I
left school I was too old for the Pony Club except as an associate member, so I
went straight into adult competition and Alison had to teach me literally everything, from the ground up, you might say. I had to learn different dressage tests
and know which one I was doing *before* arriving at the competition. I had to
learn how to walk courses, where to get your numbers from, where to find out
the times when you were starting, what sort of boots or bandages went on the
horse's legs and why. And that was all before you got on to the horse to warm it
up before its dressage. Lesson number 1 was: plan ahead and allow plenty of time
for things to go wrong. Not very original, but it's a lesson of which I am constantly
reminded – if I don't always remember it – when making my travel plans.

A very important part of equestrian activity is the role of the groom. I had
grown up under the watchful eye of the stud groom at Windsor who was almost
the most important person in my life. The most important was Frank Hatcher
who helped us with the ponies. I think I was well educated as to the importance
of the work of grooms, but I was to discover how vital they were to producing
and competing an event horse. The daily care, the daily exercise and the daily
observation of their charges were all invaluable. Even if you were looking after
your own horse, when you reached a competition – especially a three-day event
– it was impossible to manage without 'help'. For instance, when packing up the
horse box, you would find that there was so much to remember that there was
always scope to forget something.

Even now I'm still making mistakes for the first time, but I *have* learnt from
some of them. Learning the wrong dressage test can spoil an otherwise peaceful
morning; not allowing enough time to walk the showjumping course can lead to
rather obvious errors; but the scope for major nonsenses is on the cross-country
course. Over the years I managed to perpetrate quite a few, like walking a course
that had three different standards and, in spite of recognising the problem,
managing to jump the wrong fence, although I didn't realise it until I asked why
I had been eliminated.

On another, later occasion I walked the course in two halves and I thought
that, with the plan of the course, I had seen all the fences. Unfortunately, it
wasn't until I was half-way round on the horse that I noticed all the hoofprints
leaving the track that I was following. In spite of being pretty sure that I was

going the right way, I thought it might be prudent to go with the majority, and round the corner I found a fence I had never seen before but which was definitely part of the course. It was just as well that I jumped it.

The tack and the regulations that controlled its use could also cause major as well as minor aggravations. The rules for horse trials and pure dressage were different, which often led to confusion. Sometimes it was just a case of having the wrong noseband on for the dressage test, which could be changed quite quickly and, if you were lucky, could have a remarkably calming influence on the horse. The two best tests that Goodwill ever did were after last-minute tack changes. One of these was at Badminton when Mark rode him in 1977 – I was sufficiently pregnant not to be competing – and we forgot to change the crossed noseband that Goodwill always wore with his double bridle for the regulation cavesson noseband. The judges noticed and sent them out to change it. Goodwill seemed to think he'd finished and when he went back he was much more relaxed than his rider. The other occasion was with me before the Spillers Combined Training Championship at the Horse of the Year Show and again involved the wrong noseband and a quick turn-round. That was the closest Goodwill ever came to leading a dressage class, but his jumping won him the class in the end.

A more serious tack problem involved the use of a weight cloth, a leather saddle cloth with pouches designed to carry lead. The weight cloths were needed because at the higher standard of competition there was a minimum set weight of 11st 11lb, so that the lightweight girls didn't have too much of an advantage over the heavier men. I came back one day from a pretty good cross-country round which might have got me a placing, until I came to take off the saddle in order to be weighed in and realised that I had no weight cloth (it had never been put on) and therefore would not make the minimum weight requirement. I was eliminated. That was not a mistake I made again. A so-called friend of mine suggested that I should weigh in anyway on the assumption that I carried a weight cloth only to make people *think* I needed lead to make the weight – the implication being that I was heavy enough without the weight cloth.

At other times there was the disappointment of doing only some of the competition and then the horse not being quite right, and of accepting Alison's advice to save it for another day. Alison was the key. Her contribution was the fact that she could talk to me, and that I could understand what she was saying. For me she was the right person. Inevitably, with sports people, you have to meet the right person at the right time. It doesn't matter how naturally gifted you are, if you don't get that combination, you don't make the best use of what talent you have. Alison was the right person as far as I was concerned. She was very thorough, very good on basics, never in a hurry, always went one step at a time and she never built up my hopes.

There were other points that were especially important. The first was that there were no short cuts, no deliberate rule bending, and you did not argue with the judges. When things were not going so well and you were tempted to think some disaster had befallen you, Mrs Oliver had a very convincing line about every cloud having a silver lining. Sometimes these linings were very small indeed, but just the effort of looking for them seemed to lighten the darkness of the short-term gloom.

That was one of the other things I learned while working with horses: you have to develop a long-term outlook. In a sport like horse trials, unlike show-jumping, there is only a limited number of competitions to go to in the year, so if your horse isn't fit or the weather forces a cancellation, you can often miss the opportunity to gain necessary qualifications for the more important competitions – and there are even fewer of them.

Because horse trials involve galloping and jumping, the potential for damage is always quite high. Often the damage can be small cuts, bruising or strains which usually recover if given enough time. Time is always at a premium, but Alison was sure that proceeding in haste meant repenting at leisure. The worst news you can have as a rider is to be told by the vet that your horse has strained its tendon, because tendons take such a long time to regain the elasticity that the strain has overstretched. If you are lucky, your horse might be ready to start work again in a year. Alison always tried to stop before the damage necessitated that sort of treatment.

Prevention was the sort of treatment that I was taught and always had been, and not just in the case of horses. Prevention meant noticing when something wasn't normal and that meant knowing or recognising what *was* normal. With horses that meant feeling their legs regularly so that you could identify any new and suspicious lumps, bumps or just places which were hotter than usual. When you were riding, it meant noticing if they moved differently, which might be caused by an unseen source of pain in their backs or in the big muscles over the shoulders, over the hips and down the back legs.

Prevention meant noticing if they weren't eating their normal amount or were just off their food altogether; the way they moved round their stables and the rather more mundane observation of the colour of their urine and the consistency of their stools.

The source of most of this information tended to be the grooms, the farriers and the vets. Farriers put horse shoes on horses; blacksmiths are people who work in iron for agricultural machinery and in wrought iron for gates and lamps and also make horse shoes; vets came later. I learned a great deal from talking to them and asking them endless questions and just observing them at work. I also discovered that they were not always right and learnt some lessons the hard way. But when you are just starting you simply don't have the experience to know anything different.

When I was starting, vets were still more advanced than human doctors in the field of what we now call sports medicine. I imagine that this was a result of the fact that in the sport of horse racing vets had, for two hundred years, been treating what were in effect professional athletes. The development of veterinary science had actually been inspired by the successes of the racehorse Eclipse. The Royal Veterinary College was founded two hundred years ago by Professor Charles Vial de Saintbel, whose reputation in particular, and veterinary science in general, were greatly enhanced by his post-mortem of the great Eclipse.

There was a lot of money in racing and owners knew that good horses were few and far between, so the vets had to become specialists in preventive medicine. Their knowledge of the whole animal, its skeletal and muscular structure, and often their own experiences as horsemen, made them very aware of the weak points and the type of exercise that might strengthen them. Treatment was often very basic and of the handed-down variety without much scientific evidence to back it up.

There are well-known examples, like bran poultices to draw the pus out of a poisoned foot, and kaolin (a type of very fine white clay powder) poultices, applied hot or cold to the legs. To try to explain which and why would take another book. Wytch-hazel, a clear odourless liquid made from the bark of *Hamamelis*, is used on bruises and softens windgalls (little swellings just above the fetlocks which cause no trouble unless they harden up). If you had a bad cut that had healed but the proud flesh would not go, the old remedy was to put honey on it; fortunately this is not one I've had to use yet, so I don't know if it works.

Another old-fashioned remedy that I know does work is to hang a piece of gorse in the horse's box if the horse is completely off its food. The horse will often eat it in preference to anything else. Nobody can tell me why it might work, although it was our vet who recommended this course of action when one of Mark's horses went off his food completely. Persian Holiday was a soft horse but he certainly thought that gorse was the only thing he was prepared to eat, which he did for about a day before resuming his normal diet. My own theory is that saliva plays an important role in activating the digestive juices and it is the sharpness of the gorse which stimulates the saliva and the digestive processes.

Some people will put a clod of earth in the stable as a matter of course in case the horse feels in need of the minerals earth contains. Goodwill frequently ignored good grass when you took him out to graze and spent the time digging away the grass to get at the soil underneath. Acorns were another alternative that horses sometimes ate in preference to their usual diet. This is a more worrying habit because acorns are supposed to be poisonous, but they have medicinal properties for certain conditions. I don't think however you will find vets prescribing acorns.

I have to admit that I did not learn all these things in my first year with Alison, nor in my first three years, and I'm still learning. I had to learn how to ride well enough to be able to cope with the complexities of competing at the same time. That meant going to as many different competitions as possible: attending dressage meetings, combined training (dressage and showjumping), hunter trials and endless days of showjumping – only then would I be ready to go to a one-day event. Being based in Berkshire meant that there was a tremendous choice of competitions within comparatively easy reach. The longer journeys came when travelling to horse trials.

Practice was what I learned about, and that there was no substitute for experience. Getting everything right at home did not mean you could turn up at your local show and repeat the performance in front of the judges. Horses respond to atmosphere, to crowds and to arenas in as many ways as humans do, but most of them get nervous to some degree and you have to learn to control your own nerves in order to relax your horse. Perhaps that was one of the few things that I already knew about as I had spent most of my life attempting to control my nerves every time I went out in public. Funnily enough, I found it easier to manage my nerves when I was worrying about the horse. Just before the cross country it was more a question of suppressing the fear!

While I was learning about competition, I was also learning to ride different horses and I was grateful that I had had the opportunity to ride horses in the Mews as well as my own pony High Jinks. Horses like Pride, the Jordanian Arab, a gift from King Hussein of Jordan to The Queen. An elegant though not beautiful grey of about 15.3hh, he was a comfortable but lively ride and he would jump small fences. He had a curious sense of humour which manifested itself in

Slipper, a borrowed pony, at Windsor. We were generously lent ponies from time to time.

pretending to be lame when he saw me coming into the yard – I think because he knew the ride would be more varied than his usual exercise. Nowadays, with all *my* horses, it works the other way round: I have only to appear in the yard and they produce an endless variety of complications that render them unridable.

There was another of my mother's 'gift horses' that I was allowed to ride; this one came from Portugal and was bred and trained to fight bulls. He was a liver chestnut stallion who looked as if he'd caprioled out of the pages of *The Duke of Newcastle's General System of Horsemanship* (published in its original French translation, 1658). He had a great crested front with a long wavy mane, a sloping back with a square backside and a cascading wavy tail. His action was interesting too as he 'dished' more than any horse I've ever seen. That meant that his lower leg – instead of pointing the toe and the whole leg following through in a straight line – rotated outwards, which made him look like a rotary mower. You needed a saddle with a high cantle (back), otherwise you fell off over his steeply sloping bottom. Nonetheless, he was a lovely ride, but his most endearing habit was to lie down in his box and remain there if anybody walked in, so you could go and sit with him or even on him without him moving at all. He was called Busaco and he fathered a foal called Oporto who was successfully evented by Debbie West.

Another gift horse came from President Khrushchev. Melekush was an Akhal Teke, a tall, thin, gold-coloured stallion with black mane and tail and black down his legs, but with three white socks. His head was long and narrow with positively oriental eyes sloping upwards, but his most remarkable feature was his striking colour, a real golden sheen. He came from one of the Soviet Republics I visited in May 1990, Turkmenistan. Just outside the capital, Ashkhabad, there is a stud that breeds Akhal Tekes and I was shown one relative of Melekush's, but only two other horses there had the same colouring. The breed is famed for its stamina and endurance and even now takes part in 'races' from Ashkhabad to Moscow and as far as Germany. For many years Melekush was ridden by my father and was a polite but interesting hack. I don't remember being allowed to ride him, though I did ride his smaller but not so striking-looking compatriot, Zaman.

My father's polo ponies were the other source of riding experience that I gained before going to Mrs Oliver's. Although they were trained quite differently and were usually relatively small, they contributed greatly to my appreciation of what horses could do when properly trained and how competitive these creatures could be in their own right. They actually seemed to enjoy playing polo, because it was the only time they really came alive. The way they raced each other up and down the pitch and how one might lean upon another in order to prevent the other player hitting the ball were not things you could teach them.

So I was fortunate to have enjoyed considerable variety in my youth, both at home and at school, and I still enjoy the opportunity to ride different horses. But, having agreed to try to train me, Mrs Oliver did not have an easy task, and the fact that I made such comparatively rapid progress speaks volumes for her ability as a teacher. If you wanted a trainer to help you win prizes, Alison was not the lady for you. If you wanted to learn how to become a three-day event rider, then you were in very good hands.

After polo with my father and my brother Andrew and our father's ponies.

CHAPTER 3

Riding for the Disabled:

'A unique partnership between rider, helper and pony'

MY decision to spend more time riding did not mean that I was avoiding
official engagements; obviously at that stage in my public career I was not in
great demand. It did mean that I planned my life under Alison's guidance and
fitted the few requests for official functions around the competitions and training. I had received a number of requests to be Patron or Honorary President of
various organisations, but had been strongly advised by my father to wait until I
was asked by a body to which I felt I could contribute something and in which I
could take a close interest. So when I was approached by Lavinia, Duchess of
Norfolk, the then President of the Riding for the Disabled Association (RDA), to
become their Patron, it did not take me long to make up my mind. Although
some groups had been in existence for several years, it was only in 1969 that
they formed themselves into a national association, ably led by the Duchess.

The Duchess of Norfolk is a woman who has a very full life, but whose
major source of enjoyment has been horses, and she too felt there was a different
role for horses to play in their long history of working with man. I knew something about Lavinia as the wife of the Duke of Norfolk who was responsible for
all the great ceremonies of State, and I knew a little of her considerable reputation when riding to hounds in Leicestershire as well as of her enthusiasm for
flat racing – especially the breeding and the training – but I didn't know her
very well personally. And yet her involvement and invitation were enough for
me to know that this was a body to which I felt I could contribute.

A lot of people tend to think horses are just for the indolent rich to ride or
race and for no one else. I really did believe that here was something that people
with horses could be seen to be doing that was of benefit to the community,
quite apart from the value of the therapy itself. In those days people didn't
regard riding as a real therapy. It was considered rather an eccentric, nice thing
to do, but with nothing particularly scientific about it. At that stage it was
thought to be just a way for handicapped children to take exercise.

I thought – rather foolishly as it turned out – that with my own experience

Visiting the RDA Group in Handford.

of ponies and horses I might be able to contribute something to the Association. I hope that I have helped, but I definitely feel that it is I who have benefited from my visits to the groups.

Like many others, I was concerned about my own initial reaction to people with more obvious handicaps. I need not have worried. It was very easy to ignore or forget completely any of the riders' disabilities because of their own commitment to and interest in what they were doing. I also learned a great deal about how the movement of the animal affected your muscles, the training required for the animal in order that the rider could gain most benefit and the psychological impact of the comparative freedom of movement of the animal and its own understanding of the competence of its rider.

The more we did, the more we discovered how riding improved children with communication difficulties and with muscular problems, in ways that you cannot apparently achieve through any other forms of physiotherapy. Amputees and elderly stroke patients can be helped as well as those with more serious physical and mental disadvantages than the rest of us. I have such admiration for stroke victims of sixty-plus who start riding as therapy, having never ridden before in their lives. They're so brave; I'm sure I wouldn't start if I was that age. A most extraordinary range of injured and disabled people were beginning to gain benefit from riding as a therapy – not just as a way of getting them out of the hospital or school for a day or of giving their parents or 'carers' a respite.

For those with a mental handicap or illness, it is much more difficult to measure what benefits can be gained from riding. It is really only by talking to their parents and regular helpers that you can gauge the impact of their activities; an impact which often comes as a terrific boost to their morale. This is also true of those who are normally wheelchair-bound, people who suddenly are able to look others in the eye, or even to look down on them, and can at last be independently mobile; all these give equally big boosts to *their* morale. Physically they might not have shown any particular improvement, but the riding gave them a terrific fillip mentally.

So a lot of potentially valuable information was coming together through the Riding for the Disabled Association groups which nobody had expected or hoped for at a time when it was thought that riding was good for the disabled without knowing exactly why. Lavinia, Duchess of Norfolk, as President, and Verona Kitson, as Chairman, developed the Association. They made it grow intelligently and steadily, persuading new groups to sign on as members, so the movement didn't grow out of control. They established standards and courses for organisers, instructors and physiotherapists. These are expanding and developing all the time.

We now have a paid professional director. When the position was first suggested, there was a lot of humming and ha-ing from all the volunteer ladies, who said, 'We don't need a professional director. Verona Kitson did it perfectly well, so why can't anybody else?' The answer was that Verona Kitson was an amazing lady – end of story. Not many people were as capable or had the opportunity to give the time and effort that she did. Verona still had time to be one of the most respected dressage judges in the country. (There is a space on the dressage marking sheet for the judges' comments and I always made a point of reading hers.) I was even more respectful of Dame Mary Colvin, one of our best senior dressage judges, who was also one of the great leading lights of the Association in the early days. All of them did fantastic jobs.

Dressage played a crucial role in the history of the RDA, because the inspiration for the movement came from the example of the Danish dressage rider, Lisa Hartell. She was the one who set people thinking when she turned up at the 1952 Olympics in Helsinki, having overcome the not inconsiderable inconvenience of being a victim of polio, and won a silver medal. If you saw Miss Hartell on a horse you would never have suspected that she had great difficulty in walking; her balance and the strength in her back and seat seemed to more than compensate for having virtually no strength in her legs. But for some unknown reason it was in the UK rather than in Denmark that this inspiration manifested itself.

It was really extraordinary, but I suppose that having all our native ponies was a great advantage. Horses are more difficult to work with, because of their size and the need to manhandle riders on board. So there's a built-in advantage of having a large pool of native ponies of various sizes with which to work.

Now the RDA has sprung up in various countries in the world: in Germany (generally thanks to the British Army wives); in many Commonwealth countries – New Zealand, Australia and Canada are especially well developed – and a little bit in the United States. I recall that on the occasion I met President Reagan, when he came to Windsor for a couple of days, the first thing he asked me was, 'Do you know about this marvellous therapy of riding for handicapped people?' I had to tell him that I was sorry, but it was almost invented here! But he had been most impressed by what he had seen and heard. He is now a great supporter, which is very good news for handicapped riders in America, because their medical profession is much more nervous of risk-taking than any other country's doctors.

In the early days the medical profession here in Britain was very hard to convince that riding had any point for disabled people and others certainly didn't consider it a therapy. Most of them were appalled at the idea of people who were already 'high-risk' doing something more risky. The facts that the disabled wanted to ride and that riding might be good for them were almost irrelevant, because you could not measure the effect against the risk. Riding is inevitably a risk, so the doctors understandably tended to go for safety, for their own peace of mind. But their decisions were often arrived at without having taken the trouble to go and see for themselves how much could be achieved and how much pleasure riding gave to those with very limited ambitions or movement.

Things became easier when more physiotherapists became involved and began using riding as a regular form of therapy. Doctors came, watched and saw, and began to understand what was going on. Even so, we still get the 'odd one out' doctor who can't see the point. When I went to one of those rehabilitation units for accident and stroke victims, I can remember being asked by the doctor,

Above and opposite: Visiting one of the excellent Riding for the Disabled groups at Bradbourne in Kent.

'But what sort of *exercise* do you take on a horse?' When you stop to think about it, it is very difficult to define the exercise you do take, and for a moment I just looked at him. Then I said, 'Well, you try it and then tell me which bits of you *don't* hurt!'

If you have never ridden you imagine it's simply like sitting in a chair: nothing happening. One of the real bonuses of riding is the fact that you require involuntary movement to keep your balance in the saddle. You don't have to bully somebody to take exercise; if they're going to sit there and stay on, their muscles have to do something whether they like it or not.

So we've been able to put our rides together slowly in a much more scientific way. I think our training and instructing has become much better and much more targeted towards individual disabilities. Because of the RDA, my own experience has been with a total range of disabilities, mental and physical, and they can all be influenced by riding in their various ways, depending on the level of severity. So this has led me to a closer knowledge of the different sorts of problems that disabled people encounter in their lives.

There are many more children riding than adults, but it slightly depends on where you are. They ride in commercial riding schools, they ride in fields, they ride in hospital grounds, all over the place, and groups come and go. The demand changes. One riding school closes, another one opens. One special school has its own ponies; another finds it too difficult to organise. Organisers move on or run out of time, head teachers change, doctors and physios get promoted. You just have to keep going.

The success of the RDA depends on a unique partnership between rider, helper and pony. Often when the helpers start they have had no previous experience of any type of disability and they worry about dealing with handicapped people. But with the pony they have a third party, and can communicate through the pony. The rider wonders about the pony and *the helper* wonders about the pony, so somehow they start to communicate *because of* the animal in a way in which many of the disabled could never have done before.

The helpers get completely absorbed by their work and totally forget that their charges are handicapped. It's so difficult to try to educate people not to be frightened of those who suffer from having some form of handicap. Ignorance of what to expect, of course, creates concern. It's understandable, because some forms of handicap can make people look different and they can behave violently, but through the RDA groups helpers can come to terms with the handicapped in a straightforward way and can therefore relate to them much more easily. So the able-bodied helper is benefiting too. Of course, many helpers not only know little about handicapped people, but they also have never had any experience of horses and ponies either. The extraordinary thing is that a large number of them go along a little bit dubiously and wondering, and then stay for years.

The helpers are vital, but psychologically it is the animal which interests and motivates the rider. Many of those with behavioural problems, speech difficulties and so on find that it is much easier to have a *rapport* with an animal than it is with a human. So although the pony has a non-speaking role, it can be a catalyst to development in a way which people alone cannot. Surprisingly the ponies seem to know the difference between the able and less able riders. There are RDA ponies which, in the school holidays, are Pony-Clubbing like fiends with their owners on them, yet who become as good as gold when they are with their disabled group. They seem to recognise the limitations of the rider.

I remember thinking about my old pony, High Jinks, 'Well, nobody else will be able to ride him because he is too strong – he rushes off all the time.' But, to my surprise, this proved to be patently untrue. When I grew too big for him, he spent the end of his career at Balmoral for the factor's daughter and others to ride. He was ridden by all sorts of people, never put a foot out of line and never galloped anywhere – until I got back on him! The difference must have been between the level of expectancy of a rider that he knew so well and that of any other rider whom he did not know. Riders and owners do different things. Ponies and horses are astonishing like that – how they seem able to understand the difference between competent riders and those who are genuinely handicapped.

And it's not that the latter are seen as no threat, because often they have muscular spasms which can be very disturbing to the ponies. I have always thought that one of the things that worries horses most is when novice riders cling on with their legs around the girth. It's extraordinary how much RDA ponies tolerate, which they probably wouldn't put up with from anybody else.

But not all horses and ponies are suitable for disabled riders and we have to be very careful when looking for the right animals or deciding whether or not to

This is the mid-Essex Group.

accept those that have generously been offered to groups. We do occasionally have to look gift horses in the mouth. However, the majority of the horses and ponies used by RDA groups belong to riding schools and individuals and surprisingly few fail to adapt. These RDA ponies – and the big horses too, that we need for some of the adults – may be hunting for half the season. A mixture of occupation is good for them. If they are just used purely for RDA, they get so bored with slow work that they go more and more slowly, won't go out of walk and just amble round with their heads down. This is bad for them and bad for the riders, who will get less benefit from their riding.

Because our training and instructing is now more targeted at individuals and their particular disabilities, I believe that all sorts of groups – deaf, blind, physically and mentally handicapped – can and do benefit from riding in their own way. It's an education in terms of what people can cope with and of what a remarkably complex construction the human being is; how much of the body can work in spite of what we do to it, and how the body can compensate for things that are not quite right. The more you learn, the more you wonder whether anybody is born with all their faculties. We are all disabled in some way – just ask a tailor, dressmaker or members of your family!

Some of the disabled children are so much improved in themselves that their riding improves and this progress can be measured. They have their own series of tests within the RDA. But some of them also become quite capable of earning their own living looking after and riding horses. For instance, the Fortune Centre is a purpose-built centre that runs training courses, not only in riding, grooming and tack cleaning but also in stable management and related office work, thereby offering real job prospects for a few of our riders.

Some of them end up by riding very competently, particularly those who suffered from the effects of the drug Thalidomide, who, once they learn to adapt and we learn what needs adapting, can ride very competitively. There is a girl I see from time to time called Philippa Verry, who lives just outside the Park at Windsor. She has no arms, but she rides all over the Park and gives many demonstrations using her feet to hold the reins – quite astonishing.

Apart from the riding itself, there is the added benefit for the riders of getting out and meeting different people. This is particularly true for those more severely disabled people who have to live in special accommodation, and who through the RDA can meet people other than their immediate carers. But everyone who takes part in RDA benefits from this meeting and mixing.

I keep trying to persuade people that 'horses' aren't just about grotty little children with pigtails and rich parents. There is so much more to be gained from contact with horses, and indeed from any animals. In my case I was able to ride well enough to compete at an international level, which gave me the added bonus that the sport took me to places I certainly wouldn't have gone to otherwise, and of meeting foreign people I wouldn't have otherwise met. Even competing at a national standard certainly takes you out of your little corner in a way that very few other things do, unless you go and work away from home.

Sport in its many forms is very good for that, and this is just as true for those with a handicap. Competition has become an important part of the RDA's therapy, enthusiastically supported by riders of all standards, including those who are too badly handicapped to take much part, but are encouraged by the achievements of those who can. Competition at an international level is a rather different problem. The variety of disabilities, the complexity of any rules and the enormous problem of providing enough suitable horses and ponies makes international competition more difficult than in any other sport. My own feeling is that the RDA should use sport as part of our therapy rather than as an end in itself, but there is obviously a balance to be struck.

I don't know how much I have contributed to the RDA, but I do know that, like the helpers, I have gained a great deal. I now have a far better knowledge and understanding of all types of disabilities and the everyday problems disabled people encounter in their lives. The riders, the helpers, the carers and the organisers have helped me to appreciate the potential of equestrian sport and not least to appreciate my own horses a bit more.

CHAPTER 4

The Three-day Event:

'The need for all-round horsemanship'

BEFORE I go any further, I should try to explain what a three-day event is. To do that, I have to go back to the high days of the cavalry, particularly on the continent of Europe and especially in France where the competition became known as *le militaire*. Its origins were a military exercise to prove that the horses were well trained (that is, to work well in the riding school); were brave enough to take a message anywhere (that is, across any country, jumping any type of obstacle, at the gallop); but were fit to turn out for duty the following day (that is, to negotiate a simple jumping track). It was designed to highlight the importance of horsemanship, of not abusing your horse, but of protecting it as a vital part of your regiment's fighting power and for your own survival. Like the exercise, the competition evolved as a three-day event, the dressage testing the school work on the first day, the endurance phase testing the boldness and stamina on the second day and the showjumping testing the overall fitness on the third day.

The endurance phase originally evolved in five sections. Phase A was a warming-up section, setting off at a brisk trot before reaching Phase B, the steeplechase. This was to test a horse's ability to jump fences at speed. I may say that the steeplechase courses on the continent do not look anything like the ones in the UK. Solid walls and wooden bases, big wide ditches and tall green hedges require rather more care and attention from the horses than our inviting brush fences. Phase C was a cooling-off and recovery phase, but covering more ground than Phase A. I believe that Phase C originally ran virtually straight into Phase D, with no compulsory ten-minute halt to sort yourself out, to get information on the course or to have the opportunity to get yourself even more frightened. Perhaps that was not a problem for cavalry officers. Phase D was always the critical phase and the one that is most often shown on television. It is the phase where all the jumps are, and where most could, and still does, go wrong. Your pacing was also critical, because there was another phase after D. Phase E was a gallop, on the flat, to finish the endurance day. Now you know where the term 'speed and endurance' comes from with reference to the second day.

Riding Purple Star at Windsor.

If this sounds a bit sketchy, it's because, by the time I started competing, the ten-minute halt had been introduced and Phase E had been dropped. This made life a great deal easier for the scorers and for idiots like myself who had not been able to understand the scoring when it was partly plus marks and partly minus marks. The present system of all penalty-point marking started just after I did my first three-day event.

It must be remembered that, to finish the competition, you had to turn up with a fit horse on the third day – well, fit enough to jump round a small show-jumping course. Veterinary inspections were not quite so rigorous as they are today, but then the pressures were probably not the same. So the horse had to be well schooled, bold and fast, and be able to jump carefully after a great deal of exercise.

I didn't know all this when I started. I barely knew what a one-day event was. I was introduced to the intricacies of the sport of horse trials at the end of my Pony Club career. This was the condensed form of the three-day event, with the dressage, showjumping and cross country all taking place on the same day and the cross country confined to Phase D. The level of dressage test, the height of the fences and the speed required to negotiate them without incurring any penalties all depended on the standard of the competition. From Pony Club to Olympic Games, the degree of difficulty was established and well known. Those limits are constantly reviewed and some have been modified and the dressage tests are changed from time to time.

My very first experience of this type of combined training occurred at Windsor one Easter holiday when my father and the Crown Equerry put together a one-day event in the Home Park for which, I believe, they did the judging as well. The other memorable thing about it was that everybody got a prize – and I've still got my alarm clock, even if it doesn't work any more.

I wasn't so much attracted to horse trials as led. My leader, if that's the right expression, was The Queen's Crown Equerry, Lieutenant Colonel Sir John Miller, who had himself competed successfully while serving in the Welsh Guards. His good mare, Stella, was shortlisted for the Helsinki Games, where she was eventually ridden by Bertie Hill. Stella retired to stud after several more years of carrying her owner over many country miles out hunting. It was her first two sons that were to play such a crucial role in my limited sporting ambitions.

Having, I hope, explained a bit about how a three-day event works, I ought to say a few words about the type of horse that might make a good three-day eventer and some of the characteristics which it needs to have. Stella's eldest son, for example, Blue Star by Night Watch, was a tall thoroughbred, but polite enough for an ignorant sixteen- or seventeen-year-old to manage. When I think of him now I can see that he really was the 'right type', the right stamp of animal that you might look for as a three-day event horse. He had good limbs, good conformation and plenty of bone and lots of quality. How do you define quality? Difficult. To me, horses have a 'look' of quality about their heads and necks and their overall outline. 'Balance and fineness creating an impression of strength' might be a way of describing what I think I mean by quality.

My grandmother's ex-hurdler, Colman, being converted into an event horse. He went to a family in Great Somerford who all rode him, and he's been a great success.

If anybody asks me today what I look for when trying to assess a potential three-day event horse, I am inclined to simplify the answer by replying, 'a Cheltenham Gold Cup horse with a streak of independence'; or 'a balanced equine athlete with a look of eagles'. When I'm looking at event horses or race-horses, and at how they move, I think they need to be what I call 'loose-limbed and athletic'. The walk is tremendously important. I was always told that you can improve a trot and a canter, but you can't improve a walk. If you've got the basics there, and the walk is free and loose, and the horse oversteps, which means that its back feet overstep the place where the front feet were, then there is a good chance that the animal will be reasonably athletic. There's a school of thought that holds that if the horse has a short canter stride, you'll be more often right when jumping. If you're coming to a fence on a horse with a wonderful galloping stride, you must make up your mind a lot further away as to whether your stride will bring you to the fence at the right place, whether to 'kick' or not to 'kick', whereas the horse that goes a bit more like a pony and takes shorter strides will help you to be right more often.

Some people will definitely not buy a long-striding horse for that very reason. Others believe that you want a horse that covers the ground because it takes so much less out of itself. Four miles across country is wearing, and logic says that if your legs go round very quickly it's even more wearing. But if you have something that moves easily across, say, ridge and furrow – which is not easy for any four-legged animal – the wear and tear will be less. Ridge and fur-row is a medieval form of agricultural land use where the crops were planted on the ridges and the water drained into the furrows, and whose marks are still visible on today's landscape.

Big horses can be more encouraging to sit on, because the fences don't look so big. But little horses can be so much quicker to respond and easier to handle in the big, more technical combinations that it's very much swings and round-abouts. It's what suits individuals. I don't think I minded very much either way.

Whatever my answer, whatever criteria I use, my 1971 European Champion, Doublet, fitted none of them. But he possessed the 'X factor' – he enjoyed what he was doing and was on your side. All the right physical attributes, speed and jumping ability can never overcome a lack of mental appli-cation, of individuality or of bravery. On the other hand, my 1976 Olympic partner, Goodwill, was nearly everybody's idea of the ideal type of event horse, a little bit heavy-topped for some, but with excellent conformation, strong, active paces and well-developed jumping muscles. He never had a day off for lameness all the time he was competing. He too possessed that very special 'X factor'.

So, apart from the physical attributes, there are psychological qualities which a good three-day eventer needs. I don't know if you can tell whether horses are intelligent. I suppose they can be intelligent in relation to other horses of similar age and experience; however, they do have to be essentially brave and completely genuine, so that, if you ask them to jump something, they don't question your authority, logic or indeed sanity, but will always attempt to do just what you ask of them. The dividing line between being genuine and just plain stupid – that is, not having the brains to think about the problems facing them – is very narrow. You can tell fairly early on whether horses are really genuine and whether they think about how they are going to respond to your demands. Of course, if you give them confusing or incorrect commands, you have to accept the consequences.

There's a fascinating old photograph of Doublet jumping at Eridge (the final trial before the European Championships at Burghley). It's taken from head on. His eyes and his ears and my eyes – which you can see between his ears – are all looking at the next fence. I know that's true because the next fence was a corner and not directly in front of the table we were jumping, and you had to go slightly off a straight line. You can see that he's looking at it while jumping the table.

Finally, any horse must enjoy what it is doing. Good event horses have to, because unless they actually enjoy testing themselves and using their talent and ability, I see no reason why they should co-operate at all. There is no way you can make horses do something they don't want to do. They are so much bigger and stronger than we are.

You can't frighten a horse into racing, because there are far too many options for it to avoid the issue. For the same reason I don't think you can frighten a horse into showjumping. Why should it clear the fences? It would learn very quickly, if it were that way inclined, that knocking down the fences or stopping would ensure it only jumped one round. If it were less clever, it probably wouldn't jump many clear rounds anyway. And I'm perfectly certain that you can't frighten a horse into going across country. You, as an individual, are so much the weaker. You might be able to frighten it occasionally during schooling at home, when you might be having problems getting it to jump a certain type of fence. But that won't help you in the long run. It's a sort of battle initially. If the horse is testing you, then it's necessary to win the battle. If it goes on fighting battles, then that's a different problem.

Blue Star, older brother of Purple Star, both bred by Lieutenant Colonel Sir John Miller.

You can certainly frighten a horse into doing some things like loading into a horse box or going through water, but the effect is usually only short-term. One of the things people fail to understand about horses is that a degree of mutual trust has to be established between rider and horse before you can get anywhere, never mind to the highest level of competition. There are people around nowadays who think that horse-sports are cruel, but that presumes that you have an unwilling partner. A horse going across country on its own is really a freak, because it is a gregarious, herd animal. So to be able to detach itself from the herd, in its mind, and to be committed entirely for itself across country, is definitely out of character with all its natural instincts.

I would have been incredibly lucky if my first competition horse, Blue Star, had fulfilled all the criteria of a good three-day eventer. Unfortunately for us, Blue Star was diagnosed chronically unsound, probably as a result of some trouble in his back, which made him go unlevel on one circle – one hind leg was not working the same as the other – and he was therefore technically lame for the purposes of dressage. It was a great shame, because I had some lovely rides on him round hunter-trial courses and he had lots of spare ability that would have made it possible for him to go on into adult competition.

It was then that Stella's second foal, Purple Star by Flush Royal, came on the scene and I started to learn what dressage was supposed to be. Purple was not the ideal type of event horse. He wasn't very big and was short in front, which meant that, when you were sitting in the saddle, his ears were very close to your face. If he so much as sneezed, you were very likely to overtake him altogether. At the time I didn't really notice, but I did learn to hang on very tight.

Purple was good enough to interest me in the format of horse trials. He could perform a very nice dressage test, especially when ridden by Alison Oliver. He jumped carefully enough so that even I couldn't stop him jumping a clear round. But he was always an entertaining ride across country, prone to sudden changes of direction at the most awkward moments. Our very first Pony Club event was nearly successful, but for a disagreement about which side of a tree we were going to jump. He won and I hit the tree, split my knuckles and ended up under his tummy. Now why do you think I went on eventing?

The decision to pursue eventing more seriously wasn't taken until I left school, but it was a deliberate one in the sense that a career didn't seem to be an option and

Here I am riding Purple Star at Windsor Horse Trials in April 1968 watched by my father and my brother, Andrew.

Purple Star in a Pony Club One-day Event at Cowdray - the one I would have won if I hadn't fallen off.
I hit the tree.

I wanted to see if I could do something well. So I looked to sport, and to riding because that was the sport I knew best or had at least been practising for longest. Having decided on riding, I was not at all sure on what branch of equestrian activity I should concentrate.

Polo seemed the most likely to me, because I had grown up watching my father play the game and had spent many hours helping to look after his ponies. I had also attempted to hit the ball with a polo stick while riding a pony. That was only partially successful and there was not a lot of encouragement to take up what was then an almost exclusively male sport, although Mark's aunt, Flavia Phillips, told me there were more women playing polo before the Second World War.

This was where Sir John Miller and Alison Oliver came in, because between being lent the former's horse and the pair of us being sent to the latter's stables at Warfield, the decision seemed to become much more obvious. I think I already realised that showjumping would be too much of a full-time commitment, I still hadn't seen the point of dressage and the idea of going racing in any shape or form never crossed my mind. I was also attracted by the need for all-round horsemanship and the added challenge of getting a horse to be competent in three different skills.

But I think that my overriding reason for deciding to compete more professionally – with a small 'p' – was the need to test myself on obviously equal terms against other competitors. The fact that the type of competition I chose was equestrian was because I had more experience with riding horses than with any other sport. If I had spent more time sailing, playing tennis or cycling, then perhaps not only my sporting career but also many other aspects of my life would have been different.

*Lieutenant Colonel Sir John Miller's horse Purple Star in
the Cowdray One-day Event.*

CHAPTER 5

~

Competing Internationally:

'Then there was Doublet'

I had never had any ambition to ride at Badminton and therefore it was not something that Alison and I discussed until she felt it was a realistic aim. I started going to Alison's in 1968, but it wasn't until late 1970 that either of us really thought that I or my horse would be capable of tackling what was, and still is, the premier three-day event in the world. Looking back, three years was a very short time in which to learn the intricacies of such a competition; but then, ignorance has its advantages.

My route to my first Badminton must have been remarkably trouble-free, judging by most of my subsequent efforts. It started with Purple Star, who was never considered as a three-day event horse, but was a very good school-master. Not long afterwards, another horse appeared on the scene called Royal Ocean, a rather well-bred horse by Guersant (found by Sir John Miller from Sir John Galvin in Ireland). He had the class and the potential to make the grade as an eventer and we even won a novice horse trial. But he had a problem. He was a chronic head-shaker, which meant that his head was never still when you were trying to do dressage, and the judges didn't like that. We spent some time trying to identify the reason for his nodding but we couldn't find anything treatable. This problem introduced me to 'The Black Box', best described as a form of complementary medicine. To achieve a diagnosis, all you have to do is send a bit of hair, mane or tail from the affected animal and wait. If that sounds a rather inadequate explanation, it's the best I can do, because I have no idea how it works. The Black Box's answer to Royal Ocean's twitching was that he had a piece of broken bone at the top

High Jinks and Doublet (left) at Windsor. Doublet, bred by The Queen, was then an unbroken two-year-old. No one could guess what a success he was going to be.

Royal Ocean at Wembley Horse of the Year Show for the Spillers combined training final.

Osberton Horse Trials – walking the course!

of his head. The Box was right but unfortunately the injury was inoperable and therefore meant his early retirement from eventing.

Then there was Doublet. The idea of sending Doublet to Alison was another of John Miller's ideas, because Doublet had grown too big for polo. He was pretty well bred in that he was by Doubtless II, an Argentinian-bred thorough-bred who came to Britain to race. He was apparently one of those extraordinary horses that would run like an arthritic goat one week and break the course record the next. He was a black horse and normally he threw black animals, yet Doublet was pure chestnut. The dam was an Argentine polo pony mare called Sureté that my father played for many years. She was a hard chestnut colour, hadn't a white hair on her and was only 14.2hh. There was no telling how much thoroughbred blood she had in her, but Argentinian ponies are famously tough and durable.

Doublet was not the easiest of young horses, so Alison rode him to begin with, until the question of Royal Ocean's future was decided. Summer 1969 saw Doublet and me beginning to forge a reasonable partnership at a variety of competitions, being placed in Foxhunters (showjumping), and winning our first horse trial at Osberton at our first attempt. Now that really surprised everyone, not least myself, although I think I realised at the time I was having a very good ride. Our subsequent competitions also went well even if we didn't actually win them. We ended our first season with a sixth place at the Novice Championships at Chatsworth.

Chatsworth was the premier one-day event in the country, in one of the most lovely settings. We, the eventers, were very fortunate to be allowed to use the Park of Chatsworth House for our competition, thanks to the generosity of the Duke and Duchess of Devonshire. They were keen racehorse owners and the Duchess was an expert breeder of Shetland ponies and Haflingers, and their support for horse trials was very important and much appreciated by the competitors.

They were also extremely generous in their hospitality to me and I much

This was Doublet's and my first trial and our first win –
we were competing at Osberton.

'Walking the course' at the Ice Pond at Chatsworth before the Midland Bank Novices Championships in 1969.

enjoyed being able to stay in their historic house that had such a friendly atmosphere. There are many lovely things in the house but I have to admit that it is the beds I remember most fondly. I didn't always sleep in the same room, but the beds were big and very comfortable and a good night's sleep was never a problem at Chatsworth.

Jumping the course at Chatsworth well was an important marker for the future. Because of its level of difficulty and the number of spectators, Alison always considered Chatsworth a good indicator of how a horse and rider might react to the crowds and pressure of Badminton. So we ended 1969 on an encouraging note.

In the spring of 1970 I accompanied my parents on their tour to South-east Asia, which included Thailand, Singapore, Brunei, Sabah and Malaysia. In doing

Here we are in action at the Ice Pond at Chatsworth.

that I missed the start of the spring horse trials season, but Alison had arranged for Richard Walker to ride Doublet in one or two competitions to help prepare him for the Tidworth Three-day Event in May. Unfortunately, that good idea backfired when Alison decided that Doublet had sustained the sort of injury which needed a bit of time to heal properly. He would therefore not be going to the Tidworth Three-day Event which had been planned as the next important step. This was the news that greeted me on my return and I've no doubt that Purple Star was no more pleased than I was to hear it, for he was then 'volunteered' to take Doublet's place at Tidworth.

To add to the complications my trainer was heavily pregnant, expecting her first child at about the time of the three-day event. This meant that Purple and I went to a great friend of Alison's, Lars Sederholm, who lived at Waterstock, just east of Oxford. It was very good experience for me to work with somebody else, but someone whose outlook was very similar to Alison's. Purple and I made it to Tidworth and even managed to get round the cross-country course with two stops, but it was the showjumping that caused the major headache – to me anyway. Purple decided that the (in and out) combination was frightening, stopped very abruptly and shot me over his head.

Needless to say, this incident was recorded by the press, and although the photos that appeared were at least factual, the words were not. It was nothing new and something I had to learn to live with, however inaccurate, annoying or downright insulting it might be. Media interest, at that stage in my career, was very much at a novelty level where every hiccup was recorded. I certainly hadn't reached a standard that warranted any attention from the serious sports reporters who might have understood more about the competitions. Even when I did, I was referred to for years as a showjumper.

Never mind the result of Tidworth, the object of the exercise was to get me round a three-day event: to discover about the roads and tracks and steeplechase and to learn the difference of riding a cross-country course nearly twice as long as any one-day event course. The other bit of good news was that Alison's baby did not arrive in the middle of the cross country, which it might well have done, because she was being given a mobile grandstand view, courtesy of Lady Hugh Russell's Mini Moke. This vehicle was a well-known sight around the horse trials, crossing the country every bit as well as most of the horses, though Lady Hugh never quite managed to get it to jump the fences; the passengers were inclined to believe that the Mini Moke conveyed the sensation of jumping all too well and for most of the time! Lady Hugh used this form of transport because she was paralysed as the result of a riding accident out hunting. She had competed as an individual in the 1966 World Championships at Burghley on Turnstone and her husband remained an active competitor for many years, riding their home-bred horses who were all named after water birds. Lord and Lady Hugh Russell were tremendous benefactors of eventing as riders, owners and organisers and the sport owes them a great deal.

The Tidworth trials usually marked the end of the spring season as there were then no one-day events in the UK during June and July. That was over twenty years ago; the growth of the sport has meant that there are now competitions being held throughout the summer months. In 1970 I spent those months getting Doublet fit again for the autumn season and then going to events which would continue his and my education. We ended the season with Alison feeling that we had done well enough to justify planning on going to Badminton in 1971.

Doublet had his holiday at Windsor from October to the end of December and came in to start work on 1 January 1971. Starting work meant six weeks walking on the roads – very boring but considered essential after a horse had been out of regular exercise for any length of time. I often asked about the origin of this tradition, but apart from the historical observations of generations of horse copers that it toned up the muscles and strengthened the tendons, nobody knew whence it had sprung. It was also important that the walking was done on a firm, level surface.

It is only quite recently that I came across a possible scientific reason for this habit. Wearing my Chancellor of the University of London mortar board (figuratively speaking) I visited one of the colleges, Queen Mary College. They had arranged a small exhibition of their work, one aspect of which was on the long-term problems of artificial hip replacements. It had been noticed that some years after the operation there were signs of wear in the hip joint. Research led them to conclude that for bone to remain healthy and growing it needed to be load-bearing – supporting weight – but the artificial hip joint in those days was made of a material that was heavier than the surrounding bone and, because of the imbalance in load-bearing, the bone around it was dying. The College designed a composite material that is the same weight and density as bone and since then there have been many fewer problems, making it unnecessary for many people to undergo a second hip replacement operation.

I then rather confused the issue by asking the scientists if they thought there could be any connection between their discovery and the practice of road work that was supposed to be so good for horses' legs. I knew that the old stud grooms' answers to 'splints' (bony growths that were usually sore at an area of weakness as a result of overwork) was to give the horses more road work, which seemed to help. The indication would seem to be that here again was a problem related to load-bearing and density and that it was the concussion from the road work that affected the bone structure and the level surface that was important for the ligaments and tendons.

Whatever the real reason, walking on the roads went on for six weeks, and in January that was not most people's idea of a 'fun' hack. Towards the end of that period you could start some dressage schooling and then build up the trot work by going out for longer and longer hacks. By then you had added some jumping exercises – a series of low fences at related distances (convenient to the horse) to help get the horse supple and responsive. Finally you started the cantering. The distance and speed at which you cantered totally depended on the type of ground you had available. At Warfield it was one of Mrs Gold's big flat fields or the even flatter area around the polo grounds at Smith's Lawn in Windsor Great Park. That meant twice or three times a week cantering very slowly for five minutes, building up gradually to twenty minutes and only letting the horse go faster right at the end.

It was a long and tiring process that seemed to work for both horse and rider, but it did mean a lot of wear on the legs, especially the horse's. When we moved to the hills in Gloucestershire with steep grass banks and virtually no flat land, we found we were getting the horses three-quarters fit by trotting them up the banks and needed only a few short sharp canters up the valley to get them 100 per cent fit. This had the advantage of putting less strain on the tendons but the disadvantage of not giving you the opportunity to teach your horse to settle in a regular rhythm.

The horse-trial season began in the middle of March; slightly depending on when Easter was, which affected the date of Badminton – and the start of the season took its cue from Badminton. Alison selected the horse trials with the most imposing and well-built courses, not in any hope of winning them, but in order to ensure that we were up to standard and, if all went well, to build up our confidence in each other. I think they included Crookham, which was always the first horse trial, Liphook and Rushall. Suffice to say that I went to Badminton feeling that it was the next logical stop – that was before I walked the course.

At a three-day event you have more time. This is good news and bad news. You have time to walk the course a minimum of three times, but you have three whole days to think about it. The advice I was given was to walk the course and look at all the options, but to remain conscious of which approach appeared the most inviting when you saw a fence for the first time. The second walk-round was to decide on which option to go for at the combination fences and, having decided that, to select the line you would ride between the fences, in order that you could arrive in the right place to jump each one even if you could not see it until the last moment. It was also to plan to go the shortest way.

There are two points worth mentioning here. One is that the problems of combination fences are seldom their size or complexity, but the decision-making process of choosing which bit you are going to jump and then sticking with that choice. The other point is that, when you walk the course, there may be other people walking as well, but there are no spectators. I have to say that it was not until after I had ridden the course that I appreciated how different everything then looks. All the landmarks I had selected to help me find my line were no longer visible because of the crowd. This was particularly unnerving when I was relying on these landmarks to get the right line into a fence I wanted to jump on an angle, like a corner. I also discovered that the course is roped with string in order to provide good viewing for the spectators and not necessarily to keep the spectators away from the fences. This phenomenon doesn't manifest itself until the crowds appear and the effect is not always easy to foresee at the course-walking stage.

The first point didn't worry me then, because I relied on Alison to make up my mind for me. It has become more of a problem since. The other point was learned the hard way.

The first thing that hits you when you arrive at the stables at Badminton is the atmosphere. It is a tangible presence of expectation, of hopes and fears. If your nerves were under control when you arrived, it was very difficult not to be swept along in the unspoken anticipation and excitement. That was where my 'public' training helped me: keeping my outward self calm also kept my inner self under better control. It doesn't stop me feeling nervous, but it helps to hide it from my relations and the horse.

Doublet lived in the stables and I lived in the front of the big house with a magnificent view down Worcester Avenue and of the Lake. The advantage of staying there was that everything was very convenient; the disadvantage was that you were a bit isolated from the other competitors and therefore didn't get to know them. At this stage in my career, I hardly knew any of the other riders except by their riding reputations. However, it was a lovely place to be and the Duke and Duchess of Beaufort and their staff were very understanding about my erratic timetable. They were even more understanding about the disruption, the crowds, the mess and all the other inconveniences of running the most important three-day event in the world. Master (as he was known)

In the stable yard at Badminton looking after Persian Holiday after the cross country.

Competitors' briefing before Badminton.

never wavered in his support and the many successes that Britain has had in international three-day events are – in no small measure – thanks to his generosity.

The first place to pay attention is at the competitors' briefing, where you are given all the information you require – you hope. This includes maps and meal tickets, *the* most important components of a happy eventer's kit. After the briefing there is a conducted tour of the roads and tracks on wheels (that was like a mass advertisement for Land Rover), and of the steeplechase and cross country on foot. The steeplechase is usually fairly straightforward and needs only one walkround. The cross-country course, in Badminton's case, is 4–4½ miles long with thirty-two or thirty-four fences, some being combinations. There is a great deal to look at and learn.

My first impression of the course? I think I must have been in shock or making remarkable use of my public training, because I don't remember any dramatic reaction, only that Alison thought that Doublet and I were ready for this challenge and therefore it must be possible. Funnily enough, I can't remember every fence on the course, but it went left-handed with one of Colonel Frank Weldon's notorious Coffin fences as the third fence. There was no alternative to jumping the Coffin straight through, rail, ditch, rail, which sounds pretty simple but it doesn't convey the steepness or distance between the rails and the ditch, and it was usually the most influential fence on the course. There were no Luckington Lane fences, but there was a Vicarage Vee – a rail at right angles to a big ditch which could be jumped over the angle or by tackling the ditch and then the rail as two separate fences.

Course walking, Badminton, 1971. Alison trying to persuade me the Normandy Bank would be no problem!

The Lake fences were relatively straightforward by modern standards, but the price of a mistake was exactly the same: you got wet. The fence after the water was the Normandy Bank, a new fence that year (I think) that owed its inspiration to the European Championships at Haras du Pin in Normandy. The French home-grown version caused considerable dismay before it was jumped, and no little grief in the attempt, but it was a 'natural' fence: the fields in that part of Normandy were divided by low flat-topped banks with ditches on both sides and a small set of rails on one edge. The Badminton version was an 'island' fence; that is, it stood on its own as an isolated artificial bank which, no doubt, made it more impressive to look at.

Colonel Frank Weldon's briefing before Badminton.

That was followed by the Ski Jump, so called, I imagine, because the ground rose to the take-off point, thereby hiding the fact that there was no ground immediately available to land on; it was otherwise known as a 'drop' fence. As with water fences, this was when your horse really needed to trust your judgement. The Hanging Log where the Keeper's Rails now are was hung diagonally across an unmade-up ditch. It was not an attractive sight and demanded a bold

Negotiating the Normandy Bank, Badminton, 1971.

jump. The Quarry fences were relatively uncomplicated by today's standards, but still required an honest horse and a confident rider. The final combination round Huntsman's Close put a premium on steering and the last couple of fences really tested your own and your horse's fitness and your concentration: they were solid, and the final Whitbread Bar was very upright.

In between walking the course, I had to try to concentrate on the dressage phase, the importance of which seemed to have receded, if not vanished alto-

gether, as I pondered the problems of the endurance day. In my case, Doublet's dressage was good enough and consistent enough for me not to have to spend too much time 'working him in'. There tends to be a difference between the way horses behave at a competition site and the way they behave at home. Most of them react to the atmosphere by getting excited and therefore inattentive, to which the only answer is to spend as long as it takes trying to persuade them that all those tents, people, cars, etc., are no more exciting than an empty field at home. I was lucky: Doublet was one of those all-too-rare horses who went better at a competition than he ever did at home.

On the day of our dressage, which

Half-pass. Warming up before dressage on Doublet at Badminton 1971.

was on the first day of the competition, it was grey and miserable and in the practice arena Doublet was doing his famous impression of an arthritic goat (being particularly uninspiring), largely because there was nobody watching him. Fortunately, when we got into the main arena and he saw the crowd, he pulled himself together and I really had very little to do. Remarkably he transformed himself from a very ordinary equine into a top-level performer and finished the day in a creditable second place.

Keeper's Rails, Badminton, 1971.

While the second day of dressage was being completed, I walked the course for the third and final time, walking the line between the fences as well as taking in the precise place at the fences that I wanted to jump. The 'going' was firm because of a fairly dry spring. But this was Britain where we don't have a climate, we just have weather, especially in April. During the night it rained. This had the effect of leaving very large puddles in some rather awkward places, a phenomenon which, along with the appearance of the spectators, made the course look very different on the morning of the cross-country day.

Doublet jumping the Ski Jump at Badminton in 1971. We finished fifth.

My memories of my first ride round Badminton are surprisingly hazy, but perhaps that is the result of the level of concentration required to attempt to follow so many instructions. I do still remember Alison telling me what to do if I had a fall, and, if I had another one, to retire. Fortunately, I didn't have to act on either of those instructions and I enjoyed a remarkably trouble-free ride. I managed to get my timings

Steeplechase, Badminton, 1971.

right on the roads and tracks but not quite on the steeplechase. In the ten-minute halt, Doublet seemed in good form considering it was his first three-day event. More important, he was coping well with the crowds. It was crucial that he wasn't distracted by them, so that we could maintain our concentration.

He proved that he could rise to the occasion across country as well as in the dressage. Apart from dropping his hind legs in the Vicarage Ditch (where I went the long way) and suffering a moment's doubt at the Elephant Trap back into the Park over the ha-ha, he never gave me any real worries. He made the Coffin and the Lake fences seem quite easy and he jumped the Normandy Bank much better than I had dared hope. It had certainly been one of the fences that had worried me, because Doublet was not a great one for attacking his fences and you could not afford to 'fiddle' it – to go slowly and let the horse pick his way. It was on my approach that I became aware that Colonel Weldon's 'stringing' of the course and the size of the crowds had prevented me from seeing the fence when I expected to. Fortunately, it didn't seem to matter; in fact, it may have been a help!

The Irish horses had their own special problem because the only safe way to jump an Irish Bank is to trot and pop up on to it and then steady yourself on the top, before deciding at what point on the far slope to jump off. Unfortunately, one horse which tried that at Badminton ended upside-down in the ditch on the landing side, having tripped over the – to him – unexpected set of rails on the top. I happened to see that before I started, which was not very encouraging, except that it enabled Alison to point out that that was what would happen to Doublet if I didn't kick hard enough.

The fall also caused a delay on the course – while the horse was extricated from the ditch – which necessitated the other horses on the course being stopped. One of those stopped was a certain Lieutenant Mark Phillips riding Great Ovation. He was stopped for some time and there is no telling how much help that breathing space was, because they completed the course in a fast enough time to finish in the lead.

After negotiating the Bank, the rest seemed to fly by: the Ski Jump was no problem; Doublet jumped the Hanging Log so boldy I wondered if I'd jumped the right fence, and so on to the end where he finished feeling

My first time at Badminton. Family group with the Duke and Duchess of Beaufort after the cross country.

strong and I finished feeling relieved with not receiving any jumping penalties. However, we did incur several time penalties (for taking longer than the time allowed) and we finished the day in fourth place, which I thought was astonishingly good.

Showjumping at Badminton, 1971. A picture of health and enthusiasm after the cross country.

It always takes a little while for the sense of satisfaction to permeate the relief. There is still the concern that your horse may have done itself some damage and will not be sound enough to pass the vet's inspection on the final morning. Doublet was certainly a bit stiff from his exertions, but it was nothing that a little gentle exercise would not ease and he trotted up well. This was good news for me because I was not very confident about our showjumping. Doublet always jumped with a flat back, so showjumping was never our strong point. Unlike my ideal event horse, Doublet was always stiff through his back and not very supple. This made it difficult for him to perform the correct parabola over a fence which, in turn, made it more difficult to jump a fence without knocking it down.

There was another small problem in the shape of an open water jump. Neither of us had ever encountered water in a showjumping course. This was not really the time or the place to learn – in front of a large crowd – and we

Both 'on course' at the fence before the water. Showjumping at Badminton, 1971.

learned the hard way. In fact, Doublet did jump very well, until he found that unexpected obstacle. When he saw the water, he was confused. I think he assumed he ought to jump into it and tried to slow down. I kept kicking, but it was too late and he ended up by taking off awkwardly and landed on all fours in the middle of the water jump. That was our only penalty, but it cost us 10 points and dropped us to a final fifth place, behind Lieutenant Mark Phillips riding Great Ovation,

Open Water, Badminton, 1971...getting it wrong. *Open Water, Burghley, 1971...getting it right.*

Mary Gordon-Watson riding her current World and European Champion Cornishman V, Debbie West riding Baccarat and Richard Walker riding Upper Strata.

For me, to finish at all would have been satisfactory. To finish in the top twelve would have been a real achievement, but to finish as high as fifth was beyond all our wildest dreams. It was only my second three-day event and Doublet's first. The Warfield contingent returned to base more than satisfied.

Badminton Three-day Event has always been a goal in itself and some people spend years trying to get there or trying to get round it. I had already been extremely lucky in reaching that goal in just three years. What would happen next?

What happened next was that Doublet was put on the 'long list' for selection for the European Championships to be held at Burghley in Lincolnshire, along with the combinations that had finished in the top twelve at Badminton. The list was made up in April, but the Championships were not until September, so there was much that could be improved and much that could go wrong.

Something did go wrong, but on this occasion it wasn't the horse that had a fitness problem; it was me. About the middle of July we had been promoted to the 'short list', which meant that as long as Doublet remained sound we would go to Burghley. The 'short list' numbered twelve because Britain was the host nation, otherwise it would have been just the six from whom the team of four would be chosen with the other two competing as individuals. Also on the 'short

The Owner and Breeder congratulating her home-bred partnership after Badminton, 1971!

list' were: Mary Gordon-Watson and Cornishman V; Debbie West and Baccarat; Mark and Great Ovation; Richard Meade and The Poacher, who had won Badminton in 1970 and gone on to be second to Cornishman in the World Championships at Punchestown. The Poacher had also been in the Gold Medal-winning team in the 1969 European Championships at Haras du Pin, ridden by Staff-Sergeant Ben Jones. Tom Durston-Smith and Henry The Navigator had been eighth at Badminton and had also completed the World Championships at Punchestown; Michael Tucker and Farmer Giles were sixth at Badminton; Angela Sowden (soon to be Mrs Michael Tucker) and Mooncoin were seventh; Rosalyn Prout and Farewell were eleventh and Michael Bullen and Wayfarer completed the list.

About the same time I woke up one morning feeling as ill as I have ever felt, sort of grey and disinterested. I ended up in hospital having various revolting bits of me removed, after which I improved rapidly, but could I get fit enough quickly enough to do the horse and the team justice by the first week of September?

The answer was that I wouldn't know if I didn't try, so I set about trying. The first stop was so-called convalescing in Scotland, which involved some graduated hill walking and that was a lot less painful than getting out of bed or laughing. When I returned south, I was treated by Sir Charles Strong and his Faradic machine. Sir Charles had begun his career as a medical orderly in the Royal Navy and through observation and experience had turned himself into one of the finest sports injury specialists for both humans and horses. I already knew him because he had served in the Navy with my great-uncle, Lord Mountbatten, who had encouraged him to continue his work and while he was at it could he treat his polo ponies too? This he did and I would often see him in the stables working with the portable Faradic machine which he had designed and developed himself, but I would also meet him when he was treating my father for the various strains and bruises that were the inevitable consequence of playing polo.

Faradism is the use of an electric impulse to stimulate the muscles. It works both as a tool to help diagnose the seat of damage where you cannot see it and to work the muscles around an injury. When there is physical damage and pain, there is lack of use and compensation which can lead to some muscles withering. Faradism works those groups of muscles around the affected area without any effort from the patient and the impulse is varied in strength and frequency up to the threshold of pain. If I have remembered nothing else, I have never forgotten Sir Charles' great rule, 'Exercise within the threshold of pain', because pain indicated damage and if it hurt, you were doing more damage.

Sir Charles' advice was not to ride for the moment but to concentrate on general fitness and my stomach muscles in particular, so I didn't start riding until about four days before the final trial for the 'short list' horses at Eridge. As Doublet had been brought on by Alison, the final trial was more critical for me than it was for him. As it turned out, although we made a silly mistake at a ditch-bank-rail combination in the wood and I fell rather slowly over his head, Doublet went very well and the selectors forgave my sloppy fall to include us among the twelve Britons allowed to compete at Burghley.

Arriving at Burghley, with all the tents and flags and foreign riders, you immediately feel an atmosphere of something special. For reasons that were never entirely clear to me, Doublet was not stabled with the rest of the team in the tented stables, but in the huge stable block at the back of the big house, where I was also billeted at the top of one of those corner turrets overlooking the Park. I didn't know my hosts, the Marquis and Marchioness of Exeter, which was slightly daunting for me, but not much better for them. I felt somewhat cut off from the other competitors, but then I did spend most of the day around the main stable area, the main arena and the course itself, and there were a number of social events to which all the riders went and which were part of the atmosphere of the three-day event.

The Russians had a team at Burghley who spoke no English when their team manager was around, but spoke remarkably good English when he was not around. They also drank whisky like water with no discernible side effects like those suffered by members of any other team who attempted to keep up with their level of intake. Then they would produce their vodka, saying they were

With Alison Oliver and Lars Sederholm at Burghley, 1971.

now going to have a real drink. How any of them got to the start of the competition was a mystery, never mind complete three days.

The main arena at Burghley is more open than the one at Badminton, largely because there are no trees in it and the dressage arena seems rather isolated out in the middle. I remember thinking that remoteness might be an advantage in that there would be less to distract the horses' attention, though it depends on what sort of horse you are riding. Doublet seemed to need atmosphere to do his best work, so he might have missed the intensity of atmosphere that the arena at Badminton created. As it was, he once again rose to the occasion, and went one better by going into the cross-country day in the lead. Suffice to say that I have never experienced a better test, although I may have ridden better.

To go into the endurance phase leading the field is a nice but not a comfortable experience and there was still a theory that combinations who did well in dressage were bound to make a nonsense somewhere on the cross-country course, so the possibility of victory had not occurred to me. Doublet's experience at Badminton had given him confidence and from the moment I started he seemed more positive. The steeplechase course went round the outside of the golf course and rode very fast, which meant that even I managed to complete it in the time allowed. Doublet had a very economical trot which made the roads and tracks section much easier to judge; he seemed to trot at almost exactly four minutes per kilometre, which was the time you allowed in order to calculate your progress.

The cross-country course was not as intimidating as that at Badminton, but it was big and had plenty of worries for me. The Leaf Pit made the Ski Jump look like a hop, but it had no fence at the top and the horses could see only too well how far down they had to go. Doublet never hesitated and, as it was the third fence, it did wonders for my confidence. There were two water crossings and, at the first Trout Hatchery, he jumped boldly over the log into the water making rather a splash which may have unsighted him for the jump out, up a bank. Whatever caused it, he tripped up, landing on his knees and his nose. At no time did I feel we were in danger of parting company and it certainly looked more dramatic than it felt. Doublet picked himself up and galloped on even more quickly, as if he were annoyed with himself.

Quite a lot of the course at Burghley is over 'ridge and furrow', which makes it difficult for the long-striding horses to gallop comfortably, something I didn't discover until taking Goodwill there. Doublet had no such problems, having a relatively short stride, and we made rapid progress, back to the second Trout Hatchery fence which was just below the first. This one involved jumping a set of rails into the water, but with no fence coming out we managed that without trouble.

About the second last fence was a combination which could either be jumped as a corner to a single rail, a single rail to a corner or as three single rails all on the angle. Because Doublet was very honest, I didn't mind jumping

Going in...

Blundering out...

Recovery...

The Trout Hatchery riding Doublet at Burghley in 1971.

corners, and the quickest way was to jump the corner to the single rail. I liked to jump the corner first because that was the difficult bit, and if you weren't foot perfect, you had only a single rail to cope with afterwards. Doublet was foot perfect and came home with the second fastest time of the day with 18.8 time penalties. That surprised everybody!

It was a hot day and the Warfield team went into action to help Doublet recover from his exertions. The 'team' seemed to grow throughout the three days, manning the ten-minute-halt box, the finish of the steeplechase, manning buckets, sponges and scrapers and spare tack and acting as extra horse holders.

It is worth highlighting at this stage that no one can compete in horse trials single-handed, but it is only since then that I have learnt how many jobs there are for volunteers, because I have done most of them. Even at that time, though, I was already very much aware of how many people I relied on to be able to compete in a three-day event.

I spent most of the rest of the day waiting to be overtaken, but apparently I had gone fast enough to make that pretty unlikely. Stuart Stevens on Classic Chips rode the fastest round with only 4.4 penalties to pull himself up from a lowly dressage score to lie in third place, with Debbie West riding Baccarat lying second. Now was the time to start worrying about how Doublet was feeling, and the answer was: sore. I say that with hindsight because I was not told at the time

'Well done, thank you, let's get on with it.'

Struggling to get up...

how worried Alison and the vet, Peter Scott Dunn, were about the bruising that Doublet had inflicted on himself by treading on his own front leg with his hind hoof when recovering from his trip out of the water. What was doubly unfortunate, as it turned out, was that Doublet was not wearing bandages which might have protected him from the effect of the blow. This was a deliberate decision on the basis that bandages could slip and cause their own problems and that legs were better left with just a coating of grease to help deflect blows.

Alison must have had a long sleepless night but, thanks to her decision not to tell me, I slept very well and trotted him up with great confidence at the final vet's inspection, and I must say that he never gave me any indication that he was feeling any soreness from his leg. This was important for my attitude to the showjumping.

Fortunately, the order of jumping was programme order and not reverse order of merit, which meant I didn't have to wait around to see what everybody else did. It shouldn't have made any difference because I did have two fences in hand (the equivalent of 20 penalties) which increased to three after both Baccarat and Classic Chips had one fence down each. I knew, after our experience at Badminton, that I needed to be more positive in my approach, especially to the earlier fences, because Doublet took a little time to warm up too. In spite of my resolution, the way we jumped the first three fences did not encourage our

Burghley Champions, 1971.

supporters, but from my point of view I felt that Doublet was being careful if not fluent. The further we went, the better we went, and we finished galloping because I was not taking any risks with the open water jump so adopted the simple approach of 'If in doubt, kick on!' That worked, but then I couldn't slow down to jump the last fence, so I had to jump it faster than my trainer would have liked. By that point, however, it didn't matter if I knocked it down.

The noise from the crowd was an extraordinary experience and made Doublet take off round the arena as if he knew what he had achieved. Did *I* know what we had achieved? The honest answer is probably not, although I was enormously relieved not to have disappointed my parents who had taken the trouble to be there. My father didn't have much choice, because he was then President of the International Equestrian Federation, but it couldn't have been much fun for them, especially if there had been an objection to the winner! I was also relieved for and inadequately grateful to Alison and the 'team' from Warfield, whose contribution was crucial to our success.

To receive the prize from my mother and the medal from my father on a horse bred by my mother was very special, but I don't think I realised *how* special until I understood more about the difficulties of breeding an event horse and getting it prepared and chosen to run in an international competition, never mind winning it. I also became aware of how long-suffering the parents of event riders have to be to cope with the ups and downs of their offspring's fortunes.

After the prize giving there was a press conference where there were a few questions that could be answered but many more that could not, including speculation about competing at Munich in the 1972 Olympics. I had started eventing only three years before with no clear ambitions and suddenly there I was – European Champion. I had been very lucky, but would our luck last? I had always felt that it was unrealistic to have too specific an ambition with horses because of all the things that could go wrong with them. Doublet could quite easily have made himself lame coming out of the water and I wouldn't have won anything.

Holding the Raleigh Trophy presented by The Queen and the FEI medal presented by Prince Philip at Burghley in 1971.

CHAPTER 6

Columbus, Goodwill and Kiev:

'After the ups, the downs'

THE year 1972 began in the same way as 1971 with Doublet starting his normal six weeks' walking on road exercise after his holiday. Following Burghley it was decided to apply a 'blister' to his front legs to encourage the healing process of the bruising he had suffered. Alison proceeded with his fitness work to get him ready for Badminton, but it became apparent that the area of damage was still giving cause for concern. Alison was of the opinion that three-day events were not the place to find out if your horse was going to stay sound, so we set about discovering in another way if Doublet's injury from Burghley was going to stand up to the speed and endurance of this type of competition. We took him to Kingsclere to work on Ian Balding's gallops, where the Derby winner Mill Reef was trained. They are lovely gallops and Doublet did work pretty hard. The next morning the answer was obvious, unavoidable and crushingly disappointing. The way that Doublet stood in his box and the expression on his face showed that he too knew that all was not well.

So that ended any possibility of going to the Munich Olympic Games but, with her usual positive thinking, Alison was looking round for an alternative. This appeared in the angular grey form of Columbus, another home-bred horse by Colonist II out of Trim Ann. Colonist II was owned by Sir Winston Churchill and Trim Ann was owned by Princess Alexandra, who, I believe, hunted her before Trim Ann came to Windsor to be one of the more exciting hacks. I have an image of riding in the forested part of the Park with long grass rides, struggling to control whichever animal I was riding as Trim Ann quietly gathered speed and disappeared into the distance. She must have been an exhilarating hunter!

Trim Ann was not what you would describe as a good-looking mare, but she was tough and fast. Columbus was more like his dam, tall, narrow and strong, but took after his sire in being rather too enthusiastic as a young horse. It was this trait that made us decide that he was not ready to take on the bigger courses in the spring of 1972. I had started riding him in novice events in 1971

Riding Goodwill.

and as long as he never got galloping we got on quite well – well enough to be placed in novice events, even to win an intermediate event, and well enough for Alison to consider running him at Burghley in September. So I had something to take my mind off Doublet's enforced holiday.

After Badminton, Alison went with her husband Alan Oliver to watch him showjumping at the International Show in Rome. Also at the show was an owner and horse dealer, Trevor Banks, who already knew the Olivers, and in conversation with Alison said he might have a horse that would fit the bill. That was how, one day in May, a dark brown gelding with four white socks turned up at Warfield for me to try. Goodwill had been the Working Hunter Champion at the Horse of the Year Show as a four-year-old in 1969 and was snapped up to become a highly competent Grade A jumper who competed at Barcelona and Aachen. When I rode him in the indoor school, I got carted at the trot and couldn't stop; when I jumped him outside, I got carted down the line of fences; but when I took him to Windsor Great Park to try him over the cross-country fences, he was relaxed, confident and bold. He came to join the team.

If we had set out to find two more different horses than Doublet and Goodwill, we could not have been more successful. Doublet was a relatively small, slight chestnut; not a particularly good mover, but he loved the crowds and atmosphere and was a competent jumper without real scope. Goodwill, by con-

Riding Columbus who later was going to prove rather too strong for me.

trast, had tremendous jumping ability, was an active and athletic mover, but couldn't cope with crowds and loathed dressage arenas, an aversion we never managed to overcome.

Columbus remained the great white hope and, although he wasn't an easy ride, he had tremendous scope. He and Goodwill were the same age (seven) but completely different types, both physically and mentally. The former was tall (17.00hh), lean, angular, a bully in the box, a bit of a tearaway outside but lacking in confidence, surprisingly careful and very quick on his feet in spite of his long back. The latter was a 'round' horse (16.3hh), muscular and strong but a gentleman to look after, a bold and confident jumper and yet very sensitive to the atmosphere in crowded arenas.

Columbus had a reasonably successful spring season and Goodwill got off to an encouraging start in his eventing career. In August I took both horses to compete in Scotland where there were three horse trials in eight days, two close to Kilmarnock in Ayrshire and one near Lockerbie in Dumfriesshire. It was a part of Scotland that I didn't know at all and this 'mini circuit' provided an excellent opportunity to widen my knowledge of people and places, and a lot of fun it was too. Any of the competitors who came from the south were given a warm welcome and generous hospitality, being accommodated locally in spare rooms and not-so-spare rooms, in caravans and horse boxes.

Ayrshire is dairy country, giving its name to Scotland's famous milk breed. The country is largely grass fields, which made the building of cross-country courses that much easier and nicer for the horses. Perhaps my liking for the courses was coloured by the fact that Columbus was a good fourth in the Open Intermediate class at the Lockerbie Horse Trials while Goodwill was fifth in the Novice and then fourth in the Open Intermediate at the Eglington Horse Trials.

Columbus had gone well enough to convince Alison that he was capable of tackling Burghley. The big question mark was whether I would be able to hold him over the full three-day event distance. I could just about manage around a one-day event course, but I wasn't too confident about my strength lasting the steeplechase and the cross country. There were lots of discussions about what sort of bit I might try to help me brake more easily without stopping him altogether. Columbus was not an out-and-out tearaway; I just needed to make my presence felt at the critical moments, but if we put too strong a bit in his mouth, we ran the risk of distracting him and stifling his enthusiasm. It was a very fine dividing line and we tried one or two options before going to Burghley, but decided not to use the gag that we had opted for until after the steeplechase.

This turned out to have been an unfortunate decision, because I felt I was out of control on the steeplechase and pulled him up before finishing that phase and therefore withdrew from the competition.

There is no doubt that, if I had then had some racing experience, I would not have been so easily put off, because Columbus was not a careless jumper, and if I'd had more nerve and experience we could have got on quite well. As it was, Alison and I decided to look for a stronger rider; and thereby hangs a completely different tale! I did in fact ride Columbus again, a few years later, when he had grown into a comparatively relaxed ride, but to all intents and purposes that was the end of a promising partnership.

This left Goodwill as the great brown hope and he responded to this rapid promotion by winning an Intermediate class at Knowlton in Kent and coming second in the Intermediate at Chatsworth – virtually the same course that Doublet had jumped in the Novice Championships two years before. Once again, Alison and I felt that Chatsworth had done its job as a yardstick and that he had gone well enough for us to think about entering him for Badminton.

January 1973 saw the start of Goodwill's three-day event career and the

Goodwill's first time into the lake at Badminton.

build-up followed the same logic as Doublet's, leading to the same decision – that he was ready to run at Badminton. He was ready in a different sort of way from Doublet: his jumping was much more confident and mature, but his dressage was largely a case of containment, so I was not looking forward to discovering his reaction to the crowds in the main arena. On the bottom of the dressage sheet on which the judges put their marks for the movements during the test there are 3 more marks to be given for: (a) general impression, obedience and calmness; (b) paces (freedom and regularity) and impulsion; and (c) position and seat of the rider, correct use of the aids. In all honesty, the only criterion that fitted our test was 'impulsion' and rather too much of it.

We started the endurance day just over 20 marks behind the leader, Lucinda Prior-Palmer (now Lucinda Green) riding Be Fair, and with serious doubts about Goodwill's ability to gallop the full distance, partly because, in spite of our best efforts, Goodwill was still a round horse rather than the image of a lean, fit, three-day eventer. I wasn't too worried if he wasn't galloping fit as he was certainly jumping fit. The roads and tracks were hard work for me because I could not persuade Goodwill to proceed at any speed less than a smart extended trot, which didn't seem to bother him very much but was wearing me out. He didn't gallop fast enough on the steeplechase course, not because he got tired but because he just did not know how to gallop. But he still felt very strong.

The cross-country course went left-handed, in the same way as in 1971, and had several drop fences (too many, according to a lot more experienced people than me). I almost felt guilty that I had such a good ride. I certainly got tired, but I had no problems. The 'stringing' phenomenon (see p. 61) made another appearance around the Stockholm fence and was the only thing that nearly spoiled my day. The approach to the Stockholm fence involved a right-angle turn just before the fence, the right angle being created by the string which you had to ride next to in order to give your horse as much room as possible in front of the fence. It was a tight turn but looked fine on the walk-round. What I had not thought about, until Goodwill started to slow down of his own accord, was that before you turned the corner you were cantering straight at the crowd and Goodwill for one was thoroughly disconcerted by the wall of people and nearly came to a complete stop. When we turned the corner and he saw the fence, he almost heaved a sigh of relief and continued on his smooth way.

Thanks to Goodwill's talented cross-country round, he had moved up the order to finish the day in eighth place. Having passed the vet's inspection, he

Goodwill listening to my voice. The picture shows the 'gag' bit.

completed the competition with a clear showjumping round and finished the competition in eighth place behind the winner Lucinda Prior-Palmer riding Be Fair from Richard Meade on Eagle Rock and Virginia Thompson on Cornish Duke. This was a more than satisfactory result for a virtual novice and established his credentials as a top-class three-day event horse. Establishing his credentials was important, because Doublet had not yet shown that he was fit to be picked to compete in the European Championships to be held in Kiev, Russia, in August 1973. He was making good progress and had been to one or two competitions in the spring at which I thought he had gone very well, but then I wasn't a selector! We still had to be sure that his leg injury had fully recovered.

There was to be a final selection trial in the summer before the selectors had to make up their minds and Doublet was asked to take part. He seemed his normal self and I was feeling fairly confident about the course. There were three water-related fences on the course, the first of which was into a 12-foot-wide stream with 5-foot banks on each side and across it was a single rail. This rail could be jumped either by climbing down the bank downstream of it, trotting upstream and jumping it from water to water, or jumping down from the bank over the rail and landing in the stream, which was quicker but demanded more accuracy and boldness. I chose the quicker option and was rewarded with a bold, accurate jump from Doublet, but landed in a bad patch which nearly caused him to fall. We continued on our way, apparently none the worse for this experience, and after several more fences arrived at the second water jump. This one involved jumping over a tree trunk straight down into the edge of the lake. This too he jumped boldly but perhaps slightly more cautiously and once again had a little difficulty staying on his feet. This experience was immediately followed by a coffin type of fence back across the stream we had jumped into earlier: rail-stream-rail. It was at this point that Doublet thought that enough was enough and stopped at a fence for the first time in his competitive life. To say that I was surprised would have been an understatement of the highest order; when he stopped again, I didn't know what to do, and my third and final attempt was feeble, unsuccessful and meant that we were eliminated.

Whatever the cause of Doublet's lapse, he had ruled himself out of a trip to Russia. It was now for the selectors to decide if Goodwill was competent enough to allow me to defend 'my' title. In the end, they decided to let me accept the invitation to compete as an individual in Kiev and Goodwill and I were on our way to Russia.

Between the selection and the concentration period there were other horses to ride, especially Flame Gun, a real character. By the leading sire of National Hunt racehorses, Vulgan, out of the mare Hope, who had finished fourth at Badminton in 1952, Flame was a bright chestnut with a temper, but fun to ride. He had been going well during the year and had qualified for the Novice Championships at Cirencester where he finished ninth. That was not the memorable bit. One of the fences was a stone-faced bank, a stone wall up to 3 feet and a grass bank up to about 6 feet and about 6 feet across the top. The object was to jump on and off the bank and I rode at it to achieve that end in a slow, bouncy canter to give Flame the best chance to jump up off his hocks. He certainly did that, to such good effect that he never touched a blade of grass on the bank, but very nearly left me sitting by myself on the top. I can only imagine that, because he could see over the bank, he thought he could jump it in one; which he did. We may have been only ninth, but he had shown real potential.

The team got together for some joint training stabled at an estate on the edge of Windsor Great Park called Ribblesdale, very generously lent by Peter, now Lord, Palumbo. The riders lived in one of the boys' boarding houses at Eton. I could tell you about the food – if I could remember anything worth mentioning – but not about the beds, because I slept in the Castle: nobody quite knew what to do with me. These concentration periods were more designed for everybody to get to know each other rather than achieve any miracles of training with the horses. The other team members were: Lucinda Prior-Palmer (Be Fair), Janet Hodgson (Larkspur), Debbie West (Baccarat), Marjorie Comerford (The Ghillie), Rosalyn Jones (Farewell) and Richard Meade (Wayfarer). Be Fair had won that year's Badminton; Larkspur had won the previous year's Burghley; Baccarat had been fourth at Badminton in 1972; The Ghillie was seventh at Badminton in 1973 and would have been second if he had jumped a clear showjumping round; Farewell was fifth the same year and Wayfarer was seventh at Badminton and fifth at Burghley in 1972.

It was also an important time for planning. Planning what to take and what not to take in the way of food and equipment was a cause of endless discussion, frequently hi-jacked by reminiscences of earlier campaigns. One or two of the back-up team had been in Russia before when the 1965 European Championships had been held in Moscow. The reminiscences were horror stories, of course – surely they were exaggerated, and anyway things would have improved by now, wouldn't they?

The back-up team were the same people who supported all the official British teams at international competitions and consisted of a chef d'équipe, a stable manager, a vet, a farrier and sundry trainers, because, this being an individual sport, each rider seemed to have their own guru without whom they felt they could not function. It was nonsense, of course, but I certainly hadn't reached the stage of being able to cope without Alison's cheerful and positive presence. The mysteries of how much hay or corn to give the horse, when to take the water bucket away before the cross country and many other finer points had not yet been revealed to me, or perhaps Alison felt I had enough trouble remembering the dressage test.

The day of departure dawned so early that, in spite of its being August, it was dark when we set off for the journey to Luton. The 'we' in this instance were horses, people and supplies, and the loading process took some time. For the flight, the horses travelled two to a pallet and these were built up to make them like stalls with a sort of canvas pram hood to protect their heads or protect the aircraft. It became apparent that the airline staff were much more frightened of the horses than the horses were of the aircraft. Somebody had no doubt told them the story of what happened when a horse kicked its way out of the wooden stall and went to sit with the human passengers in the back. No doubt if it had had the sense to sit still, it might have survived the flight.

Fortunately the loading process and the flight all went remarkably smoothly. There was a refuelling stop in Vienna, because all aircraft flying into Russia had to have enough fuel to get to their destination and back, in case of misunderstandings. This made our aircraft very heavy indeed and for me almost the most worrying part of the whole exercise was taxying further and further down the runway, wondering if we were ever going to get airborne.

The arrival in Kiev was without incident and the offloading process was completed safely, if not quite so fluently as the loading, because the airport did not appear to be equipped to manage pallets; the only answer was a forklift truck. From my point of view the arrival was unusually relaxed – there was no

Training in Russia under the watchful eye of Alison Oliver.

official reception party and I was allowed to hang around and make (un)helpful suggestions, just like the other riders.

The drive into Kiev was fascinating, the airport being some way out of the city on the steppes. The city is situated on the high west bank – up to 300 feet high – of the Dnieper River, but the country is essentially flat. We drove past vast apple orchards, with rings of rotting apples lying round the base of the trees. Every now and again you might see one person putting an apple into a crate but the impression was one of disinterest and waste on a massive scale. This was further reinforced when we discovered that the cross-country course went straight through a field of steadily rotting tomatoes, again with lots of crates but only one person who obviously saw no point in doing the field all by himself.

The route to the stables went right through Kiev and gave us the opportunity to observe the city of seven hills and its people. The stables were situated in what I think was described as the Cultural Park, a curious combination of gardens, paved roads, plots of trees, glasshouses and large sculptures. The stables themselves were in a large building and, from the horses' point of view, quiet and comfortable. The Park was spacious, with a series of sand arenas, but nowhere except the roads on which to exercise. Not for the first or last time the chef d'équipe's job was to find somewhere where we could give the horses a gallop. After some fierce negotiation we were allowed to use the trotting track on the other side of the road, which turned out to be where the Russian horses were stabled. It also turned out to be the place where Goodwill learnt to gallop.

There is a subtle but crucial difference between a horse whose legs just go round faster and one that can lengthen its stride and cover the ground more easily and efficiently. So far Goodwill had not appreciated the difference. I took him for a canter in the company of The Ghillie, Marjorie Comerford's great old horse, who did know the difference. Towards the end of the second circuit, Marjorie asked if I would mind if she went a bit quicker up the straight. I didn't mind, but Goodwill did when The Ghillie strode away from us as if we were standing still. I could tell from his ears that Goodwill was mystified by this disappearing act and annoyed that he couldn't keep up. He learned quickly; he didn't get any time penalties on the steeplechase course in Kiev or anywhere else thereafter.

Having seen the horses settled in, we went to find our own accommodation. This was in a large hotel in the centre of Kiev – a Russian tourist-class hotel for Russians, which was very different from a hotel for foreign tourists. All the visiting teams were billeted there, but for some reason the Russian team was not allowed to be there as well, which was a great shame. On the other hand, perhaps they knew what to expect. It was a multi-storey block with central lifts and one central stair, all of which arrived at the same place, and were over-looked, you might even say guarded, on each floor by a woman of fearsome appearance. The one on our floor bore a striking resemblance to the notorious character from an early James Bond film, Rosa Klebb, and nobody felt like argu-ing with her. The rooms were functional and the advice to take your own bath plug turned out to have been very pertinent, as did that to take iron rations, because Russia's culinary achievements proved to be every bit as bad as we had been led to believe – except in the case of Chicken à la Kiev and the butter, which came from an EEC butter mountain.

Rumours and stories of bugged rooms with which we had been regaled by the Moscow veterans were tested by my policeman, who more or less took his room to pieces, including removing the mirror from the wall which he then had great difficulty in putting back. He did find a device eventually, in the telephone. As telephoning was a long-winded and expensive business, I doubt if 'they' heard anything very interesting.

I was, of course, treated exactly the same as any other team member, which wasn't too difficult as nobody in Kiev knew what I looked like, even if they had somehow discovered that I was there. Well, that was what we all thought until I was accosted by the floor maid in the hotel corridor, while attempting to do some ironing. She watched me for a moment before approaching me with outstretched arms, chattering away in Russian and then planting three of the wettest, smelliest kisses on my cheeks that I have ever encountered. I have to admit that she might have mistaken me for somebody else, somebody more famous like Lucinda Prior-Palmer for instance, but then we shall never know.

There was another incident that also seemed to indicate an active form of bush telegraph. The competition was not widely advertised and there seemed to be no reason to suppose that any spectators would turn up for the dressage, given that knowing about the event was unlikely but that finding out that it was taking place was even more difficult. The organisers didn't seem to be expecting many as the dressage arena was in an area not much bigger than the arena itself and surrounded by bushes and trees. However, I was told afterwards that, shortly before my test, people started to appear around the arena, mostly elderly women in black. When I had finished, they melted away into the park as if they had never been there. I wonder whom they thought they had come to see?

In spite of my anonymity, there was a 'man' who accompanied me everywhere, claimed to speak no English and was not a policeman. I was also given the use of a car and driver who definitely did not speak any English, but whose driving was international; he was nicknamed 'Fangio'. Although we had a language problem, we always managed to get where we wanted to go, which led us to believe that our 'man' did indeed speak English and that was not altogether surprising given that, as a KGB officer who had been posted to London for six years, it would have been astonishing if he had not. He was a great help, even if he was convinced we were all mad.

Driving to and from the stables meant going through the middle of the city and it was there you could feel and see differences: the food shops with the long queues and empty shelves, the colourless clothes and unsmiling faces, and the feeling that there was an age group missing. You saw very few school-age children and virtually no student age group as they were either at university, in the services or in State-run cultural groups. By the side of the road you would often see people selling vegetables that were the produce from their own 1 hectare ($2\frac{1}{2}$ acres), to which everyone was entitled. Nearly 80 per cent of the fresh fruit and vegetables sold in the USSR came from those sources. As all agricultural workers were paid low wages for whatever they did or did not do, that partially explained the lack of interest we had witnessed in the orchard and the tomato field.

One of the nice things about international competition is that, with only one horse to ride, there is time to look around and enjoy sightseeing, shopping or eating out. Sightseeing included a visit to the Russian Orthodox Cathedral which still dominated the Kiev skyline with its elegant, gilded, onion-shaped domes. Religion was not banned as such, but you could not be a card-carrying Communist and a practising Christian. The reason for not banning the Church was a historical one in that post-revolution observation indicated that only old women went to Church, and that under the new order everything would be catered for so there would be no need for religion. The assumption was that religion would die out. Judging by our observations, that was a serious miscalculation. The Cathedral was still being used for services by old women (probably different ones) and young children, and there was a choir of old men with rich voices. The interior and exterior of the Cathedral were in amazingly good condition compared to the rest of the city, and it turned out that the domes were re-gilded every twelve years. It was a classic example of just one of the paradoxes that went to make up the Union of Soviet Socialist Republics, and a vivid reminder of the power of the spirit which cannot be accommodated by the purely material.

Another outing was a picnic beside the River Dnieper which ran through the city. At that time of year the water was relatively low and there were plenty of sandy banks to sit on. It was hot and sunny and most of the good citizens of Kiev seemed to be there as well. This allowed us the opportunity to observe the men and women at play – mostly women, I have to say, and they were all anxious to acquire a sun-tan. This involved changing into swimming costumes on the beach. Anybody who has ever tried this on a crowded English beach will know the difficulty of not offending other beach users, but this was not a problem in Kiev – nobody seemed to mind. The other thing we noticed was that there were very few thin Russian women but they all wore two-piece costumes of the black jersey variety which seemed, if not inadequate for the job, positively overwhelmed by gravity.

Shopping was much more difficult. Because of the weakness of the rouble and the desire for foreign currency, tourists and visitors were supposed to shop only in the hard-currency shops that sold the usual standard souvenir merchandise – Russian standard, of course – which, apart from the nest of wooden Russian dolls, quite like the one that I had grown up with, was largely unattractive and badly made. This, combined with the total lack of interest shown by the women who took your money, meant that they got very few pounds sterling to ease their hard currency problems. Thanks to our KGB friend, I did manage to get to a more Russian gift shop where the atmosphere and service were completely different, possibly because it was a tiny shop run by a family.

Eating out was a decision taken on the basis that it could not be any worse than eating in the hotel, which could not be described as a gastronomic experience. The choice of restaurants was again restricted by currency, so we went to a restaurant where Intourist regularly took their package visitors from overseas. On the night we went there was a group of students from England and a party of Russians. We came a poor third in the serving stakes and it was an hour before we got a menu, but the food when it came was an improvement on our normal fare. Some team members had suffered from not wanting to risk the food or from just not being able to eat it and were therefore not feeling their best when the competition started, in spite of having had emergency rations brought out by later arrivals. I have to admit that I didn't suffer very much and barely lost any weight. This must have been the result of my upbringing – no, not the culinary standards but from drinking unpasteurised milk and eating free-range eggs and food on lots of picnics where it sometimes had to be retrieved from wherever it had perversely landed with, no doubt, some interesting bacteria attached.

I don't want to give the impression, however, that all the food in Russia was not very appetising. My father, who was then President of the International Equestrian Federation, was staying in a foreign tourist-class hotel and he said the food was more than adequately good.

In between all these interesting experiences we concentrated on the competition which included learning our way round the roads and tracks in case the direction indicators went missing. The roads and tracks showed us more of the Ukrainian countryside, which is mostly very flat, and land use, which was a source of amazement to the Lincolnshire farmer and owner of The Ghillie who was a member of the party. His amazement was based on the apparent waste of land that, had he been farming there, would have ensured his having to find an alternative form of income.

The cross-country course itself was not all that far from the stables, beyond the park and through a spindly wood to a valley. Using the contours of the valley, it made for an interesting and demanding course, though just how interesting and demanding was perhaps somewhat underestimated. Walking the course, I don't remember feeling very worried, but I already had enormous confidence in Goodwill. The infamous second fence had not caused me as much concern as many, but I made a classic error from which I learnt a pretty painful lesson. I, and many others, thought there was only one way to jump the fence, based on its shape and on the lie of the land, which meant approaching it and jumping it across the angle where the offset parallel sections met. Although I looked at the rest of the fence, I did not pay nearly enough attention to the alternatives. The rest of the course had its problems and it did not appear to be a case of: jump the second fence and the rest would be relatively straightforward.

My dressage was unimpressive but calm, which was all I could ask of Goodwill as he had already decided that dressage arenas were not his favourite place. Being an individual, I was drawn in the middle of the running order and set off on the first section of the roads and tracks, trying to convince myself that I had worked out my time schedule properly. (I always had done, but I still went on working it out in my head. I have since decided that that was my way of not getting bored on the long trotting sections.) Thanks to Goodwill being outspeeded by The Ghillie and so learning to gallop properly, we got inside the time allowed on the steeplechase. So I set off on the second and longer section of the roads and tracks feeling very positive if not confident.

On my return to the ten-minute-halt box I noticed gloomy faces. While Goodwill was being washed off, I was told of the problems at fence number 2. It transpired that several horses (Baccarat included) had stopped at the ditch which ran under the fence, and in stopping had caused the edge of the bank to crumble a bit, enough to make our chef d'équipe tell me that I ought not to try jumping it there. This was the moment when, with a bit more experience, I would have said 'no', because I had not walked the alternative well enough.

However, I accepted the advice and tried to visualise what I was going to be doing. The approach to the fence was up and down a shoulder and along the side of the hill just above the ditch line over which the fence was positioned. To jump the fence straight meant traversing the slope higher up and then turning

About to fall at Kiev on 8 September 1973.
Plenty of height but not enough distance!

right 90 degrees downhill to the parallel part of the fence. I nearly got it right, but when I turned downhill I discovered that instead of being able to fit in three good accelerating strides, Goodwill was going to fit in only two and a half. Horses can't work out halves – and as they have four legs, who can blame them? – so he took off sooner rather than later. The result was fairly spectacular, so I'm told. Goodwill's leap very nearly succeeded in that he got everything over the fence except his back feet, but they unfortunately were tucked up underneath his bottom which meant that when they hit the back rail of the fence they effectively stopped him and pitched him on to his nose, at which stage I left, rapidly ejected out of the saddle, and landed heavily on the point of my hip and the tip of my shoulder on what felt like a road.

I had barely come to a halt, as it seemed to me, when I was surrounded by people, shouting, talking, waving, and all in different languages. It was difficult enough to establish my own state of health, never mind Goodwill's, but when I stood up I discovered that my right leg was completely numb between my knee and my hip. The leg didn't seem to want to support my weight. I felt this would be a disadvantage to my being able to maintain my balance in the saddle if I got back on. On being able to see Goodwill through the throng of people, it struck me that he looked positively shocked by what I suspect for him was a very rare occurrence. Both these observations, although still valid, might have resulted in a different decision if I had been competing as a member of the team. As it was, I was there purely as an individual competitor, and because I saw no point in risking either the horse or myself I decided to retire with both of us more or less in one piece. In hindsight, I don't believe I would have decided differently. My mistake came before the fall and from that I did indeed learn the hard way.

I was not in the same position as Janet Hodgson and Larkspur, who were members of the team. It was therefore important that they finish the course in order for Britain still to have a team after Baccarat's elimination. Janet continued in spite of two crashing falls, the first at the second fence where she landed on her face and the other about three fences from the end. Her true team spirit did a lot to silence those critics who felt that women were not tough enough to fulfil their team role.

I made my way back to the start-and-finish box hanging on to the nearside stirrup leather with my right hand, because my right leg wasn't working very well. By the time I got back to the stables, the feeling was returning to my leg, but the end of my collar bone was causing me very serious pain and it appears that I had been very lucky (a) not to have broken my collar bone and (b) not to have dislocated it. The pain was the result of the end of the bone sinking back into the socket from whence it had nearly been ejected. This information was not available to me at the time, so I was perhaps not as grateful as I might have been that the pain and inconvenience could have been worse. If it had been a little bit worse, I would have been unconscious and therefore relatively unaffected.

I'm not sure what happened after that, but I suspect that the vet must have given me something for the pain and I returned to the hotel to sort myself out. I had only just got back to my room when our friendly neighbourhood floor maid appeared in my doorway. She followed me in and, with much wailing and weeping, tried hard to help me undress. Touched though I was by her concern, I was not that badly damaged and it was only by retreating to the loo and locking the door that I could convince her that I didn't really need her help.

The next morning I returned to the stables to find Goodwill apparently no worse for his experiences, which was a great relief, but the casualty rate for the rest of the field was quite considerable. The vet's inspection didn't take very long, but I seem to remember that it was just as well the riders didn't have to pass a medical test. I know I was very glad that I didn't have to do anything more strenuous than watch the final showjumping phase and the ultimate success of the Russian riders. The individual champion, Alexander Evdokimov riding Jeger, was a thoroughly worthy but narrow winner – he and Herbert Blocker, riding Albrant for West Germany, finished on the same score, Evdokimov being declared the winner because he was closer to the optimum time in the cross-country phase. Sadly, he was never seen again at any championship events. West Germany won the team event from the USSR, with Britain taking the bronze. I seem to remember that the Russians gave Janet a special prize for her bravery.

I returned with my father to Balmoral, where he very kindly arranged for Sir Charles Strong to come and treat my shoulder and leg, which got me back on an even keel a lot quicker than if I'd been left to my own devices. As it turned out, my shoulders have never been even since then – the right is marginally shorter than the left, but not enough for anybody except the dressmaker to notice!

CHAPTER 7

~

Accidents and Injuries:

'Character-building!'

AFTER Kiev it was time to take stock. The horse was all right, I was all right; what next? This was a moment for Mrs Oliver to be at her most positive, and she was. There was a three-day event in Holland in October, which would give us the opportunity to find out how much, if at all, our confidence had been affected.

Getting to Holland would be a lot easier than getting to Kiev – well, it should be: it's a lot closer – but it involved a bit more driving and a boat trip. It was an unofficial team event with several British riders wanting to get some international experience over a course that had received good reviews from previous British competitors. Because it was an international and not a championship three-day event, competitors made their own entries – with the approval of the National Federation and/or the selectors – and their own travel arrangements. This meant that those with horse boxes offered space to those who either did not have a horse box or whose box was of such an age that a trip to the continent might prove fatal. Filling a horse box also meant that you shared the cost.

This was fine in theory, but horses being the animals they are you would just get your wheels organised, your passage booked and your vet papers in order and the horse would develop stage fright in the shape of any equine condition that would prevent it from competing. This was disappointing enough for the erstwhile competitor; it was also extremely awkward for the fellow travellers whose financial contributions would have to rise proportionately.

Although we used 'my' horse box, I had not yet gained my HGV licence, so the driving was done by a very important lady who worked for The Queen called Marie Wood; she knew more about horses and especially the transporting of them than most people ever will. Before joining The Queen, Marie had worked for Mrs Cynthia Haydon, at that time Britain's leading whip (the term used to describe the driver of a carriage). Part of Mrs Haydon's success in the showring – where she was almost unbeatable – and later in the three-day driving

Riding Flame Gun at Tidworth where he was second.

competitions was her attention to detail, and with a carriage and four horses in harness there is a great deal of detail to attend to. Marie was entrusted with that job and she never lost her eye for detail. Also she never panicked, which, when you are moving horses around, is an essential quality. This admirable trait may have developed from coping with Mrs Haydon's hackneys, a breed renowned for their tendency to get excited quite quickly.

Having seen the horses off, I drove myself to the ferry for the overnight crossing from Harwich to the Hook of Holland and on to Boekelo. On arrival we went to see the horses and generally get our bearings. Fortunately, everybody had had a comfortable crossing, which was just as well because the extensive social programme organised by our Dutch hosts started almost at once. Not only were we made to feel very welcome, but we had the opportunity of getting to meet and know our fellow competitors too.

Surprisingly, this would be my first visit to Holland. Boekelo, which was the nearest town to the event, lies in the east of the country. The area is flat but attractive, with a generally light soil and plenty of woodland dividing a mass of small farming enterprises: a few pigs here, a few cows there, a little maize here and a root crop there. Designing a cross-country course with the permission and co-operation of some thirty land owners requires special skills from the course builder. The soil was mostly sand or peat, which was a great advantage in October when it could get very wet. The free-draining land, criss-crossed by ditches of all sizes – and some were like arms of the sea – meant that you could run the cross country in almost any weather conditions except a monsoon.

Goodwill seemed to have travelled well and also seemed to enjoy being in a different place. Unfortunately this enthusiasm for his surroundings didn't appear to improve his dressage, which was one of his 'usuals' – that is, he couldn't get through it quickly enough.

The cross-country day was more memorable because it dawned to a blanket of thick fog. It was one of those very still, damp, autumnal mornings, when the mist clings to the trees. As the sun usually managed to burn off the mist as the morning wore on, they started us on the roads and tracks at the scheduled time and we trotted off into the mist. The steeplechase didn't seem quite so bad, although you couldn't see all the way round the track. I was enjoying my ride until Goodwill just brushed the top of one of the fences. He landed perfectly safely and quite straight, but with his centre of gravity too far forward which meant that his momentum eventually tipped his balance on to his nose and his knees. He slid along the wet ground, still going in a straight line, with me sitting surprisingly securely, waiting for him to recover his balance and get up off his knees. He slid to a halt on his tummy some 15 to 20 yards from the fence and I sat waiting for him to get up. He seemed to feel that this was an unnecessary effort, so he simply capsized to the right where he remained, unconcernedly, lying on his side. I had to get off to avoid being rolled on. A young Dutch girl ran up to catch him and was obviously mystified by his lack of interest. I was definitely unimpressed by his want of effort, especially as it incurred 60 penalties for a fall. As neither of us was damaged, we continued on our way via the second lot of roads and tracks to the ten-minute-halt box.

It was not until we got back to the box that I discovered that the fog had created rather more trouble than originally envisaged. The first hint of that trouble was that the box appeared to be somewhat overcrowded with an unusual number of horses in it. The reason was obvious, or rather not obvious, because

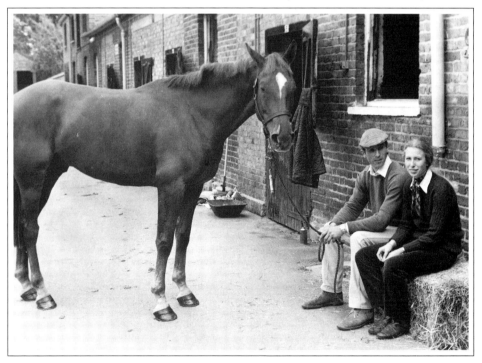

With Mardi Gras outside the stables we converted at
Sandhurst when Mark was at the Royal Military Academy.

the jump judges and officials couldn't see far enough, never mind the riders not being able to see from one side of a field to the other. The potential for losing competitors was considerable, so the decision was taken to postpone the start of the actual cross-country course, a postponement that eventually lasted for an hour.

It was difficult for both riders and horses to have to wait so long and then gear themselves up again for the most technically demanding part of the competition: tackling the obstacles. But it was the same for nearly everyone. My problem was setting off on a very fresh horse, ridden, as Goodwill was in those days, in a jointed snaffle and drop noseband. By the time I had finished my satisfactory but arm-stretching round, I was convinced that, as brakes, they were wholly inadequate. Even the water obstacle, which involved crossing two 50-yard stretches of water with an island to jump on and off, didn't slow him down very much. We finished with one of the relatively few clear rounds, which made our grass-skiing episode on the steeplechase course even more annoying. We managed to jump a clear round in the final showjumping phase and finished twenty-second. We might have been fourth without the 60 penalties for Goodwill's little lie-down.

So the 1973 season ended there and Alison and I had plenty to talk about on the ferry home concerning Goodwill's future and mine. My life was about to change – well, my domestic arrangements were – for I was to make the transition from being a carefree spinster living at home to a careworn wife looking after her own home (this is written with hindsight!) and neither Alison nor I could really know what to expect.

I would be living in a house in the grounds of the Royal Military Academy, Sandhurst, not far from Winkfield, but with stables and grounds that made it possible to keep horses there. So would I be riding and training on my own for the first time since I started competing? Was I going to manage to plan which competitions I needed to take Goodwill to? Was I going to go completely independent or share responsibility? Was Goodwill the right horse for me?

The answer to the last question seemed to revolve around finding a more effective system of control, which meant finding a bit that would allow me to have greater stopping power without worrying the horse. There was no doubt that Goodwill was a very good horse and, even with his boring habits of leaning on his bit and therefore on my hand, his honesty and power gave me tremendous confidence. He was certainly capable of jumping the biggest courses, even if his dislike of dressage arenas was always going to be a handicap.

So that was one decision taken; I would have to learn to ride him better.

The other questions were much more difficult to answer, but I was looking forward to seeing how much I had learned. I would not really be 'on my own' as Lieutenant Phillips, as he then was, had been competing since he started riding, which was a bit before he could walk, according to his mother. What I didn't appreciate at the time was that Mark hadn't been completely 'on his own' before, because his mother, Anne, and his aunt, Flavia, had done some of the riding and most of the organising. As it turned out, nothing much changed except that I then did some of the riding.

The stables that we were allowed to have at Sandhurst were a short walk from where we lived, but required some work to make them usable for our rather large horses. They had been the carriage horse stables and were two stalls with one door. Tying horses in stalls is fine for those that spend a lot of the day out, but, except for the days when they are competing, horses used for sport seldom spend more than an hour or two a day out of their stable. So we set about turning the stalls into boxes, which involved some fairly Heath Robinson structures to allow us to use all the floor space and still get the horses in and out.

The scope for the animals damaging themselves and each other was considerable, but with no options available they all seemed to survive. Goodwill was probably the only horse of ours which suffered as a direct consequence of these arrangements when, as a result of an argument with his close neighbour, he threw his head in the air and hit a metal bar that I imagine had been used in the past to hang up a headcollar. The bar had a rounded end, about $\frac{1}{4}$ inch across, which made a hole right through Goodwill's head into his sinus cavity about half-way up his face. Fortunately, there was very little blood and no great problem apart from little

I passed my HGV licence while living at Sandhurst. The week after I passed, a young horse put Mark's back out at a show in Gloucestershire and I had to drive home to Sandhurst.

bits of bone, although anybody who has ever had any trouble wth their sinuses can imagine the discomfort.

Having the horses on the doorstep did mean that I learned a lot more about observing and treating their various physical and sometimes mental problems. I was getting to know the 'normal' so that I might be able to recognise the 'abnormal'. This was made easier by being lucky enough to have very good staff who were observant, conscientious and remembered to tell you what they had done.

We had a lot of problems with the horses' feet because of the gravel and flinty consistency of the main exercise area. We learned to identify and treat the poisoning caused by the tiny gravel particles working their way up the inside of the hoof, and the cuts and bruises caused by the larger flints. If identified early enough, the poisoning could be halted by the farrier cutting out the affected area so that the poison could drain out of the hoof. If not, you had to wait until the poison worked its way out of the hoof through the coronet band at the top edge of the hard wall of the hoof.

The cuts were not always very obvious, which made the picking-out of the horses' feet an even more critical part of stable management than usual. Your mind tended to be concentrated by the fact that if you missed the early phase, you could spend a lot of time 'tubbing' the foot. This meant persuading the horse to stand with its foot in a bucket of warm water and salt. The remedy for the bruised foot was equally old-fashioned: a bran poultice. But it was not that easy to keep in place as many of the horses regarded the lengths to which you went to keep the poultice on their foot simply as a form of initiative test to see how long it took them to get at the bran and then eat it.

We went to Sandhurst in December 1973 and Alison and I had decided that I should have Doublet and Goodwill to work them towards Badminton as there were a few hills behind Sandhurst, unlike the area around Winkfield, although we still had to go to Windsor Great Park to canter them. It was an enjoyable period for me, having the opportunity to get to know the horses so much better. The build-up progressed more or less as planned and I joined Mark, who was in the habit of taking his Badminton horses down to Devon to be sharpened up by Bertie Hill.

Going to stay with Bertie and Mary had two major advantages. The first was Bertie and Mary themselves, who were the most marvellous hosts, treating us as part of the family on what is a working Devon farm. The second advantage was the countryside itself, just north of South Molton, where the grass-sided valleys are very steep and made it positively easy to get the horses to peak fitness.

Bertie had also been one of the leading British three-day event riders in the 1950s, lured from his first love of riding in hurdle races. His wonderfully relaxed approach to life and his natural horsemanship had made him a very successful rider of all types of horses in all types of competition. One of his rides was Stella, the dam of my first event horse, Purple Star, and he rode her in the 1952 Helsinki Olympic Games to finish seventh. He was the best-placed Briton, but there were only three members in a team and all three had to count and one member was eliminated. He was in the Gold Medal team four years later in Stockholm riding Countryman, but that rather bald statement covers an extraordinary story that is told elsewhere. Bertie then completed a rare hat-trick when riding Wild Venture in the Rome Olympics in 1960. He *completed* three successive Olympic three-day events on three different horses.

Along with all his other talents, he was a very good instructor. His greatest strength, certainly from my point of view, was the way he rode the cross-country courses – fast, but relaxed and accurate, something I found very difficult to do. Cross-country schooling down at Bertie's was for me, in quick succession, nerve-racking and exhilarating. I was never good at practising over competition-size cross-country fences, but at a competition I was much bolder.

Bertie and Mark had a habit of rushing out and building a copy of the latest Colonel Weldon 'jockey stopper' from a photograph that appeared in the pre-Badminton issue of *Horse and Hound* magazine just the week before the competition. It wasn't always a very accurate reconstruction and didn't always achieve the hoped-for result, which was to encourage the rider, if not the horse, to believe that this novel example of an obstacle was indeed jumpable. I'm afraid I learned to say 'no' to this form of training and learned more from watching other people's attempts.

Course walking at Badminton.

But overall I benefited enormously from my sojourn with the Hills: a time to relax in a lovely part of the country with very nice people, no outside interference and just your Badminton horses to concentrate on. It was like taking a deep breath of fresh air, which allowed you to arrive at Badminton feeling ready for the fray.

In 1974 I reached Badminton with two fit horses and feeling reasonably pleased with my own fitness, because to ride two horses on endurance day would be hard work. You could choose which horse you wanted to ride first and I chose to ride Goodwill first for two reasons: (1) he would do his dressage early on the first day when there were fewer people and less of an atmosphere and (2) I didn't fancy riding him when I would probably already be feeling tired after riding Doublet, though Doublet was a much less tiring horse to ride. In hindsight it was a good decision for a third reason as well.

Goodwill's dressage was a little bit better than the previous year's, but not much. Doublet's was the better. I set off on cross-country day to give Goodwill a good ride with his new bit, a roller gag, but using two reins. I'm not sure I can describe how a gag works, but the action of the pull on the reins which run down through the middle of the large bit rings tends to make the horse lift its head to avoid the pressure on the bars of its mouth. My hope was that this would make it easier for me to balance Goodwill in front of a fence without having a battle or having to slow down too much. I was warned that this type of bit, if used too often, would make Goodwill jump with a hollow back and therefore spoil his natural round jumping action. Priorities being what they were, I decided to take that risk and see what would happen.

The answer was that he went extremely well and I enjoyed my ride. I don't believe we had any anxious moments, or at least none that I can remember now, but then my memory of that Badminton is of what happened to Doublet that year. After such a good ride on the relatively inexperienced horse, I was looking forward to riding Doublet and I set off on the roads and tracks feeling that he seemed well and even enthusiastic. I thought at the time that that was unusual but encouraging.

Doublet never pulled but he did that day, and on the steeplechase I found I could not really hold him – he was trying to run away. This would have been manageable if he had also concentrated on jumping the fences. Unfortunately he seemed to have lost all sense of self-preservation, which was bad news for both of us.

Approaching the open ditch for the second time, I could see we were not going to meet it on the right stride. I tried to slow him down and got no response, which was unusual, so decided to be positive and kick, which should have made him do something. He did nothing, but just galloped through the bottom of the fence. Of course, you can't do that to a solid obstacle without something having to give and, not for the first time, the fence won.

Doublet and I passed each other in the air. I came off over his right shoulder but landed some way to his left, and we were both a long way from the fence, which was looking decidedly the worse for wear. I caught Doublet, who was looking a trifle wild-eyed, remounted and finished the phase, checking to see if he was still sound before setting off on the second roads and tracks.

When we returned to the ten-minute-halt box, there were many anxious faces – not surprisingly, because what I couldn't see was that Doublet's hind legs were covered in blood from where he had nicked a blood vessel. Peter Scott Dunn, the vet, and Alison decided that Doublet should be withdrawn and I could only agree, but I was desperately disappointed.

Doublet still seemed wild-eyed and unaware of the damage he had done himself, and I finished the day with very mixed feelings. Goodwill had vindicated our belief in him and went into the last day in fourth place, giving The Queen some more good news, because Columbus was in the lead ridden by Mark. We were all concerned about Doublet, who needed some nursing, but Goodwill was the one who had to do more work.

He pulled out sound in the morning and caused us no worries for the vet's inspection. Both he and I made a better job of the showjumping and, with no further penalties to add, we finished in fourth place, to Columbus, Larkspur and the American Bruce Davidson riding Irish Cap, a result that none of us would have dared hope for. Yet there was still an air of disappointment in the horse box going home.

Soon after Badminton the selection committee published its 'long list' for the World Championships to be held at Burghley in September, in which they had included Goodwill. This news, although it didn't completely dispel the air of disappointment, did give us something to look forward to and plan for while we were worrying about Doublet.

We watched Doublet very carefully over the next two weeks to see if he showed any signs of ill effects from the damage to his hind legs. He never took a lame step and seemed remarkably bright considering the shock he must have had to his system. I now knew, because Alison had told me after Badminton, that Doublet had been given some 'bute' – phenylbutazone, a widely used anti-inflammatory medication – before the competition and that we would need to allow him a good two weeks to make sure that any pain-killing effects had had time to come out of his system before deciding if he was all right to start competing again. The decision to carry on was given careful consideration based on the advice of the vet and the fact that Doublet felt all right to me.

After three weeks I took Doublet and Flame Gun to the Great Park to give the former a quiet canter to prepare him for the Tidworth three-day event, to which I was already taking Flame. I rode Doublet first and was cantering round the outer extremities of the polo grounds. The furthest end of the ground from where we unboxed was relatively rough – that is, not mown, with a few mole hills and so on – and we were still going steadily over this when I heard rather than felt his hind leg break. I knew it as certainly as if I'd seen it go. I pulled him up as quickly as I could and jumped off. What I saw was sickening: he had shattered his hind leg through the hock. There was nothing that could be done for him except to put him out of the misery that he would be in when the pain took over from the shock which, for the moment, allowed him to put his head down and graze without apparently feeling that he had broken his leg.

I was completely on my own at this point, nearly a mile from where Alison was waiting with Flame, and it took them some time to realise something was wrong. Even when they eventually reached me and the full horror of what had happened hit them, we still had to get to a phone and call the vet.

I suppose it didn't take that long, but it felt like an eternity, and my own form of shock was beginning to wear off by the time the vet did arrive and I was told what I already knew – that there was no hope of saving Doublet. I was in no mood for polite conversation, so I got on Flame and took him for his canter up the other end of the polo ground. I couldn't really see where I was going, but Flame knew what he was doing. Just once I looked back, to see Doublet collapse to the ground.

Almost the worst part was going to Windsor to tell The Queen and then pulling myself together to visit an RDA group in south London that afternoon. My late and much-loved mother-in-law used to point out at moments when things had gone badly wrong that it was 'character-building'. I hoped in this case that she was right.

Was there anything for me to learn from this agonising episode? The answer to that was yes, but not immediately. I think I felt that I had not discharged my responsibility to the horse who was my partner in a challenge that was my choice. Although you have to be prepared for accidents to happen, there are preventable accidents, and I needed to know if Doublet's fatal injury could have been avoided. I'm afraid the answer to that was also yes, on two counts.

One was more obvious and easier to correct and that was to have had his leg X-rayed after his fall at Badminton, irrespective of the fact that he was not lame. We might have discovered what I later found out was a possible cause of the break – a star fracture, which would probably not have caused any more pain at the time than the bruising had done, but which would have left an area of weakness.

This bit of knowledge was put to good use just two weeks later at an event where somebody's horse came backwards down the ramp of a horse box too quickly and fell off the side, doing itself what looked like superficial damage to its back leg. Alison was asked what she thought they ought to do by way of treatment and whether it would be all right to ride in the competition. Her answer was to take it home and get it X-rayed. They rang to thank her when a star fracture had been identified and the horse was given time to recover, which he did perfectly well.

The second thing I learnt was the effect of bute and this turned out to be the real cause of the problem. Doublet had rather narrow feet and it was felt that he didn't like the firm ground, therefore restricting his normal positive approach to jumping and possibly worrying him enough to make him perform badly or even refuse to jump altogether. In those days bute was not a banned or even restricted substance and was often used on a 'just-in-case' principle. Because it was first and foremost an anti-inflammatory medication, it would be beneficial for any minor damage sustained on endurance day, and its pain-killing qualities would be an added bonus. The trouble with that principle was: what was the right amount? There was a danger that you kept on giving a little bit more 'just in case'. As I mentioned before, I had not been aware of the fact that Doublet was given bute or how much he was given. I fear that, on this occasion, for lack of any evidence to the contrary, Doublet was given 'a little bit more' and it had unexpected results.

It was only as a result of discussing the fall as the cause of the possible star fracture, and my comment that for the first time I could not stop Doublet, that I learnt about bute's pain-killing properties. I was informed that of course the effect of bute would deaden the feeling in the bars of the horse's mouth, as well as relieving any sense of discomfort caused by his feet. The bars are the sensitive

With Alison Oliver riding Goodwill, me riding Flame Gun.

areas behind the front teeth that the bit rests and acts on when pressure is applied through the reins; they are therefore vital to your ability to control the horse's speed and direction.

To say that I was not impressed by this rather casually given information would be a major understatement. But I was even more annoyed with myself for not having paid greater attention to that aspect of my horse's welfare. Needless to say, the experience has coloured my view of the use of medications. Since that day I have hardly ever used any medication for any reason other than treatment of a specific condition.

The other question I had to ask myself was whether to take Flame Gun to the Tidworth Three-day Event which started less than two weeks after losing Doublet. How affected would I be by the accident and what I had learned since – would I be able to ride the horse well enough to do him justice? I don't remember ever contemplating giving up riding in events, but I was perhaps wondering if Tidworth came too soon. Equally, I had been brought up to get on again as soon as possible, and if I was serious about the sport, then Tidworth was an excellent opportunity to pick myself up and carry on.

So I took Flame Gun to Tidworth, where he excelled himself in his dressage test to finish the first day in second place to Aly Pattinson riding her very successful mare, Olivia. The endurance day had three new experiences for me to deal with.

The first was the most worrying and nearly brought our participation to a premature halt. Flame was galloping enthusiastically around the steeplechase course and was about half-way round on the second circuit when, in the process of landing over one of the fences, he must have struck into one of his front legs with one of his hind feet. This had the effect of making him go suddenly and very obviously lame. My immediate reaction was that not only had I lost my best horse, but that I had now also broken down poor Flame. I pulled him up to a trot as quickly as I could and to my astonishment he trotted out perfectly sound, so I kicked on and finished the steeplechase course, but incurred 5 time penalties as a result of those few moments of concern.

We completed the roads and tracks and passed through the vet check without any problem. Flame certainly seemed to be feeling well and was still very full of himself. Then, towards the end of our ten-minute halt, I was called to go to the start. When I got there I was told there was a delay on the course.

The delay grew longer and longer, the reason for the hold-up turning out to be a certain Lieutenant in the King's Troop (Royal Horse Artillery) who was riding one of the Troop's gun team horses – brave, but short on galloping stamina. Baffler, as he was called, had successfully baffled everybody by running out of steam and jumping into the Hayrack which the rest had managed to jump over. Baffler was a troop horse, so he didn't panic but just stood there while the fence was taken apart around him. Needless to say, the delay was extended while the fence was rebuilt.

Walking round at the start waiting for a course to be re-opened is not designed to improve the rider's state of mind or the horse's physical condition. When the message comes, you have quickly to get yourself and the horse back to a state of readiness. Fortunately, Flame was always on the go and he didn't need much encouragement to be ready for the off. He was always a pleasure to ride across country and that ride at Tidworth stands out in my mind as probably the most enjoyable I have ever had in a competition. It included another, fortunately unique experience.

Part of the course followed a cut track through an area of scrubby thorns. One of the fences, a white gate, came about 50 yards after a blind corner, and when we came round the corner, we found a number of spectators between us and the fence. A surprised 'Look out!' from me and a blast from the steward's whistle sent them scattering into the bushes. While this was going on, Flame was marking time, literally. Seemingly on his own initiative, he appeared to slow down and was almost cantering on the spot until the 'hazards' had removed themselves. Then he just set off and jumped the fence as if nothing had happened.

We then had some time to make up and he galloped for home across a large field where I was conscious of a small green mechanised object overflowing with arms and legs, apparently heading for the same gap at the other side of the field where the course went. I knew instinctively that it was Lady Hugh Russell in her Mini-Moke, but I was determined that I was going to reach the belt of trees, where the next fence was situated, before this motorised amoeba. Flame seemed to be of the same opinion. We made it and went on to complete the cross-country course with no further penalties to add to his dressage and the 5 on the steeplechase. We also ended the day in the lead from Olivia, who was less than a showjumping penalty behind, which meant that Flame and I had no room for error in the final day's showjumping.

In spite of the fright that I had had on the steeplechase course the day before, Flame trotted up perfectly sound and bursting with vigour at the vet's inspection. Unfortunately, my horse's enthusiasm got the better of him during our showjumping round and we had one fence down, so that it was Aly Pattinson who collected the first prize, with Flame as the runner-up.

The 5 penalties from the steeplechase proved critical, penalties I might well have avoided had the traumatic experience of Doublet's accident not made me especially cautious when Flame had felt so lame. In all other respects Tidworth had been better than we might have hoped and did wonders for my confidence and enthusiasm.

We returned from Tidworth to prepare Goodwill for Burghley and once again went north to the Scottish events where we finished third in the Open Intermediate section at Annick. Because the World Championships were in the UK, the home team could enter the six from whom the team would be chosen, plus another six who could run as individuals, and it was as an individual that Goodwill was selected to compete while Columbus and Mark were selected for the team. This meant that I was allowed to 'share' Mark's team accommodation at the George in Stamford, which was comfortable, convenient and good fun.

For some unknown reason, I seem to remember more about this visit to Burghley than I do about my first, successful one. No doubt it is because I was more relaxed and knew what to expect. The stable lay-out had all the horses living in tented boxes at the bottom of one field, the caravans for the grooms' accommodation were just beyond them and the stables' administration was grouped around the old black barn which served as the canteen.

The rest of that field and the one next door had practice dressage arenas and practice fences for schooling purposes. To exercise the horses you could ride up to the main arena – just to look around, of course – or hack round the roads and tracks section. If you wanted somewhere to gallop your horses, there was probably a field set aside as long as you asked first. Depending on how far you had come, how long before the competition you had to arrive and when you did your last 'piece of work' (the maximum speed and length of gallop required to achieve full fitness), you might need a big field or just a short, sharp 'blow-out' up the schooling field. This was not always appreciated by those who still had their dressage to do. By 'blow-out' I mean going fast enough to make the horse take a really good deep breath.

The British team on this occasion consisted of: Richard Meade on Wayfarer (who had finished fourth in Russia and sixth at this year's Badminton); Bridget Parker and Cornish Gold (who had finished tenth at the 1972 Olympic Three-day Event in Munich); Christopher Collins and Smokey (who had finished ninth at this year's Badminton) and Captain Mark Phillips and Columbus (who had won this year's Badminton). There was a very strong cast of individuals led by Janet Hodgson on Larkspur; Lucinda Prior-Palmer on Be Fair; Hugh Thomas on Playamar; Barbara Hammond on Eagle Rock and two of the only three horses I ever really coveted during my eventing career, Toby Sturgis' Demi-Douzaine and Virginia Thompson's Cornish Duke.

Goodwill did not like the main area at Burghley where all the space around the dressage arena seemed to make him even more nervous. With the leader on 45.67 points, our 69.00 didn't look too hopeful, but with a big cross-country course to jump and some luck there was always a chance of improving our placing.

What is luck? The bad news was that Goodwill did to himself very much what Flame did at Tidworth. He jumped the open ditch on the second circuit of the steeplechase really well, nodded his head on landing and then nearly pulled himself up in three strides, feeling to me as if he were on three legs. I let him come nearly to a standstill and then asked him to trot on to find out what the damage was, bearing in mind my experience with Flame when his lameness had been like the effect of a human hitting a 'funny bone'. To my intense relief, Goodwill trotted out sound and we galloped on to the finish where he pulled up still sound and Alison told me to carry on round the second section of roads and tracks and that we'd examine him in the box at the ten-minute halt.

I was encouraged to discover that he felt his usual tankworthy self, but was a bit worried about what we might find back at the box. The good news was that he passed the vet check on returning from the roads and tracks and the team vet Peter Scott Dunn could see no reason for him not to continue. So off we went across the horrible ridge and furrow to the first fence. He jumped the first four fences well, so that I was unprepared for what happened at the fifth, the double Coffin behind the main arena.

The approach was downhill to a palisade, one stride to a ditch, land and take off again immediately over another ditch and then up a steep bank to a palisade on the top. One of Goodwill's great strengths was his commitment through a combination; once he had jumped the first part, his ability to think on his feet made progress remarkably smooth. On this occasion we jumped in perfectly well and over the first ditch, but he was not making ground in his usual powerful way so that he landed too close to the first ditch leaving himself too far from the second ditch to jump it cleanly. His hind legs dropped in the second ditch which brought him almost to a standstill. He had insufficient impetus to climb the bank and jump out at the top; where we stopped. I turned back far enough to get a reasonable run at it and he jumped out easily at the second time of asking.

I thought perhaps that both he and I were guilty of being over-confident or had not woken up enough, but as we progressed around the course I realised that he was probably feeling very sore and just not wanting to stretch out with that bruised front leg. Usually Goodwill jumped fences with 'drop' landings lower than the take-off point just as easily and smoothly as the ordinary fences, but on this course each one felt like going down in a lift. I found it very alarming, but in hindsight it was extremely brave of him to jump them at all.

We had rather an exciting experience at the Lower Trout Hatchery. There was a set of rails on the edge of the water, not something that would normally have bothered Goodwill, but on this occasion he suddenly lost his enthusiasm and, instead of picking up both front feet at the same time, he tried hurdling it. I thought that I was going to get very wet, for one second we were perpendicular, but in the next he had recovered his balance and we survived to jump the rest of the course clear.

Although we were disappointed with his performance, we soon realised, when we took his bandages off, how lucky he had been. He had struck into himself right on the back of his tendon, and if it had been to one side or the other, he would probably have been seriously lame. If he hadn't been wearing bandages, he would have severed right through his tendon.

The immediate concern was to limit the bruising, which meant hosing the leg with cold water, then wrapping it up in a hot kaolin poultice and repeating the process every four hours. These are the moments when looking after your own horse single-handedly becomes a nightmare and the grooms really earn their keep. Amazingly, after some gentle exercise, Goodwill passed the vet's inspection on the third morning without giving his connections too many worries.

He then proceeded to jump a competent clear round to finish the World Championships in twelfth place, curiously enough exactly the same result as a certain Mrs Alison Oliver riding Foxdor in the 1966 World Championships, also held at Burghley, as I discovered recently. The World Championship was won by Bruce Davidson riding Irish Cap on a score of 71.67 penalty points from Mike Plumb riding Good Mixture with 71.93. Both were from the USA. Hugh Thomas was less than 1 point behind on 72.47 to win the bronze, with Janet Hodgson and Larkspur finishing fourth.

What is luck? The best clear round in the fastest time of the day was achieved by Mark riding Columbus, but he finished the course knowing there was something wrong because he felt him falter just after the second to last fence. In fact the main tendon on the horse's leg had slipped off the 'groove' in which it normally ran over the point of the hock.

Slipping the tendon off the hock is sufficiently uncommon not to be recognised by many vets. The majority of riders who might work with horses all their lives never see that type of injury. What you discover very early on is that there is no cure and that horses vary widely as to how they adapt to this re-routing of the 'mainspring' in their back leg.

Columbus had always been prone to over-reaction when he thought he was injured. If he received even a light tap anywhere on his legs, they immediately became impressive lumps which you couldn't touch, and as his manners were never very good, you needed to call for volunteers to carry out any treatment. At Burghley he nearly shortened the career of the team vet by aiming a kick at him, which – if it had connected – would have severely damaged Mr Scott Dunn and the wooden partition of the stable, if not the whole row of boxes. Rumour had it that the tendon had only partially slipped and there was some hope that Columbus would be sound enough to compete the next day – until, that is, the vet tried to feel his hock and the kick finished the job of removing the tendon from its groove.

In the morning Columbus was still unlevel behind and, even if it had been possible to get him to trot up sound, the chances of him being able to jump off his damaged hock were not good. So the sad decision was taken to withdraw him when he was in the lead with 1 showjumping penalty in hand for the 1974 World Three-day Event Championships. For Mark it was a devastating disappointment that was impossible to mitigate, except that the horse lived to fight another day, a fact that Columbus' owner (The Queen) was probably more comforted by than his rider.

It was quite difficult to pick ourselves up from the anti-climax of Burghley with a bad short-term outlook for both horses. Goodwill would need a longer holiday than usual to ensure that he suffered no ill effects from the bruising he had inflicted on himself. At that stage we really had no idea how long it would be before Columbus would be able to be ridden again, never mind become sound enough to compete again.

At that time the weight of veterinary opinion suggested that Columbus' eventing days were over because his hind legs would no longer be able to 'track up' evenly and he would therefore be judged technically unsound for the dress-age phase. It was because of this consideration that advice was sought to see if there was any alternative to just leaving the tendon to settle and function in its new position. There was a highly respected French vet, Dr Edouard Pouret, who had had some success in pinning the tendon back into the groove on the top of the hock, and it was decided to take Columbus to the Equine Research Centre in Newmarket for Dr Pouret to operate on him there.

Columbus travelled to Newmarket with my girl groom, Bryony Tucker, who stayed to look after him. The operation was carried out and a pin inserted through the tendon into the centre of the groove. The horse was then left in the recovery box, which was very large with a well-padded floor and walls and very bright lights. Bryony very sensibly asked if the lights could be turned off and if she could remain in the box with him, because she knew what a big baby he was. Her requests were turned down on the grounds that they needed to be able to observe him from the outside and they wouldn't let her stay because of the risk of him thrashing about while coming round from the anaesthetic.

Bryony's instincts told her that, being on his own in a strange, brightly lit box, Columbus was bound to struggle to get up before he had fully recovered from the anaesthetic. My own experience in coming round after an operation was very similar in that, with a bright light shining in my eyes, I struggled to come to, tried to take the drip out of the back of my hand and was violently sick.

Unfortunately, Bryony was quite right about Columbus' reaction. He did thrash about while coming round, to such an extent that he bent the pin that Dr Pouret had just put in and they had to repeat the operation the next week. This time Bryony was allowed to stay with the horse and have the lights dimmed – and he came to quite quietly and got up sensibly. For a while progress seemed promising, but after a week or two Columbus started to lose condition and was obviously in some pain from the pin, so the decision was taken to remove it and leave the tendon to its own devices.

This set-back was rather depressing, but I was beginning to learn from other people's experiences with this type of injury that the long-term prognosis might not be as bad as we had first thought. For instance, in other horse sports, like National Hunt Racing, there were examples of horses returning to success on the racetrack after suffering the very same injury.

I didn't discover that until meeting Fred Winter at the Horse of the Year

Show in October. When I asked him what sort of treatment they had carried out in such a case, the answer was none; the horse had just been left in the field for a year to allow the tendon to settle and the animal to come to terms with this new sensation of the tendon running down the outside of the hock. Columbus was turned away and forgotten – not literally, of course, but just in terms of being an event horse.

Curiously enough, not long after that, one of Marjorie Comerford's horses suffered exactly the same injury on the steeplechase course at the Luhmühlen Three-day Event. Even more surprising was an example Mark and I encountered while we were staying with my great-uncle, Lord Mountbatten, at his home, Broadlands, in Hampshire. He still kept a few horses, mostly retired polo ponies, so that he could ride and take his guests riding round his lovely estate. He took us to the stables and showed us a horse that had been lame behind for some time but the vet had been unable to diagnose the problem. The horse was standing with his back towards us as we walked in and it was immediately obvious to us that the tendon had slipped off the hock. What was different about this case was that the tendon had divided, with about one-third now running down the inside of the hock and two-thirds running down the outside.

Slipping the tendon off the hock is still an uncommon injury and probably indicates a weakness in the conformation of the hind leg – Columbus did have rather straight hind legs with not enough angle at the hock – and yet, when you consider the pressure that the hind joint is under so much of the time, it is a wonder that this kind of injury doesn't occur more often. Humans and horses suffer from a very similar range of injuries as a result of the strains of specialised sports, the most commonly affected parts being the tendons, ligaments and muscles. All can be treated, but the best treatment for tendons and ligaments, because of their structure, is rest.

Columbus returned from the vet for a lengthy rest. Nobody knew how long it would take before he could be ridden again, never mind if he would ever be capable of competing. Goodwill was in the field enjoying himself before he came back into work to be prepared for Badminton. We paid special attention to his early work, keeping a close watch on the leg he had bruised at Burghley. He showed no ill effects and his fitness programme progressed according to plan – a very rare occurrence.

Unfortunately, Flame Gun's did not. I collected him from Warfield one morning to take him for a slow canter at Smith's Lawn in the Park. Flame didn't like cantering slowly and his legs seemed to go all over the place in a form of frustration. But we certainly hadn't gone very fast and I returned him to Warfield with his ears pricked and apparently quite sound. The next day he walked out of his box in his usual bouncy way, but when they tried to get him to trot he just didn't seem to be able to. He was sore on the tendons of both front legs. Poor old Flame's season stopped before it began. I was extremely annoyed with myself for not having discovered until afterwards that he had been on walking exercise the previous week and probably shouldn't have been cantering at all: another lesson learned the hard way.

But there was another horse in the yard, Mardi Gras, a six-year-old chestnut gelding by Manicou out of Easter Day, bred by Lord and Lady Abergavenny who owned and lived at Eridge, where the final trial had been held before the 1971 European Championships. He was an extremely generous wedding present and I think he joined us as a four-year-old. We hadn't done a lot with him the year before because we thought him immature, although he might just have been idle to the point of being ungenerous, so we gave him plenty of time. We also took him to a new form of equestrian activity called a cross-country team race. We didn't really know what it was, but we thought it might encourage him a bit.

This 'race' was in North Yorkshire, run by the Zetland Hunt, which was a long way to take a box-load of two young horses and one Army Saddle Club

A painting of the Zetland Hunt Cross-Country Race.
I'm riding Mardi Gras who finished in front.

faithful, hoping to find another team member up there. After we had walked the course, we all wished we hadn't bothered! The good news was that it was all on grass. The fences were solid and mostly inviting. The bad news was that some of the fences were also very big. The stone wall was at an immovable 4 feet, 'The Chair' was around 5 feet and one of the hedges had a 6–7-foot drop.

While we were walking it and getting ready to go – which was all a bit of a rush – very few teams seemed to be completing the course clear. Indeed very few teams were completing the course at all, and this was in spite of their members who had had a fall making every effort to catch their horses, remount and follow on behind. Some that did even managed to overtake their struggling companions.

We eventually set off with a sort of plan for who was going to lead and who would take over if they had a stop or fall, etc. – otherwise we just kicked and hoped for the best. I was not optimistic about my chances of getting round, but I had seriously underestimated the effect on Mardi of going 'in company' with other horses. I started at the back, thinking he might not keep up, but very soon found myself being pulled to the front, just in time to race over 'The Chair' fence. We all seemed to land on top of each other in the water, but survived. From there it was uphill all the way home and it was then that Mardi's breeding showed. I gave him a kick and he galloped past his team mates. We were all astonished to get round, but we were even more astonished to discover later that we had won.

The spring of 1975 was wet. This was not so much of a problem for getting the horses fit as for the organisers of horse trials. They were faced with difficult decisions about the mess that would result from the number of vehicles, especially horse boxes, leaving long-term damage. And they worried about the point at which the going underfoot was made too heavy to be safe. Several competitions were cancelled, which didn't affect Goodwill's preparations, but proved very awkward for those who needed to qualify or prepare for their first Badminton.

I was rather proud of the fact that Goodwill was fit and ready to run in his third consecutive Badminton. I felt that he would cope with the wet ground better than many of the other horses. Goodwill was a very strong horse and I was confident that, whatever the state of the going, he would still be jumping the fences as well at the end of the course as at the beginning. I also felt that there was a chance that his dressage might be slowed down by the wet ground. Unfortunately for me, Colonel Weldon had made sure that the going in the arena didn't get so deep that the horses had trouble remaining balanced and

Goodwill charged round with his usual 'the faster I go, the sooner I get out' approach to his dressage tests.

As it turned out, it didn't matter. In spite of Colonel Weldon taking even more trouble to ensure that the cross-country course remained ridable under any conditions, the incessant rain and the possible presence of 200,000 spectators made the cancellation unavoidable. The dressage days and the movement of all the trade vehicles on to the show ground had already created a considerable mess and everyone could sympathise with the decision. Even so, the news was greeted with a mixture of relief and regret.

This created a major problem for the selectors, who tended to rely on the results from Badminton to help them make up the short list for that year's championship. Instead they decided to wait until the end of the spring horse trials season, hoping that this would allow time for at least some of their questions to be answered.

I decided to take Goodwill to Tidworth, which I remember very little about, except that it was also very wet and that I went round the cross country in a shower-proof jacket. I think it must have been the wettest cross-country ride I ever had – without falling in the water – and we both finished looking like filthy drowned rats. The best thing about the competition was that Goodwill's leg never gave us a moment of concern. He went well enough to finish sixth and was put on the long list for the European Championships at Luhmühlen in north Germany.

The team that was finally selected to compete in the 1975 European Championships at Luhmühlen consisted of: Lucinda Prior-Palmer with Be Fair; Janet Hodgson with Larkspur; Sue Hatherley with Harley, who had been ninth at Badminton in 1973 and third at Burghley the same year; and Goodwill. There were two reserves who would run as individuals: Carolan Geekie with Copper Tiger, who had finished twelfth at Badminton in 1974; and, finally, the only man, Mike Tucker, with Ben Wyvis who had been thirteenth at Badminton in 1974. Nobody quite knew whether this was good news or bad news for Mike.

Luhmühlen was reached by a night crossing from Harwich to Bremerhaven and a two-hour drive almost due east to an area on the edge of the Lüneburg Heath, south of Hamburg. As you drove east, the land became lighter and sandier until you came to great blocks of forestry on the poorest soil. Luhmühlen was situated close to one of these heathland areas, which was where the cross-country course was built. The town was attractive and friendly and we stayed in the Gasthaus, a handsome wooden traditional north German building.

The British Horse Trials team at Smiths Lawn, Windsor, before going over
to the European Championships at Luhmühlen.

There was room only for the British team and a few of their regular clients, but
the restaurant was popular and usually full. I thought the food was very good,
the roe deer and wild boar being particularly tasty, but the rest of the party
tended to stick to steak and French fries.

Most of the horses were stabled at the local riding club where there were
also some small working-in areas. The competitive site was a ten-to-fifteen-
minute walk away, in the centre of a racecourse. It wouldn't be fair to describe it
as a rustic racecourse, because the course had white-painted rails all round it, a
wooden grandstand and permanent fences, which were to be our steeplechase
fences. The ground was very sandy but mostly covered with old heathland turf,
which is tough and quite springy. The dressage arena was in the grassed main
arena, surrounded by permanent mini 'Derby-type' fences (the stone-faced wall,

bank, ditches and hedge that are a feature of the Aachen and Hickstead show-jumping classics).

The steeplechase course was designed to confuse the poor British and Irish. Most of our 'chase courses run round two plain circuits, which makes it easier to remember where you are going and where half-way is. At Luhmühlen the course, viewed from above, looked like a circle with a cross in it and we rode over every bit of it.

I had two problems during the competition. One was the press, who were everywhere and who chose to interpret Goodwill's relatively good dressage score as the result of doping because they had seen Mark give him something immedi-

Luhmühlen. Goodwill being quite quiet for him.

ately before his test. It was a lump of sugar to try to take his mind off the competition.

My other problem was that I woke up on the morning of the cross country with a humdinger of a cold. My nose was completely blocked and my head felt much the same. The last thing I felt like doing was dragging myself out of bed in order to jump on a horse for nearly two hours. They started the competition very early by British standards. I was due to start about nine and I was second to go for the team, which meant that poor Janet Hodgson on Larkspur had set off at sun-up.

I have to say that I was not showing much enthusiasm for my task, although I did remember to wake up and concentrate on not getting lost round the steeplechase course. It turned out that Goodwill gave me the best and most exciting ride round a 'chase course anyone could hope to have. The different fences – wooden and stone bases with a sort of privet hedge either growing or placed in the top – kept his interest and the constant turning and changes of direction kept him in a better balance. I think I was actually on the course when I heard the commentator say something about Larkspur having a second fall on the cross country. Now that did wake me up and I started to take life very seriously.

I had a wonderful ride, or rather Goodwill gave me a wonderful ride, in spite of my attempts to strangle him jumping into the water, part of a complex of combinations where you had at least three routes to choose from – a practice that seems to have got rather out of hand recently. The course was big, very well built and full of combinations. There was one, right out in the country, built like a farmyard, where the distance between the first two fences on the direct route was either for two long, galloping strides or three much shorter, slower ones. Goodwill and Ben Wyvis, ridden by Michael Tucker, were the only two horses even to try to go in two strides and they both succeeded. But I think Goodwill made it look easier.

Goodwill finished inside the time allowed so he had no penalties to add to his dressage score. I went into the lead and stayed there until Lucinda Prior-Palmer and Be Fair overtook me and we went into the third day lying first and second.

It was my habit to let the groom trot the horse up at the vet's inspections because I felt it was a way for them to show off their work. For some reason Lucinda wanted to trot up Be Fair herself, so our chef d'équipe decided that we all ought to trot our horses up ourselves. I was not keen on the decision, because

The water combination at Luhmühlen.

'Running up' at the European Championships, Luhmühlen.

Goodwill's approach to the vet's inspection was rather like his approach to the dressage arena – the faster you go, the sooner you finish – and he was much quicker than me. My only worries were whether I could keep up with him and keep my feet out of his way. In fact, after trotting very sensibly away from the stables, when he turned for home my worry became whether we would run over the inspection panel on our way back.

The team had only three members left as a result of Larkspur's being withdrawn, but we were in the lead with three fences in hand from the Russians. Goodwill jumped an accurate but slightly slow clear round to finish on his dressage score and secure the Silver Medal. Sue Hatherley was our third member riding the ex-Australian horse, Harley, which I had nearly bought from Bill Roycroft after Munich. Sue and Harley appeared to be going well, if a bit cautiously, when Harley suddenly stopped at the first part of a combination and shot a very surprised Sue over his head. They finished the course but their score dropped our team below the Russians with one rider from each team still to go.

Lucinda went clear to win the individual Gold Medal and Pietr Gornuschko and Gusar jumped a clear round to ensure the team Gold for Russia and the Bronze Medal for himself.

It was cruel luck for Sue; we all know that, with horses, that sort of thing can happen to anybody, though we all hope it won't occur at a championship event. But the team of *Amazonens*, as the Germans called us, had not disgraced themselves. The token male didn't do too badly either; he finished seventh.

For a variety of reasons the Silver Medal I won at Luhmühlen gave me a greater sense of satisfaction than winning the individual championship at Burghley. I didn't really appreciate what Doublet and I had achieved, I suppose, because I was so new to the sport and hadn't had to make any of the decisions about training. It might so easily have been a flash in the pan, as more than one person pointed out to me that women were very seldom successful on more than one horse. At Luhmühlen not only had I been successful on another, completely different type of horse, but I had also achieved it with much less help. Goodwill and I may have won only a Silver Medal, but the glow of satisfaction was golden.

Goodwill. Germany: Luhmühlen.

CHAPTER 8

The 1976 Olympics:

'The lights were on but there was no one at home'

GOODWILL went on his holiday after we had treated his suspensory liga-ment, which had shown signs of slight damage after Luhmühlen, but it was a purely precautionary exercise and it never gave him any problems afterwards. We were conscious that with his form and as long as he stayed sound, he would be a strong contender for the short list to go to the Olympics in Montreal. I tried not to think about it on the basis that there were far too many things that could go wrong.

The plan was the same as usual, to start work on 1 January in order to be fit to run at Badminton. As it turned out, the selectors asked that Be Fair and Goodwill should not compete at Badminton, a decision that was much discussed at the time. It was one that I wasn't too happy about because I felt it was import-ant for our confidence, but I had to admit that not competing avoided many of the potential risks involved with tackling a course of that standard.

I hardly noticed the difference in the run-up, because Mark had three horses to get fit, Favour, Persian Holiday and Brazil. As a result of a change in the rules, he could ride only two, but the selectors asked that he be allowed to run Persian Holiday *hors concours* (that is, his score wouldn't count). Brazil was retired after falling into the Lake, Persian Holiday was withdrawn on the third day after a reasonable but slow round and Favour finished third.

The final day was marred and the whole competition somewhat over-shadowed by the sudden collapse and death of Wideawake after his successful showjumping round which won Lucinda Prior-Palmer the coveted Whitbread Trophy for the second time. Hugh Thomas and Playamar were second and Richard Meade, riding Jacob Jones, was fourth.

Meanwhile, Goodwill was being kept occupied and I was taking Mardi Gras and Candlewick, a home-bred mare out of Trim Ann by Night Watch, to various horse trials. After Badminton I took Candlewick to the Portman Horse Trials in Dorset. She was a good-looking, well-built but rather suspicious mare who had been going reasonably well, if rather slowly. On this day, I came through a gate

The fall at Montreal.

Riding Candlewick at Tweseldown.

very steadily in order to jump a rail that was angled away from us. I have no idea what happened next, except that I eventually regained full consciousness nearly twenty-four hours later. I remember nothing of the journey to the hospital in Bournemouth, which is probably just as well because the ambulance was described as pre-war vintage and had some difficulty in keeping up with the police car that was escorting it. It may have been the influence of this unstable ride that brought on a bout of violent illness which certainly spoilt the unfortunate accompanying St John's cadet's day – and his trousers as well. (I met this cadet some time later at a St John's conference at Sandhurst when he gave me back my gloves which I thought I had lost.)

I vaguely remember being moved and being in an empty room and then moving again. I was aware of arriving at Sister Agnes' in London, which was late morning the day after the fall.

I had been very lucky. From what I have since discovered, the mare went to stop, didn't, shot me over her head and then rolled over the top of me. Fortunately, I was already unconscious and therefore completely relaxed when she fell on me and, considering how hard the ground was that year, the fact that I broke only two of the wings of my vertebrae and not any of the vertebrae themselves was a minor miracle.

Concussion is still unpredictable and, if not taken seriously, can lead to difficult complications later in life, sometimes much later. I was only too happy to stay in the King Edward VII hospital for a few days and do what came naturally, which was to sleep. Even when I went home, feeling fine physically, I would fall asleep whenever I sat down, but that seems to be nature's way of giving the brain time to recover.

I did not suffer any noticeable ill effects, so Goodwill and I worked our way towards the final trial to be held at Osberton – the home of Michael Foljambe, another generous horse trials supporter and competitor – where the selectors would choose the seven horses they were allowed to enter for the Olympics. They included the four team horses, two reserves and one spare. The 'competition' was designed to find out if their first choices were fit, sound and going well. Goodwill was never at his best at one-day events, but he gave me a very confident ride round the cross-country course, was fit and trotted up sound at the vet's inspection the following morning.

The selectors made their decision on the short list that day, but they didn't decide on the actual team members until after the concentration period at Wylye, the lovely home of Lord and Lady Hugh Russell. Goodwill was in the team along with Lucinda Prior-Palmer and Be Fair; Richard Meade and Jacob Jones; and Hugh Thomas and Playamar. The reserves were Jane Starkey with Topper Too and Mark with both Favour and Persian Holiday.

Horses and riders flew separately to Montreal, the riders joining a flight with many other British athletes, most of whom were living in the Olympic village. We headed south to Bromont, where all the equestrian disciplines were to take place. This was nearly a two-hour road journey from Montreal – a great shame for those who would like to have had the opportunity to watch other disciplines. We had our own village which had been specially built as a housing development and was completely surrounded by a high wire fence with only one entrance and exit, manned by the local provincial police, who, although technically bi-lingual, made a point of speaking only French. All the tight security was a result of the terrorist attack at the Munich Olympics, but apart from the mental discipline of remembering your pass I don't believe it was too obtrusive.

The Canadians felt it necessary to give me my own protection: a team of Royal Canadian Mounted Police (RCMP), the national force with individuals taken from all over Canada. They were a very interesting group with a wide variety of experiences in plain-clothes work. I felt really sorry for them being taken off what was serious police work to look after a nonentity like me. Certainly I had been to Canada twice before and had received police protection, but those visits had been official ones with Federal and State personnel and a very public programme where security was a more obvious problem. The RCMP were used to protecting VIP visitors, but I don't think they had ever been faced with so many in so many different places, all at the same time.

On my first visit to Canada, when my brother and I accompanied our parents on a tour that included the North-west Territories and Manitoba, we did some of the travelling on the train. The RCMP still have horses and, after one overnight stop, since we did not need to move on until late morning and as it was apparently not far from the RCMP's depot, they offered to bring some of their horses out to the train for us to ride. It was grain-belt country, miles and miles of flat, open farmland, but it looked more interesting from the back of a horse than it did from the train. Their horses were well trained and well behaved, or at least they were until my brother went to get on. His horse took an instant dislike to him and set off back down the road when he still had only one foot in the stirrup, but fortunately he did manage to get properly mounted and pull up before they got to the end of the train. By comparison, the rest of the ride was positively boring.

The country round Bromont was very different from the prairies – hilly and, after one of the wettest summers on record, a mass of variegated greens of trees, crops and grass as this was an important dairying area. The equestrian centre had been carved out of nothing, the stable blocks looking down on the racetrack, the main and practice arenas in the valley below. There were also plenty of practice arenas near the stables and you could canter around the out-side of the racetrack, which was where the steeplechase course was to go.

The horses had arrived the week before the start of the three-day event, which was the first of the equestrian disciplines to compete. Our horses were fit to run when they left Britain in order that we didn't have to do any hard fitness work after we arrived. Goodwill was fitter than he had ever been and carrying less weight, so I was completely confident that he would cope with the hills and the humidity which were worrying some of the others. The team vet was not so confident, but for a different reason. He felt that Goodwill was not quite level when taken straight out of his stable and trotted down the alley between the stables. I was asked if they could give him some bute 'just in case'. I refused on the basis he had never had it before and I wasn't prepared to find out at the Olympics, and round such a twisty course, what effect it would have on my ability to control him. It was suggested that they might not feel able to keep him in the team without the bute safeguarding his passing the first vet's inspection. I replied that that was my problem. I remained in the team.

I was not as confident about my own state of fitness as I was about Goodwill's. It had seemed perfectly adequate until I saw how much extra exercise my team mates were taking. Having only one horse to ride does limit the amount of mounted exercise you can take and although I was prepared to play badminton – with racket and shuttlecock – I drew the line at running.

Our accommodation was in houses, but our feeding was in what was to be the sports centre, a large building with tables at one end and a variety of games at the other. Badminton is a good game for exercising you as it requires fairly quick reactions in a small area. I had played the game, off and on, since I was quite young with my father and brother, but we never seemed to progress beyond the average level as a result of my brother and I suffering from the apparently insurmountable handicap of laughter, which rendered us both incapable of continuing to play. As he wasn't in Bromont, I played a lot better, but it wasn't so much fun!

Meal times and, to a lesser extent, evenings were for meeting other competitors from the other two disciplines, whom we rarely met at home, and competitors from other countries, some of whom we might have met at international three-day events, but many of whom we would never have seen before. This was where the lasting effects of the Olympic Games would be started, with new friendships across many boundaries.

There was no shortage of volunteers to go to the Opening Ceremony of the Games, and on the day we set off back up the freeway to Montreal. It was a long day with a great deal of waiting about, first at the village and then at the stadium. Comfortable shoes would have been sensible, but most people had not worn their uniform shoes before and were not used to standing for long periods. I was marginally better prepared, but I can't say that my feet were feeling quite as they had been in the morning.

Whilst waiting in the village, we had had the opportunity to meet athletes from other sports, including some of the yachtsmen who had come from even further away than the riders as they were based at Kingston, on the shores of Lake Ontario. For both groups that was almost the only chance we had to share the atmosphere that is the heart of the Olympic Games. Marching into the main stadium was certainly an experience that I am unlikely to forget. Part of the experience was sharing it with people who were complete strangers but with whom you felt an instant empathy and who were feeling very similar emotions. We were graded according to height and I found myself surrounded by our women's rowing eight, nearer the back than the front of our contingent. They were a very good group to be with.

I don't remember the ceremony very clearly, but that is probably because the sound system was not designed to be heard in the middle of the stadium, so we couldn't hear a lot of what was going on. By today's standards it was a relatively simple opening, although we couldn't see what went on before we marched into the stadium. I found it impressive, but I was already getting the feeling that the athletes were not the main concern of the ceremony's organisers, a problem that seems to have got worse rather than better as the years have passed. Still, we all returned to Bromont feeling much more a part of the Olympic Games and ready to get on with our competition.

The main excitement of any new site is the first walk-round of Phase D, the cross-country course, to see what problems the course designer has set for you. Bromont was a mixture of narrow tracks through woods and open country that started off downhill. The whole of the second half of the course was gradually climbing back up the valley. I thought the course looked different and interesting but not ideal for Goodwill because it was very twisty in places. This meant I was slightly more worried about my ability to present him to the fences sufficiently balanced to be able to jump them than I was about the fences themselves.

The second fence was at the bottom of a very steep bank – and I mean steep, the sort on which you can stand only at the top or the bottom; the bit in between was a lottery. The fence was a simple set of rails placed on flat land about 9 feet from the bottom of the bank. The horse had to come down the bank straight and balanced, which meant that you had to approach the bank very slowly to make it understand that there was something that it couldn't see but over which it needed to take great care. For me it posed serious problems, because it was so early in the course that Goodwill would be wanting to get into his stride and would assume that it was much too early to have a difficult fence.

Later there was a combination, not only in the trees, but on the side of a hill as well. If you overshot any part of the fence, it could take you some time to extricate yourself from the undergrowth. The trees also played a crucial role on a stretch of the course between two fences. Our route went through a section of pine trees, but not courtesy of any recognisable track. You had to find your own way between trees that were sometimes only just far enough apart to allow the unbattered passage of a horse *and* rider – the horse seldom makes allowances for your knees or your head. Just to make it a little trickier, these trees were not planted in straight lines.

There was one other obstacle that caused some head scratching. It was towards the end of the course and looked like an open water, but it was in the bottom of quite a deep gulley, which meant that you couldn't really gallop at it. A tired horse might well think it ought to jump into it and not over it, in which case the fall would be painful for both parties.

The running order of the team had been settled so that Playamar went first, followed by Goodwill, Jacob Jones and Be Fair. We had all decided what sort of information we would like from the number of British observers placed at strategic points around the course. I wasn't too worried about how other horses jumped the course, but I was interested in hearing if the going was affecting the way horses were jumping the fences; whether it was slippery or very soft. There were several combination fences where the decision about where to jump them would depend entirely on the condition of the ground in and around the fences. One particular combination consisted of two fences quite a long way apart but related because of the angles at which they were built and the trees and bushes in between the alternatives. There were two ways of approaching the problem: my first choice was 'A' but, having learned my lesson in Kiev, I felt that 'B' would be just as good if I received information that indicated that my first choice was not riding well.

But first we had the little matter of a dressage test to negotiate. The main arena had been divided by temporary stands to create and surround a smaller arena for the dressage. There were stands on two sides and the other two sides were steep banks. One of the banks was high enough completely to obscure the arena from the practice arena, so that on the day of the competition none of the horses had any idea of what they would see when they walked round the end of the bank. The sight that greeted them was an amphitheatre of people and noise. It was this sight that completely demoralised Goodwill, to the extent that he tried to turn round and leave.

The fall at Montreal.

The atmosphere when we got down to the bottom was intense. The crowd had gone very quiet, which, if anything, added to Goodwill's discomfort. We could hear every whisper and every click of every camera. Goodwill's big ears were working overtime and, instead of being annoyed, he was a very unhappy horse. He was so sensitive that I could hardly move a muscle without getting an over-reaction. Even in his extended trot, which was his best movement, his attention was so much on the crowd that he caught his toe on the sand across the middle of the arena and broke into a canter, something he usually managed to avoid. It was not a good test, but I kept saying to myself that it wouldn't matter on endurance day.

It rained heavily the night before the cross country, which didn't worry me at the time but later was to ruin my day. Concussion is a strange thing, and if my memory is never very good, it is almost non-existent for that day. I vaguely remember the start of Phase A, the roads and tracks. I remember being very pleased to get inside the time allowed on Phase B, because the rain had made the going on the steeplechase course like a wet beach, which made it noisy – the horses' feet slapping into the wet surface – and hard work. Many people decided to accept penalties on that phase so as not to tire their horses before Phase D.

I don't remember being in the ten-minute-halt box or what I was told about Playamar's round. But I was not told anything that required me to alter my approach to any of the fences. My memory hereafter is highly selective. I know I was thrilled with the way Goodwill coped with the bank and rails that were the second fence and recall being very impressed at how sensible he was going through the trees. Even more remarkable was the way he nipped in and out of the combination on the hillside as quickly as some who had taken the more direct route.

He was going really well, using his head and listening to me. I was having a great ride. That's all I remember. I have mentioned that there was one fence which I would have been happy to jump in either one of two ways. Because I had heard nothing to the contrary, I stuck with option 'A'. I jumped the first part quite quickly and swung easily on to the line for the second part – the zig-zag rails over a ditch. I saw my stride a long way out and gave Goodwill the message that he could accelerate towards the fence. The last thing I remember was a ghastly sinking sensation, as if all four of Goodwill's feet were stuck in treacle. Then, as far as I am concerned, the lights went out.

What happened next is, as they say, history. Goodwill did his best to

Other views of the fall at Montreal.

remain upright, or I wouldn't be here now. Becoming bogged had completely destroyed his rhythm, and the combined effect of being so close to the fence and going quite fast meant that there was no time for him to get his balance and momentum back before reaching the point of no return when he would have to try to take off or simply run into a stationary object. What was amazing was that the impact of hitting the fence didn't turn him over. As it was, he landed on his side and I landed with him.

All my information comes from the official video of the day that I didn't see until the next day and from Bertie Hill, who picked me up. Poor old Goodwill lay winded for about a minute, but seemed to be all right when he got to his feet. Bertie apparently asked me if I wanted to continue to which I'm assured I replied 'Yes'. I find that hard to believe, as I had always told the chef d'équipe that if I had a bad fall I did not want to be thrown back on because I evented for fun. However, I am in no position to argue with Bertie; but, having seen the film, I know I did not look right. The expression 'The lights were on, but there was no one at home' describes my condition at the time very accurately. I have

since discovered that if the Jockey Club doctor had been there, there would have been no danger of my being allowed to ride on.

I was given a leg up and nearly set off in the wrong direction. After that, I can only tell you what I saw on the film, and when I saw what happened at the fence coming out of the water for the first time, my heart nearly stopped. Goodwill jumped in a bit too boldly, cantered over the fence in the water and on to the fence that was clear of the water on the grass bank. The fence was a set of rails with a sawn half-log, flat side up, set immediately in front of it like a small seat. It was supposed to help the horse sight the fence after splashing out of the water and to stop it getting too close to the fence and hitting it. For some mysterious reason Goodwill didn't take one of his bold leaps, but put in another stride for which there wasn't room. One of his front legs went between the half-log and the fence, which should have made it impossible to get over the fence safely. Equally mysteriously Goodwill managed to extricate his leg *and* jump the fence without breaking his own leg or dislodging me. By now I was being about as much help to him as an umbrella in a hurricane.

Not long after that narrow escape we had to negotiate that tricky section of closely planted pine trees. There is no visual record of our passage, but as we were not eliminated for going the wrong way, I imagine we must have succeeded, although not quite unscathed. When the doctor was checking me over that evening, we discovered some painful bruising on the outside of my left leg whose presence could not be explained by the fall because Goodwill and I had landed on our right-hand sides. It took me a very long time to work out where the bruises could have come from – fourteen years to be precise; I only realised it while writing this.

Goodwill completed the course in quick time because he knew he was headed for home. His sense of direction was extremely efficient. I still have no idea whether we jumped into or over the open water in the gully, but he jumped the last few fences and finished galloping strongly as if nothing had happened. One of the most satisfying and exhilarating moments in a three-day event is when you complete the speed and endurance phases. The most disappointing aspect of my Olympic experience is that I do not have that satisfaction because I don't remember finishing the course. After dismounting and weighing out, several people spoke to me, including Hugh Thomas who passed me as I was leaving the box to return to the stables. He asked me how I had got on, to which he received the slightly surprising answer that I did not know. How did I know I didn't know?

Some time later, up in the stable block, I can remember hearing Mark's voice talking about the course, but I was in total darkness somewhere above him. I could also hear myself asking him questions. He said something about a fall which I didn't realise I had had and then he mentioned mud – it was as if somebody had turned the light on as I came to sitting on the tack box where he was pulling off my riding boots. At that moment I didn't even remember having started and was astonished to discover what I had been doing. We went to look at Goodwill who appeared to be in remarkably good condition, but minus a front shoe which he must have torn off before the fall, tearing some of the hoof wall at the same time.

I then went to find the members of my family who had taken the trouble to come and watch: my parents and three brothers. I don't think my mother had really wanted to come and my brothers didn't really know what was going on, but it was nice of them to turn up, even if it meant my enduring such comments as: 'You went so much better after your fall, we ought to bang you on the head before you start next time!'

It was about then that I discovered that a messenger had been sent to tell me to use route 'B' at that fence, but that the chain on the bicycle carrying the messenger had broken and the messenger failed to arrive in time for me to change my plans. That part of the course had become waterlogged after the overnight rain and what had looked and felt like a perfectly sound grass surface had turned into a sponge. My father went to examine it later in the day and found four deep holes, not just hoof prints. Poor Goodwill – what an unjust reward for going so well! He had proved himself a class horse and a brave horse and he would receive precious little credit for his performance. That night there was no guarantee that either of us would be fit to continue in the morning.

I did not wake up in time for the early inspection of our horses by the team vet. This turned out to be unfortunate, because it was apparently decided that Goodwill might not pass the official vet's inspection if he didn't have some help. The foot that had lost the shoe seemed to be the only problem he had and that could have been helped by a bucket of ice. The help that he got was the kind I had refused before the competition started, a dose of bute which was administered intravenously so that it would take effect more quickly. I didn't discover this for some time, but why should they tell me? I was only the rider. At the final vet's inspection, Goodwill passed and nearly ran away with poor Bryony all the way back to his stable.

Whether we jumped on the final day had become an individual decision,

Both these photographs show me going round concussed after the fall.

because Britain no longer had a team. The other dramas I had not been aware of the previous day were that Playamar, who had jumped a clear round, had strained his tendon too badly to continue and that Be Fair had also jumped a clear round, only to slip the tendon off his hock (the same injury suffered by Columbus) within sight of the finish. Richard Meade had conjured a remarkable round out of Jacob Jones to stand in fourth place going into the final day.

Goodwill was extremely strong in the showjumping where he jumped a very good clear round, but with time faults because I had such trouble controlling him. It was after that uncharacteristic display that I discovered about the intravenous bute, which made me quite angry but completely vindicated my decision not to allow the vet to give him any before our cross country. We finished in twenty-fourth place, the lowest in Goodwill's career by some way, but in the best traditions of the sport we had finished. 'If' is a little word with a big meaning – as my governess always used to tell me – but without that fall I'm convinced that Goodwill would have finished very close to Jacob Jones which would have been a truer assessment of his ability. He was a real Olympic athlete.

That was my Olympic experience and I shall always be grateful for having had the opportunity to take part in what is still a unique occasion. Why is it still unique? It may have something to do with the fact that a majority of participants are pleased to be just that, and the number of personal best performances would

seem to indicate that the taking part continues to be important. People still devote years of their life, at considerable personal cost and sacrifice, in order to compete at an Olympic Games, and for some only a Gold Medal will do. It demands personal discipline, long-term commitment, determination and support from family and friends with no guarantee of a pay-off at the end. I believe that all participants can benefit from the experience if they make good use of the knowledge about themselves that they have gained on their way to the Olympics.

Some people discover that the special atmosphere inspires them to greater

Showjumping on the final day of the Montreal Olympics.

heights than they had previously thought were possible. Others, sadly, find the opposite – that they cannot even reproduce their average performance. In most sports, if you miss one of the major championship events, you don't have to wait four years for another opportunity. Living with success or failure is an equally important experience and sometimes more difficult to manage than the success or failure itself. Some who were set on a career in sport that would have been enhanced by a good performance at the Olympics find that there is a lot less help around for those who don't live up to expectations. I was fortunate because I had always been able to regard my sport as my hobby and therefore only a short-term involvement. I had other things to do that would not be affected by my performance, good or bad.

I had already decided that my serious competitive career would probably end after the Olympics because of pressure of time and the possibility of starting a family. I could continue to have a lot of fun and satisfaction riding Goodwill, who was still in his prime and completely sound, but it would be at a different level. I had no idea what other roles might be waiting for me. I was to discover that my equestrian career was going to involve me in a variety of new experiences.

The final showjumping phase caused some changes to the placings. The leader after the endurance day was Karl Schultz riding Madrigal (West Germany), but he knocked down two fences to drop to third. Mike Plumb, riding Better and Better (USA), also had a fence down, but he moved up into second place. His error allowed a little breathing space for Tad Coffin, riding the mare Ballycor (USA), but they didn't need it and won the individual Olympic Gold Medal, while the performance of Bruce Davidson, riding Irish Cap, made sure of the team Gold Medal for the Americans from West Germany and Australia.

At that stage I don't remember feeling terribly disappointed, probably because I was just relieved that both of us were still in one piece and had completed an Olympic three-day event.

Our competition had taken up nearly one week of the two-week period of the Games and the dressage and showjumping took up most of the rest. Those of us who had finished stayed to support the other disciplines, which effectively left us with no time to go and support any of our fellow Britons competing in Montreal. We did go to the Closing Ceremony as spectators, where I got the feeling, at the moment of the handing over of the flag, that the quietness was more reflective than sad – a sense that it was we, the athletes, who had made this extraordinary festival possible.

CHAPTER 9

Riding Overseas:

'I thought you said you could ride!'

COMPETING in international three-day events was not the only time I had the opportunity to ride overseas. My 'international' riding experience – if that is the right expression – began back in 1965 when I accompanied my father on a visit to Germany to call on some of his many relatives. I remember that first ride as I would a bad nightmare; with a shudder. It was raining and I had no gloves. We rode on forestry tracks on a steep wooded hillside. I was generously lent a little horse that I don't think had been out of his stable for at least a week. The result was severe fright and very sore fingers and knees.

This experience placed a considerable dent in my confidence in general and my attitude to 'spare' rides in particular. It was my first and very nearly my last invitation ride, which would have made this a very short chapter, but I recovered. I'm not sure what that proves – either great stupidity or a very short memory – but I went on to take the opportunity to ride in many countries around the world and to enjoy a view that was available to only a few people.

In August 1966, Prince Philip, as President of the Commonwealth Games Federation, attended the Games in Kingston, Jamaica, and took my brother and me with him. Prince Charles played polo, during which there was a 'shower' of such ferocity that the spectators couldn't see the pitch and they had to stop playing. When we got back to where we were staying and eventually pulled his boots off, we emptied at least a pint of water out of each one. I was luckier when I went riding, which was early in the morning up in the hills above Kingston on a very well behaved ex-racehorse. It was certainly the best time of day and we were treated to a wonderful variety of bird sightings and sounds. The hills were steep and tree-covered and the track we followed wound to and fro as it made its way to the top of the hill. We didn't have time to go all the way to the top but high enough to be treated to a wonderful view of Jamaica.

Visiting Jamaica, watching the Games, meeting some of the athletes and experiencing a few of the exclusive holiday facilities for which the north coast of Jamaica is famous was an amazing adventure for a teenager who turned sixteen

Riding Siglavy Bona in the Spanish Riding School in Vienna.

the day we left for home. I recently returned to Jamaica, to the Mona Campus of the University of the West Indies, which was where the athletes were housed for the Games. I did not ride during this visit, but I did go to a demonstration by some of Jamaica's disabled riders who are supported and helped by some of the country's racing and polo enthusiasts. I would not have seen that in 1966. I hope I've learned something in twenty-four years.

The first offical overseas visit on which I accompanied my parents was to Austria in 1969 – and I nearly didn't make it because of a bout of flu. The State Visit was due to last from Tuesday to Friday. On the Monday evening the day before I was in Newcastle, after having launched my first ship from the Swan Hunter ship yard. A super-tanker, she was the biggest ship they had ever launched into the Tyne. She was so big that she could not be launched from opposite the top of the bow, so I had to break the champagne over the huge bulge that is normally below the waterline. That all went fine and I found it a very impressive occasion, especially the obvious pride of the workers, their families and the whole community. A ship launching is an event that has never lost its excitement for me.

VIENNA

That evening I had to attend a reception and dinner. During the reception I felt very strange and began to have difficulty with my vision. I had to ask for a chair so that I could sit down before I fell down. I also discovered that the Lord Lieutenant's wife was wearing an identical dress to mine, but I don't think that was what made me feel faint. I returned to London on the train after the dinner and barely slept at all. My high temperature removed any question of my going with my parents later that day, but a quiet day and a normal temperature might see me joining them on the Wednesday.

I made it, but not in time to join them at the Spanish Riding School for a gala performance of the Ride. I was allowed to visit the School, on my own and with my riding clothes. To my astonishment Colonel Handler was prepared to let a complete novice ride one of their precious horses. I accepted only because of what I had learnt from riding Roman Holiday and from what Alison had already been able to teach me.

The Lipizzaner is a stocky type of horse with a lot of muscle bulk that is needed for the complicated movements called the Airs Above the Ground. The origins and history of the Spanish Riding School are covered much more comprehensively elsewhere, but perhaps I ought to point out that the original

On Siglavy Bona in Vienna.

purpose of the training was to make the horse in war more useful to his rider than as just a mobile platform. Some of the movements were defensive and some offensive, although I have my doubts as to how effective the training or the movements were in the heat of battle. Much of the flat work is what you will see in an advanced dressage test and the sort of practical training that is used by mounted police units for crowd control.

I had watched a short demonstration before I was offered the chance to ride one of the White Stallions, Siglavy Bona, under the watchful eye and helpful instruction of Colonel Handler. The make and shape of the horses does not make them smooth movers and I found it took me some time to be able to find a rhythm so that I could sit still enough not to interfere with the horse, who knew far more about what he was supposed to be doing than I did. I was astonished by how much we did manage to achieve in spite of my ignorance, which says a great deal for the training and the temperament of the stallions.

Rather like that of the military and the police, the Spanish Riding School saddlery is of traditional design, very firm and broader than a modern sport saddle. I felt as if I were sitting on top of a small square-topped table – even if it was covered in doe skin – which did nothing to improve my deep seat (an expression that is used by dressage trainers to indicate if you are sitting deeply enough in the saddle). This didn't matter too much while I was attempting movements that I recognised, like half-pass and flying changes, but when it came to the passage (elevated trot) and piaffe (stationary trot) I found it more and more difficult to stay in contact with the saddle. Once I had employed the right aids to do passage, we were off. As Siglavy got into the swing and rhythm I bounced higher and higher until I finally became completely out of synchronisation with him, which he didn't seem to mind very much as I had to stop him before I fell off.

If the saddle was traditional, so was the double-bridle: the bits in the horse's mouth were a plain bridoon and a curb with fairly long side pieces. But the reins were held differently. I seem to remember that you held one rein – the bridoon – in the right hand and the other three in the left. That could depend on how strong the horse was, because you would then use the curb in your right hand. I imagine the reason for that was the necessity of carrying your sword in your right hand, and therefore you had less to rearrange if you had to move only one rein across to your left hand.

If I had had to choose between the chance to see a full ceremonial perform-ance of the Spanish Riding School of Vienna and the experience of actually rid-

Riding in New Zealand on a visit to Sir John Acland's Mount Peel station.

ing one of the famous White Stallions, I know what my choice would have been. I have always been grateful that, in spite of my flu, the programme allowed me a very rare 'hands-on' experience of a unique form of living history. Later in the week we also visited the Piber Stud, where all the Lipizzaners for the School are bred. This is where the mares live, where the foals grow up, where they are selected and disposed of and where the stallions return when they have proved themselves worthy to continue the historic bloodlines.

I believe I learned a great deal from that short visit, but I'm afraid I was not converted to pure dressage. While appreciating the skill involved in breeding, training and riding a horse to that level of discipline, I still remain a strong supporter of the all-round horsemanship that is demanded of the three-day event rider.

New Zealand

In 1970 I was invited to join my parents on an official visit to Fiji, Tonga, New Zealand and Australia to celebrate the travels of Captain James Cook two hundred years before. It was referred to as the Cook Bicentenary Tour, retracing his wake for some of the time on board the Royal Yacht *Britannia*, the most appropriate way of doing so. It would take another book to cover the tour which, not very surprisingly, visited many of New Zealand's ports.

At the end of the first week my brother and I travelled to the central region of the South Island to stay with the Aclands at Mount Peel, their farm in the foothills of the Southern Alps. We were strangers to them, but they opened their doors to us and demonstrated the hospitality for which New Zealanders are justifiably renowned. It was and still is a sheep farm, and the best way of seeing a sheep farm is from the back of a horse. The horses we rode were the station's own, but all had had at least one career elsewhere. The horse that I rode had been a racehorse, on the flat and over fences, and had retired to do some show-jumping and earn his living working with the sheep. Unfortunately, it was a very wet day from the moment we got mounted outside the house, but that didn't stop our hosts taking us for an extensive and interesting ride.

Although there were plenty of trees around the house, there were very few on the hills. There were scrubby bushes along the streams, but the trees were largely conifers planted as wind breaks. The hills did have a rather bleak appearance, yet it was an attractive, rolling countryside with tussocky, tough grass that was a pleasure to ride across.

My memories are coloured by a rather exciting homeward trip. My dear brother was riding another ex-racehorse and, as we turned downhill for home, we were told we could canter on this apparently endless grassy slope. My brother set off at what he swears was a canter, but it didn't feel like that from where I was – just behind him. It had never stopped raining and by now my fingers were numb. This handicap, combined with the effect of heading for home and being at the back, resulted in my horse building up his speed without my having any noticeable effect on his ever-quickening progress. As I drew alongside my brother I seem to remember asking him how fast he thought he was going. His answer was to ask a rhetorical question – 'I thought you said you could ride?' (shades of our childhood) – to my receding backside as I overtook him, heading for what was revealing itself to be the end of the grassy slope and the beginning of an escarpment. I was saved by the home team turning off towards the gate and my horse realising that he was on his own, which meant that he slowed down of his own accord.

The two days we spent at Mount Peel had been a welcome and necessary break on my first major tour. This was very different from a four-day State Visit and it wasn't until I had the opportunity to pause for thought that I realised how tired I was.

We were given a second chance to enjoy New Zealand hospitality in the North Island. This was very different sort of countryside from the South Island, warmer and wetter, with lots of forestry, lots of grass, cows and dairy farming; pretty country, green but enclosed compared to the wide-open spaces of the South Island.

In spite of the fact that the fencing is all wire, there are packs of hounds in this part of New Zealand and the mounted followers train their horses to jump wire. We were given the opportunity to test this claim while being taken for a ride round the property on two experienced hunters. They jumped wire as safely as most horses jump any type of timber fence, but I still don't like jumping it on my own or anybody else's horse.

The whole visit to New Zealand lasted about two weeks and, apart from learning about Captain Cook and his travels, we saw a lot more of the country than many Kiwis do, including some of the many we met and stayed with. They had been relaxed and generous hosts and we were sorry to move on.

AUSTRALIA

The tour moved on to Australia, passing through Sydney on the way down to Tasmania, where we rejoined the Royal Yacht which had pursued us from Auckland. In Sydney I was offered a ride in Centennial Park in the centre of the city – it was big enough to hold a three-day event in, which used to happen annually. I was expecting to ride a police horse, but on the day it turned out to be Dépèche, belonging to Brian Cobcroft; the horse had finished thirteenth in the three-day event in the Olympic Games in Mexico ridden by his owner. I believe he had been the Australian team's reserve horse and was the youngest in the competition. I felt very honoured but nervous. I would have been even more nervous if I

Sheep mustering with Bryan Parkinson, son of the stallion owner,
Mr Don Parkinson, on the Parkinsons' 'Talbea' sheep station
at Cunamulla, West Queensland.

had realised that there were cross-country fences in the Park and that it would
be suggested that I might like to jump them. Dépèche turned out to be not only
very capable but also very amenable and well trained. So much did I enjoy the
experience of jumping him over some of the advanced fences that he became
one of the few horses I ever really coveted.

Dépèche was again in the Australian three-day team in Munich in 1972,
this time ridden by Richard Sands, where they finished seventh. Because of the

limited funding available to the team, most members had to sell their horses after the competition in order to pay for the trip. I was going to try to buy Dépèche when they came to the UK, but unfortunately he was sold to an American while still in Germany and was never heard of again.

The tour was still following in the wake of Captain Cook and, having rejoined *Britannia* in Hobart, we sailed from Launceston, Tasmania, to Melbourne and from Melbourne back to Sydney where the waterborne reception was really spectacular. We continued to sail north, stopping at Cook's known landfalls as far north as Townsville, Queensland. There was a stop-over in Brisbane, which gave my brother and me the chance to get into the Outback, about 500 miles west of Brisbane, near to Cunamulla — well, near by Australian standards.

When we arrived, the country was red and dusty; the soil was red and the dust covered everything. The second night we stayed on this cattle station, it rained, very unusually. In the morning the country had gone green. All the apparently dead or dying scrubby bushes and trees had sprouted green leaves. Grass had appeared where there had been nothing. It was an astonishing transformation and went some way to explaining why and how people could live in what had appeared the day before to be semi-desert.

On the preceding day we had done the obvious thing and been taken for a horseback view of a tiny part of that enormous (by British standards) cattle station. These were work horses that used to be known as Walers and were tough professionals who knew their way across this very treacherous landscape. The soil was light and often full of holes, dead branches and ant hills. If you didn't know what you were looking for, you were no help to the horse, so we just tried to sit there and let the horses avoid the dangers, going much faster than I felt was safe. It was exhilarating stuff and yet very necessary in order to be able to control the cattle and manage a station of that size.

Once again, our hosts were generous in their hospitality and also arranged a barbecue for us. I had read and heard that at a party in Australia the men all stand down one end of the room while the women stand at the other. I had always assumed that to be a gross exaggeration of the truth; but it wasn't at Queensland barbecues. At that stage in my career I was not very good at talking about or listening to tales of things domestic, so I'm afraid I abandoned the ladies' end and went to talk to the men about farming in Queensland, breeds of cattle, problems of lack of water and so forth.

Water is crucial to the ability to live in that environment, very similar in many ways, climatically, to East Africa. So why was there less pressure on the land and less degradation of the soil and desertification here? One answer could be energy – electric, solar or wind power to cook with and to heat water and buildings during the relatively cold nights. All these requirements would otherwise have had to be met by the burning of wood. In many less-developed countries it often is, creating enormous pressure on the stock of available sources. The pressure of domesticated livestock, from which the less-developed countries also suffer, is mitigated in places like Queensland by the availability of food concentrates for cattle to tide them over the dry times when natural feed has been exhausted: expensive but worth it if you have relatively stable demand and realistic market prices. Even with all the modern conveniences of hot and cold running water, plumbing and power, life in the Outback is not for the faint-hearted or for those who want to get rich quickly.

Our trip to Cunamulla had given us some idea of the sheer size of Australia, something which James Cook could only guess at as he charted the endless coastline with remarkable accuracy. To follow in his wake was a wonderful introduction to the southern hemisphere, a history lesson in every port, but my brother and I were also fortunate that our ability to ride had ensured that we had the opportunity to see more than just the coastline. Our excursions up-country had enabled us to meet people whose grandparents had taken such risks in just travelling to these unknown lands and then making their homes there. The country we saw in New Zealand had changed a great deal from the virgin forests that greeted the new settlers there, but the vast spaces of Australia had changed much less. I was now sure that my decision not to go to university had been the right one. No books could have substituted for the experience that I gained by being part of that tour.

KENYA

In 1969 I was invited to succeed Lord Boyd of Merton as President of the Save the Children Fund (SCF) and on 25 November the announcement was made. It was the first such appointment that I took on. To this day I don't know why they asked me, as my only connection had been through my great-aunt, Edwina Mountbatten, who had been their President for some years. I don't think my own attempts at knitting squares or fund raising for the child that my House at school sponsored were sufficiently noteworthy to have attracted their attention. I mention this because it was a major landmark in my life and also because, just over a year later, I was experiencing equestrian activity in Kenya entirely because

Visiting villages in Kenya on horseback with Valerie Singleton, presenter of BBC Television's Blue Peter.

of my links with the work of the Save the Children Fund in Nairobi.

The curious connection was made by the BBC's *Blue Peter*, which offered to make a programme about the SCF's work for fund-raising purposes. This would give me my first opportunity to see the Fund in action overseas and they chose one of their oldest and most successful projects to illustrate the importance of long-term development. The project started as a soup kitchen, on the initiative of one man, to take young and sometimes very young children off the streets of Nairobi, where they had been attracted, like many others in many other parts of the world, by the 'streets-paved-with-gold' syndrome. Making the BBC programme was also my first real experience of 'journalistic licence'.

That early scheme was successful, but it wasn't the answer. The next step was to introduce education – training for life, as my dictionary defines the word – with basic skills being taught. The scheme had greater success in that it attracted more and more young street children. With the support of the SCF the scheme grew into the best school in East Africa, catering for all levels of ability. *Blue Peter* filmed me touring the school and talking to the pupils, accompanied by the head boy. The academic standards are high, but so are the trade training standards, so that whatever the abilities of the pupils they will be able to make the best of their talents. The success of the school could be judged from the fact that employers were very keen to give them jobs.

The SCF was only too aware that the school was attracting children from all over Kenya, and it was still not the answer. As far as possible the SCF would try to discover where the children came from and try to evaluate if there was anything that could be done to encourage those children to stay in their own communities and with their families. Schools and health care were seldom readily available outside the city, so it was not hard to understand why many set off for the bright lights of Nairobi.

In an attempt to show the sort of conditions that these children came from *Blue Peter* hit on the idea of visiting one or two villages on the outskirts of the city. Then they thought it would be nice if we arrived on horseback. That was fine by me – except that it seemed rather incongruous – but I don't think it was deemed such a good idea by the presenter, Valerie Singleton, who would not have described herself as a horsewoman. I think the theory was that we were riding between villages – nonsense, of course, but it made for prettier pictures. We were filmed riding through various locations, discussing the Fund's work and then arriving at one of the villages to see the living conditions for ourselves. I remember being impressed by the general cleanliness of the basic structures that were people's homes and the healthy state of their garden plots.

The horses that were generously provided had started life as racehorses, become polo ponies and hacks and were used to most things. They were fairly small and very narrow, but were very good until the producer wanted a shot of Miss Singleton and myself cantering across the horizon. I'm afraid the canter ended in an unscheduled dismount for Miss Singleton. Fortunately there was no serious damage done, except that standing up became more popular than sitting down; artistic licence can be painful. It also took us out into some of the lush farmland around Nairobi, which didn't look anything like the dry, dusty vision of East Africa that the tourist brochures portray. Much of the high plateau of Kenya was very productive and the well-farmed plantations of coffee and tea were the backbone of Kenya's prosperity.

The level of equestrian activity was quite high, with Pony Club and all types of competition, including a thriving polo club and racing. Apart from riding during the filming I did not get the opportunity to watch any of the disciplines in action, but certainly the horses were well looked after and very busy.

If I thought that the inclusion of the horses was incongruous, I was mystified by the appearance of some cheetah cubs in a sequence shot in the Nairobi Game Park. We were filmed taking photographs of wildlife in the Park, which included some cheetahs, but they did not have any cubs. They turned up after I had left for home, but the film crew were still there and returned to the Park to film them. I pointed out the error when I saw the nearly finished production, but was told that if I didn't say anything, nobody would know. Unimportant? Probably, but a classic example of the myth that the camera never lies.

There is no doubt that it was a very educative trip. Not only did I learn a great deal about the SCF and about the art of film making, but I also had the opportunity to join my brother for a three-day safari in the Mara Game Reserve, living in a tented camp. Each day we made an excursion in a Land Rover, rather than on horses, which might have been too tempting for the lions. The noises of the night in the African bush were numerous and loud, and appeared to be delivered from just outside the tent door. I don't believe I slept a wink during the first night and only forty or so during the second, but by the third night I could have slept anywhere and I doubt if a herd of elephants would have disturbed me.

The serious aspect of the trip was the introduction to the problems of balancing the needs of the nomadic people with the needs of the wildlife that shared their environment. The Park Ranger in the Mara was already aware that the two should not and could not live in isolation. The pressures on him to allow certain favoured people to hunt otherwise forbidden quarry were very great, in spite of the official non-hunting policy. His refusal to bow to those pressures finally cost him his job. It had highlighted for him the contradiction of having to cull many species to stop the growth in their numbers damaging not only the Park itself, but also the crops of the tribes who lived and farmed around the Park. These tribes would otherwise have been living a more nomadic existence within it, culling the wildlife themselves, but they had, sadly, begun to destroy the vegetation with their own domestic livestock. It was a lesson that has been brought home to me, time and again, ever since. You cannot relieve human suffering without establishing an environment in which both humans and wild-life can survive. However, I can sympathise with a Kenyan tribesman who regards the nocturnal plundering habits of a leopard or the passage of a herd of elephants as more of a nuisance than a British hill farmer might regard the noc-turnal plundering habits of a fox or the passage of a herd of ramblers.

I saw a great deal that was beautiful and healthy, and contributions that were appropriate and positive. I also heard declarations of a desire to help, but all too few satisfied the essential requirement that the help be understandable, affordable and repeatable, the main principles of the Fund's work.

IRAN

In the autumn of 1971 there was an extraordinary celebration taking place in Iran: the 2,500th anniversary of the Shah's dynasty. Even if it wasn't, strictly speaking, true that such an anniversary had been reached, it was a good excuse for a huge international party. My father was asked to represent The Queen and took me along as his partner.

We spent four days in Iran, two in Tehran and two in Persepolis, where the main celebrations were held. While in Tehran, I was invited to ride from the Shah's stables on the north-eastern outskirts of the city. The stables were quite isolated and faced to the east a large plain, which is the beginning of the Great Salt Desert, and to the north the foothills of the Elburg mountains, which run east-west across northern Iran and are bordered to the north by the Caspian Sea. We were to ride the Shah's own horses, which were a mixture of Persian Plateau and thoroughbred. All the riding horses were stallions. This was normal for the Middle East, where it was considered unmanly to ride geldings; the mares were too precious to ride into battle, but were tested for their stamina and temperament when the families moved their camp sites. The Persian Plateau is not an Arab horse and has none of the features that distinguish the breed to Western eyes. It is narrow, light-boned and very tough.

We were taken on a tour of the stables before being introduced to our respective horses. They were all stallions, but you could walk into any of their stables and they merely greeted you with mild curiosity; none of them made a grab for you or tried to bite you. They were looked after by men and there was a firm rule that none was fed by hand – that is, that they were not offered any titbits by hand as we might give a horse a lump of sugar – so that they never even looked to be given anything. I was impressed by the stallions' manners and sought to instil the same sort of discipline at home. It didn't work, because our girl grooms were always slipping our horses the odd Polo mint. I achieved greater success with the Shetland pony we had later, who, although cheeky, never tried to bite. It was very difficult to persuade the grooms and all other passers-by that there was some sense in the 'no titbits' rule, but his early discipline has passed the test of time and he is still a relatively polite pony.

In the group that went out that day, two riders were mounted on Caspian ponies. These small horses are famous for their size and toughness. They are pony size – 12–14hh – but they look like miniature horses with fine heads and legs. On this day one was ridden by a child of twelve and the other by an adult. We set off towards the hills and rode up the dry bed of a stream wending its way through a barren-looking valley. This was the end of the dry season, so it looked even drier than usual.

We reached the top of the escarpment that we had seen from the stables and were greeted by a spectacular view out over the desert. Behind us the mountains stretched towards the north and the Caspian Sea, getting higher and higher. Below us was a near-vertical scree slope, becoming less steep as it reached the edge of the plain. I was a little disappointed that we would have to return the same way, but the ride had been worth it for the view. You might be able to imagine my surprise and trepidation when our guide walked his horse straight off the edge of the escarpment, followed by the other members of the party. This was obviously not the moment to demur as my horse seemed very keen to follow his friends. I assumed that he had done this sort of thing before, so I let the reins go loose and shut my eyes. Apart from keeping him straight, the rest was downhill.

We regained the floor of the valley without any mishap and made our way back to the stables at an extended canter led by the Caspians. The nearest we

The amazing 'campsite' at Persepolis.

The parade of thousands at Persepolis.

came to an accident was when I and my lady-in-waiting, Mary Dawnay, were chatting as we rode back, side by side, having completely forgotten that we were riding stallions. It didn't take us too long to work out why we were being shouted at and we went our separate ways just before the 'rude-faces' phase turned into a more serious teeth-and-feet attack.

Once again, thanks to the horse, I had had the opportunity to see something more than just a city. Even in the short space of time available I had observed a little of the vast country that is Iran and had met a few of the people who live in it. The rest of the visit involved flying south to Shiraz and then driving about 32 miles north-east to the 'tented' campsite below the ruins of Persepolis where the main celebrations were to take place. These ruins, which can be traced back to the fourth century BC, represent the Persepolis that was captured and partly destroyed by Alexander the Great in 330 BC, possibly the earliest general whose understanding and appreciation of the value of the horse – as a horseman – helped him to achieve the victories that he did.

If Alexander could have seen the campsite, he could have been forgiven for thinking that not much had changed. Our accommodation was a hard-walled, round, fabric-covered, three-rooms-plus-bathroom, luxuriously appointed tent. All the Shah's guests had one, even if they would have preferred the small hotel down the road where the spare staff went.

The whole event was like an enormous picnic. There was a huge marquee where the meals were served, a sit-down banquet the first night and a less formal buffet the second. There was a *son et lumière* amongst the ruins after the banquet to which we were transported in a fleet of luxury coaches. Desert nights do get cold and I was grateful for the number of layers of clothing that I had on, but that in no way detracted from what was a spectacular evening. Persepolis may be in ruins, but they are very impressive remains. The sheer size of the columns and the blocks of stone with their carved panels were a real wonder, and the light and sound effects of the dramatic spectacle created a spine-chilling atmosphere of excitement and history.

The next day we were treated to a three-hour pageant of Persian history portrayed through the use of costume, traditional and military, and mostly on horseback. They must have used thousands of horses unless they were using the same ones over and over again, going past in front of the stands and then going round the back to join in with a differently dressed rider. Opposite our stand were two much higher ones containing the musical accompaniment in equally colourful and varied costumes. There appeared to be hundreds of them as well, with the majority playing some kind of drum. I have an abiding memory of the incessant but highly appropriate drum beating. It was another remarkable performance, but what it really highlighted was that without the horse, their ability to ride it and their respect for it, the Persians would have had a much quieter and less colourful history.

The horse plays the main supporting role in the history of many countries, not least in Britain, but it was fascinating to see in Iran that it was still considered to be part of the fabric of life and not just a historical curio or plaything for the rich.

Hong Kong

After four days in the company of heads of governments and heads of State – a heady experience – my father and I flew on to Turkey to join The Queen at the start of her State Visit to that country. After another highly educative four days I flew east on my own for my first visit to Hong Kong. I was to be there for five or six days, fulfilling a number of military and civil engagements.

The image of Hong Kong would seem to suggest that every available inch is built on. The reality confirms that image, but also shows you that there are hills and paddy fields and lots of islands. There was a racecourse too called Happy Valley, completely surrounded by the crowded buildings of Hong Kong island. (There is now another racecourse on reclaimed land on the mainland at Sha

Tin.) The racing was extremely popular with the Chinese who have a tendency to bet on anything – even two flies crawling up a wall. The standard of racing was not their main concern but the first horse past the post most definitely was.

The other horse sport in Hong Kong required even more room. Polo was played on the mainland in amongst the British military barracks, mostly by Army officers and some ex-patriot British living in Hong Kong and riding ponies from Borneo. These Borneo ponies were very tough but not very big and riders had as much trouble keeping their feet out of the way of the ponies' legs as they did trying to hit the ball. Fortunately I was not asked to play polo, but I did get a ride in order to have a better view from the top of one of the ridges overlooking the Chinese border. Once again, I was able to gain a perspective enjoyed by very few visitors to the Colony, a much better picture of the geography of the region and how it was lived in. On this occasion it gave me a very clear insight into the problems the police and Army have in trying to stop illegal immigrants.

The landscape I found rather hard, steep and angular with a sameness about the vegetation that gave everything not being farmed a uniform look. The farming was largely paddy fields, whose pattern and colours created a much more interesting patchwork of linear shapes. There was also a contrast between one side of the border and the other, both the intensity of colours and the number of fields being noticeably greater on the Hong Kong side. But then everything in Hong Kong is about the maximum use of the space available, which produces its own unique appearance and atmosphere.

After trips to Iran, Turkey and Hong Kong, I was pleased to get home to finish what had been a remarkable year in relative peace and quiet.

YUGOSLAVIA

October 1972 brought another chance to accompany my parents on a State Visit, this time to Yugoslavia, as guests of President Tito. A charismatic wartime leader, Tito had withstood the pressures of Russian-style communism and kept Yugoslavia a relatively independent socialist country that looked as much towards Europe as towards the Soviet bloc.

Yugoslavia is a large and geographically diverse country, from the heavily forested north, through the huge central plains to the sheer, desolate mountains of the south. The capital, Belgrade, overlooks the confluence of the Danube and the Sava, a historically favourable position because of its land and river communications and its dominating situation overlooking the Pannonian plain to the north-east.

I did not have the opportunity to do any riding during this visit, but included in the itinerary was a visit to the State Stud at Lippizia. Some say that the ancestors of the horses here provided the original horses and bloodlines for what has become known as the Spanish Riding School, whose stud we visited at Piber in Austria. You can certainly see the similarity in type, colour, make and shape, for both types are stocky and powerfully built. The reason for their conformation became clear when we were told that in this district of Yugoslavia, originally part of the Austro-Hungarian Empire, these Lipizzaners are working draught horses and their criterion for breeding requires all the mares, who belong to farmers, to prove their physical and mental suitability in the fields. The stallions have a rather easier life, but they are all ridden to establish that their temperament, too, is suitable.

The stud itself was not on the scale of Piber, with neither the number of horses nor the size of the buildings, but the pride and determination of the workforce to keep the stud and the bloodlines going in spite of severe difficulties were evident everywhere. Some of the stud workers were well past the age of retirement and had no doubt been mending the plain boarded buildings with care and skill for a number of years.

There were many interesting things to see in Yugoslavia, but the history of the stud at Lippizia reflected much of the territorial turmoil that has existed in this region of Europe. That it has survived is amazing and, although it is not as famous as its Austrian neighbour, its contribution to the history of the horse in Europe is still important. I'm hoping to return there – perhaps not the most accessible of sites but a spiritual home of the ancestors of the modern dressage champions.

ETHIOPIA

February 1973 saw me undertaking my first solo overseas visit on behalf of the SCF. The country was Ethiopia and the reason was to view the expansion in the long-term work of the Fund after an earlier famine. This was my first opportunity to see the Fund at work in the field, practising the principal aim of their long-term development programme: mother-and-child health care, dispensed from a clinic which then became the hub of the community for a variety of health, nutritional and educational activities. The SCF had been in Ethiopia since 1970 and was well established in the central and northern regions. At that time there was no civil war, although there were areas where bands of armed Eritreans were fighting for their independence. I was still able to get to the port of Massawa, but only by flying via Asmara, because the road was considered a security risk.

Ethiopia is a large country whose topography makes internal communications very difficult and journeys a nightmare for those who suffer from travel sickness. I had never been a good car passenger and I was an even worse aeroplane passenger – I regard flying as an occupational hazard – and when we flew to Lalibela we were treated to the worst of both forms of transport. The 'airport' was in a bowl created by mountains over 10,000 feet high; the runway was at 7,000 feet. To reach it we flew in ever-decreasing circles with the Andover being heaved about by the thermals. The landing came just in time and I climbed out relieved but rather shakily, only to discover that we then had to drive 2,000 feet back up the mountain to the seven sunken churches of Lalibela. I sincerely hoped that the journey would prove worthwhile.

I need not have worried. We were greeted by the monks of the Coptic Church in their long, flowing, black robes and with gaily coloured umbrellas. The churches were invisible on arrival, and even if you knew what you were looking for your first view might have been a fleeting one as you fell on top of one. They were created by carving into the rock of the mountain, starting with the roof and working downwards. We had a guide, a particularly tall and thin monk who wafted along the solid rock passages at great speed. If you spent too long admiring the stone work, he had disappeared around another corner. Occasionally you would catch a glimpse of the end of his flowing robe, or he might notice he had lost you and reappear long enough to beckon you with a seemingly disembodied bony finger.

Six of the churches were linked together by a network of passages. At intervals along these passages were what appeared to be hollows, about 3 feet long, 1 foot deep and 1½ feet high, scooped out of the walls at about waist height. At first sight most of them appeared to be empty, but they usually turned out to contain bones. On catching our guide long enough to ask him the question, we learned that they were human bones, for these hollows were where they used to 'bury' the monks. That meant that they had either been very small monks or they used to fold them up and wedge them in the hollows to save space. Our guide laughed a lot at this point, but then with his height he thought he was in no danger of being 'buried' in one of those hollows. I hope he was right.

The return journey was a lot less nauseating than the arrival and we flew on to see one of the SCF's clinics at work. Here I found a team of four people who ran the clinic: a doctor, two nurses and a hygienist-nutritionist. The main task was mother-and-child health care, which meant a pre-natal and post-natal clinic and then regular visits for vaccinations and weight and height recordings, the most accurate way of monitoring a child's reasonably healthy development.

One of the team's major problems in this predominantly dry and dusty environment was infections of wounds and eyes. The incidence of any kind of infection can be greatly reduced by early treatment and hygiene in the home, by which I mean the use of clean water and dressings. Changing the dressing is easier than producing clean water, because in order to get that you first have to find your water, then you have to boil it, and to boil it you need a fire; to make a fire, you need wood, and to get wood means destroying another bush or tree that might otherwise grow to produce more ground cover, to create more moisture in the atmosphere which in turn might possibly produce more rain. This was my first experience of the apparently endlessly inter-connected problems facing the highly motivated and practical aid worker who understands the need to promote long-term solutions.

I was then able to see at first hand the degradation of land that had taken place as a result of the pressure of an increasing population and traditional pasturists. To do this, I rode a mule up into the Simien Mountains. The Ethiopians had arranged a three-day trip with two nights under canvas and the possibility of seeing some moufflon, the wild mountain sheep, on the escarpment of

Learning to ride Gracha, my mule.

the high plateau. The high plateau was at about 13,000 feet and the trek started at a height of about 8,000 feet, hence the need for the mules.

These mules were not quite what you might imagine if you visualised an animal like the ones that pulled pioneers' wagons across the American prairies. The Ethiopian versions were about the size of the average British donkey and you didn't so much ride as balance on them with your feet dangling just above the ground. But if they were lacking in size, they were infinitely more capable of coping with the thin air than I was. They were also used to much larger loads than the average human, even if the British versions were slightly heavier than their normal Ethiopian riders. There were one or two horses included for this trek, but they were hardly any bigger than the mules.

The saddles were wooden cross-frames covered in an array of blankets to cushion the imprint of the mule's backbone and the woodwork. The bridles were heavy leather halters with a piece of metal that went in the mouth and served as a brake. Steering was achieved with a stick that you used to tap the right side of the neck if you wanted to turn left and the left side of the neck if you wanted to turn right. Any lack of response required harder taps further

My policeman David Coleman on the mule which fainted under him!

towards the nose. Most of the time it worked, but every now and again the animal liked to remind the rider that it had a mind of its own.

The Metropolitan policeman who had been with me since I left school had never had any ambitions to be a jockey, which was fortunate, given that his physique was more suitable for rugby football. I'm not sure whether it was his weight, the girths being too tight or just the fact that he was hanging on so tightly with his legs, but whatever the cause, the effect was that his mule fainted. It was noted that the mule made no effort to get up until his recent rider had walked out of sight over the horizon!

The 'Thunder Box' being carried up the Simien Mountains.

There seemed to be a great number of people involved in this trek. Many were armed with old .303 rifles and most were travelling on foot carrying various bits of camping equipment. The most important person was the one who was given right of way because he was carrying, balanced on his head, the 'Thunder Box'. This was an impressive structure, a wooden armchair with a hole cut out of the seat. I wondered where it could have come from – it was hardly a traditional piece of furniture – but I suspect that my hosts may have had previous experience of taking overseas visitors on such an expedition.

The Simien Mountains are of the sierra type – flat on top dissected by very steep valleys – and our path wound its way, to and fro, down one side and up the other side of one valley after another and then across the open ground on the top. We spent a night under canvas on the way up, which was a very welcome break but it also gave us the opportunity to talk with our guides. They highlighted the changes that had already taken place in the environment as they talked about the lifestyle that the nomadic people used to follow.

The lifestyle was based on livestock, mostly sheep and goats which could graze on the long tough grass that grows at altitude. They also needed a supply of water and of trees for their cooking and heating. When the supply of water, wood or grass ran out, everybody moved on and the land would have time to recover before they might come back. But in recent years the interval between

The 'Thunder Box' prominent in our campsite in the Simien Mountains of Ethiopia.

tribes revisiting these sites has become too short for the vegetation to recover. The trees are the first to suffer, because they take longer to re-grow than the grass, but with them goes a lot of the stability of the soil which, combined with the loss of moisture, results in steady wind erosion of the topsoil, transforming what was fertile and productive land into a barren waste.

As we went from the valleys to the plateaus, we could see the very obvious difference between the presence of vegetation on the steep slopes of the valley and the almost complete lack of any on the virtually flat tops. In fact, much of the surface was pure dust and it was difficult to imagine what it must have looked like before the degradation. And this was 1973, when the pressure and effect of population on the environment was not as severe as it is today. At least now the problem is more widely understood and readily accepted than it was then, but it is no nearer a solution.

On the second day of our trek we climbed on up to about 13,000 feet and stopped at midday on a much grassier plateau; it was covered with very thick, tough grass that was less popular with the sheep and goats, but the altitude also made it much colder for the humans and therefore less popular with them too. This was good news for the moufflon and other wildlife. Getting to see moufflon is not easy, even if they are there, because they tend to pick their way along the near-vertical face of the escarpment on the edge of the Simiens. Seeing them means having a good head for heights and not minding leaning out over the edge of a cliff. All this after walking a very slow half-mile and still puffing like an out-of-condition walrus. We lay on what appeared to be the edge of the world

The start of our trek into the Simien Mountains.

and finally managed to spot the wild horned sheep in amongst the rocks 100 feet below us. Needless to say, they were well camouflaged but surprisingly big for their precarious environment. Thanks to the human pressures, the moufflons' environment is also under pressure and they have to spend more and more time on the steep slopes, steadily reducing the vegetation that holds the slopes together. I hope the descendents of the moufflon we were lucky enough to see are still able to live on those dramatic escarpments.

Before we left the Simien Mountains, we were treated to a rare sight. On a wide-open expanse we were met by a mounted mass of the local tribes, some of whom had greeted my parents in the very same place nearly twenty years before. Horses had been part of their history and heritage too and they were as keen as ever to show off their skills. I have to say that I don't think they were skills that the Pony Club would have wanted to encourage or that military skill-at-arms instructors would have recognised, but it had been a spontaneous request and they were very proud to show their visitors their horsemanship. The colour, the noise, the movement and the dust cloud made it a memorable occasion.

A welcoming party of Ethiopian horsemen at Debarek.

The three days in the Simien Mountains were geographically fascinating. The dramatic topography, the harsh lifestyle and the pressure on the environment, wildlife and humans were all there. The need for appropriate aid, sensitively applied with the understanding of the indigenous population, was very apparent, as was the obviously difficult balance that needed to be struck between the 'we-know-best' lobby and those who were more interested in the survival of themselves and their children. The need for and the role of the SCF in both the short and the long term were brought home to me, but so was the importance of not working in isolation.

One of the SCF's strengths, as I saw it, was that they had concentrated on the needs of the most vulnerable group, the children, and had learned that, in order to achieve long-term benefits for them, it was necessary to involve the mothers, the family and the community. Specialising in the needs of children had highlighted the importance of continuing development programmes involving hygiene, education, nutrition and income-generating schemes that could improve the lives of the whole community. If this can be achieved, then all children stand a better chance not only of surviving, but also of developing into responsible adults capable of contributing the best of their own individual talents.

Perhaps the most important thing that I learned from the trek up the Simiens was not to underestimate the values of local religions, traditions and cultures. Most people were content with their life because they were used to its harshness, but not so content that they wouldn't accept changes that might make their life easier in the short term, even if they didn't understand why the changes worked or whether they would be able to sustain them. Taking short cuts with aid is tempting but, as I was beginning to discover, seldom achieves more than cosmetic improvement.

Ethiopia was an important part of my education in all sorts of ways. Ethiopian cuisine appeared to be a limited variety of stews, one of which contained some very old eggs, but it was the bread that I remember most clearly. It was grey in colour and bore a remarkable resemblance to a piece of tripe. I also discovered the quickest way to lose weight, but I don't think it had anything to do with the food and would be difficult to repeat – unfortunately. The day after returning from the mountains I was struck by a bug – well, several hundred of them, I rather suspect, for as well as my eating Ethiopian food, I think the local flea population was eating me. Apparently I wasn't the only thing that was pleased to climb into my sleeping bag for three nights. Fortunately, my condi-

On a tour of the late Emperor Haile Selassie's stables in Addis Ababa.

tion did not affect my itinerary, although it did require me to leave an official lunch rather rapidly.

I returned from Ethiopia via the Sudan, which was extremely hot and meant there was no danger of my regaining my appetite before getting home. I had lost some weight, a feat I wish I could achieve as easily before riding in a competitive flat race. As it was, my own horses were the only ones who really appreciated the lightening of their load, unfortunately only temporarily.

ECUADOR

In late November 1973 there were more travels to South America and the Caribbean. The equestrian experience came in Ecuador, where the fact that I was known to be able to ride gave my hosts the opportunity to extend the usual official programme into the rural areas. Ecuador straddles not only the equator from Colombia in the north to Peru in the south, but also the Andes mountain range from the Amazon basin in the east to the Pacific Ocean in the west. The capital, Quito, is situated in the sierra region at an altitude of 9,300 feet on the lower slopes of the volcano Pichincha.

In Ecuador the Spanish traditions were very strong, including bullfighting. No, we were not taken to a bullfight, but we were invited to visit an estancia north of Quito, where, amongst other crops, they bred the black fighting bulls. It was a working ranch and most of the cattle work was done on horseback.

Before we went to see the cattle, we were shown the types of horses and the different forms of training that they needed to perform their different roles. This was done in a small, open-air, walled arena. Here we saw horses very similar to those you would find in Spain. They were being trained in very much the same way, Spanish High School – one-handed, sideways movements, pirouettes, pass-age and piaffe – less technically correct than in Vienna but useful in moving cattle and avoiding trouble. Trouble usually came from the cows who were much fiercer in the fields than the bulls and therefore the breeding policy for the cattle depended more on the aggressive temperament of the former than on the fighting qualities of the latter. We were allowed to walk in the field with the bulls but were not allowed to get out of the car when in the field with the cows. In fact they did admit that nobody would fight the cows because they were much quicker and more dangerous.

I could see there was a role for a similar organisation to SCF to improve the delivery of health care to mothers and children in isolated rural communities as well as in the overcrowded 'instant' suburbs that inevitably spring up around large towns and cities. Obtaining the optimum nutrition from the available food-stuffs is part of that care to promote long-term improvements for health and development. It would be a shame if the natural resources with which Ecuador is blessed are neglected to the detriment of her own people.

SPAIN

Where does the English word sherry come from and what has that got to do with horses? The common denominator is Jerez. The English word sherry comes from the sixteenth-century pronounciation of the name Jerez and the horses of the region – of mixed Arab, Spanish and English blood – were and still are highly valued. The reason for this goes back into history. Bullfighting developed from the peculiarities of the savage cattle that inhabited the forests of the Iberian peninsula. The Carthaginians and the Romans were said to have been amazed at tales of games, held in what is now the province of Andalucia, in which men exhibited 'dexterity and valour' before dealing the death blow to a savage horned beast.

Conquest of the Iberian peninsula modified the customs of the people. The

Muslims from Africa, who over-ran Andalucia in AD 711, were great horsemen and they decided this was an exciting game but that it would be more in keeping with their traditions if the matador were mounted. Hence the *rejoneadores*. Threats of Papal excommunication of the gentlemen who pursued that form of manly exhibitionism and the social changes in Spain fundamentally altered bull-fighting in favour of the professionals: it was apparently all right to be paid to fight bulls but not to do so as an amateur. In Portugal the *rejoneadores* were retained. The skill in this kind of bullfighting is in the training of the horse and, once again, it is very similar to that practised at the Spanish Riding School of Vienna.

In Jerez the tradition is maintained by the family of Domecq and while I was on a visit to Spain they very generously invited me to Jerez to see their horses and to ride one of the stallions at their training stables. As I had not been expecting to ride I didn't even have a pair of boots with me, so the Domecqs had to lend me those as well. They were extremely comfortable and, to my great embarrassment, were given to me at the end of my ride. I wore them for years. I managed to wear out them, and a second pair, through constant use as the most comfortable boots I have ever owned.

But first I had to concentrate on the Domecqs' Andalucian horses. I knew a little about these animals because, as I mentioned in Chapter 2, The Queen had been given a stallion called Busaco on the occasion of her State Visit to Portugal in 1956. In Jerez I spent some time watching the trainer put one of the older stallions through his paces and I tried to pick up what sort of aids he was using in order to achieve the various movements. (Aids is the term employed to des-cribe the use of hands, heels and balance to convey to the horse what it is you want him to do – everybody does it slightly differently.) This was made more difficult for me by the traditional bridle and saddle. The bridle had a bit with a large port (high centre piece) and long side pieces, which meant that I would have to be very light with my hands. But the saddle was going to be much more difficult to adjust to. It was a basic cross-tree frame with a high, ornate pommel and cantle at the back, the gap in the middle being covered in layers of blanket which made it very wide and smooth. Just to add to the problems, the stirrups, which were flat metal with sharp ends, were attached to the frame so that they hung down from under the bottom of the blankets, making them very difficult for my short legs to reach.

Goodness knows what my hosts thought of my attempts; I just had to laugh. The horse was very sensitive and it took me some time to relax my own

At the Domecqs' stud, Jerez, Spain.

seat enough for him not to jump every time I tried to apply an aid. In the end we did achieve a reasonable level of understanding, although if there had been a bull about, I would have left him entirely to do what he had been trained to do – his reactions were a lot quicker than mine.

After being shown the Domecqs' stables, which included their own horses as well as those which displayed their skills in the bullring, I was introduced to their carriage horses. The stables were situated on the outskirts of Jerez and we were to have lunch in the Domecqs' town house, which was the centre of their sherry business. It seemed wholly appropriate that we should travel in their carriage pulled not by two or four but by five horses – two wheelers and three leaders – and driven by a very impressive figure of a man, perched on the box above us, with the fortunately very diminutive groom squashed beside him. I have an abiding memory of sweeping round three sides of the square at a spanking trot, between cars parked on both sides. It was an extremely skilful display that far outshone anything that he performed when the Domecqs' Sherry horses came to the Horse of the Year show at Wembley some years later.

CANADA

In November 1974 I was invited to visit the Toronto Royal Winter Fair in Canada. This is one of the biggest, longest and most comprehensive agricultural shows in the world. It lasted about ten days and included classes for all forms of livestock and agricultural produce as well as a whole host of apparently unrelated activities and artefacts. One of these activities involved a very small ice rink with a couple of skaters performing rather restricted pirouettes. We were asked to stop and watch for a little while, during which time the young lady, dressed in a classical ballet-style tutu, attempted her pirouettes. She achieved these with commendable aplomb, especially as, half-way through her revolutions, the strap on her tutu gave up the unequal struggle and left her partially exposed and no doubt wondering where the sudden cold draught was coming from. We left – quickly.

The Winter Fair is an institution in Canada. I was slightly surprised to discover that the dress for the evening performance was 'white tie, decorations, long dress and tiara'. Added to that was being driven into the arena in a carriage and then inspecting a guard of honour drawn up in the centre. The carriage was drawn by four hackneys belonging to our host, Mr McDougald. As we were about to step aboard I noticed a familiar face exercising her usual calming influence on this rather excitable breed. It was Marie Wood, The Queen's horse-box driver, who had spent her early career with Mrs Cynthia Haydon who had gained her reputation driving hackneys, also belonging to Mr McDougald. This was Marie's idea of a holiday – ten days at the Royal Winter Fair. Whatever I may have thought, I was very relieved to see her there.

We then watched the final judging – by judges in white tie and tails – of hackney, Western riding and international showjumping classes. The standard and variety was every bit as good as anything in the UK, although I thought the British breeds of cattle on show were much more impressive there than their cousins back in the UK. Everything in Canada seems to grow bigger, but perhaps that is because it is such a big country.

While in the province of Ontario I was invited to go hunting; on this occasion it was a drag hunt. I was very generously lent a large but well-proportioned horse and thoroughly enjoyed the opportunity to have a gentle gallop and jump around a rather flat part of the province. The fences were man-made, because there are very few 'natural' fences, such as hedges or walls, in Canada. The farming is mostly large-scale arable with some trees as wind breaks and big paddocks containing livestock fenced with wire. It was a grey November day, but it was an example of Canadian hospitality at its best.

UNITED STATES OF AMERICA
Ledyard

Over the years I also managed to get some riding in the United States of America. The first time was at a three-day event at Ledyard, north of Boston, Massachusetts. Ledyard had already achieved a reputation not only as a friendly event, but also as one that was very well organised with an interesting and testing cross-country course designed by the site owner and organiser, Neil Ayer. Neil went on to gain well-deserved recognition as an international course designer and builder.

The competition took place in the summer and was an ideal event for up-and-coming young horses, especially British ones after a full spring season of one-day events. I had what I hoped was going to be a good horse called Arthur of Troy – no, I did not name him – who was a thoroughbred with some previous showjumping experience. Many people thought he was brilliant; he was certainly a flamboyant negotiator of obstacles, but I was not so sure that his undoubted talents were enough to compensate for his almost complete lack of a brain. I found him very difficult to get on with because he could be very touchy and you just had to sit and suffer. He was a stiff horse in spite of his ability to gallop and jump, and that didn't help him to relax in his dressage, but because he had a nice outline and active paces he could achieve reasonable dressage marks. Across country he shied at everything and was often not paying much attention to the fences so that his jumping felt like an animated pogo stick and was very tiring over 3 miles. Anyway, in spite of my doubts he had progressed well enough to qualify for an overseas event and it was to Ledyard that we went.

Flying horses to the USA is relatively easy in theory but fraught with problems in practice. The first difficulty you encounter is presented by the handlers at the airport of entry, who insist that they are the only people who can touch the horses and make sure everyone, including the grooms, are safely grappling with Customs before they start to offload the animals. That's fine as long as the animals are perfectly behaved, but at any sign of trouble the handlers go for their syringes and fill them with dope. This happened to one of the German horses which reacted violently to this treatment and whose neck swelled up so badly that he was unable to compete five days later.

There is a forty-eight-hour quarantine which all horses from Europe are supposed to undergo, but that seems to vary in both length and conditions depending on how valuable the horse is. The grooms are not allowed to go with the horses but can pick them up at the end of the period when they may well find that all the tack and rugs, etc., have been soaked in disinfectant and left in a pile of wet equipment belonging to everybody who came that day. Then there was the long road journey to the event. The British horses travelled better than the Germans'.

Ledyard was situated in a lovely area not far from the coast. Low rolling hills were hidden by trees divided by small fields that were fenced with rough-cut planks, unbarked pine poles or regular white rails. The houses were traditional, boarded, American colonial style, many of them originals rather than

At the start of the Ledyard Horse Trials, USA.

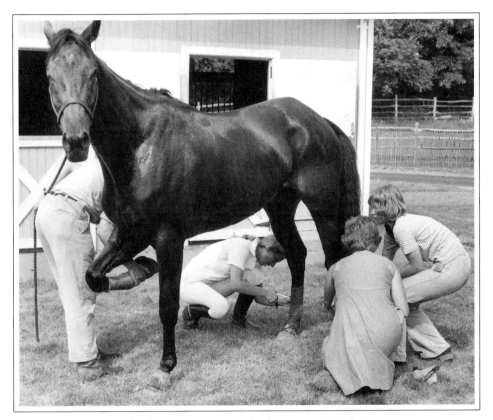

After the cross country at Ledyard, USA, everybody helps.

modern reproductions. Something I noticed about the housing which made it look very different from the UK was that there were very few garden fences or enclosures around the houses, I suppose because space is not at the same premium as it is here. It left me with the impression of an unfinished landscape, and I have been struck by that impression on subsequent visits to different parts of the USA.

East Coast America is where you find the concentration of equestrian activities of racing, breeding, hunting and competing, although horse sports of every kind are pursued all over the country – trotting, pacing, rodeo, long-distance riding, to name but a few.

The stables where our horses lived were what is now described as 'American barn' type. This is the modern equivalent of a traditional barn, which, like its European prototype, was designed for cold winters when livestock was housed in stalls facing a central passage, with the fodder and bedding stored overhead, partly for convenience and partly for insulation. In the coldest areas the family lived over the livestock to benefit from the heat that the animals produced. The modern horse barns were, on the whole, single-storey, still with the central passageway, but also with stable doors opening to the outside. This allowed for better ventilation in the summer for the horses that needed to be stabled during the hot weather. Our horses certainly appreciated the comparative coolness of the barn, because the outdoor temperature felt very hot to us.

The unaccustomed heat forced us to ride very early, usually about six o'clock in the morning. It was a very pleasant temperature then, but unfortunately we would not be competing at that time of day. Once we knew the order of starting, it was important to work the horses at the time of day we would be competing. This was not such a problem for the dressage, but might prove critical for the cross country.

The competition was based at the grounds of the Myopia Hunt Club – its insignia was a fox's mask wearing spectacles – which included a polo ground and had plenty of room for the dressage and showjumping phases. The stables were not on site but were within hacking distance. The cross-country course, on the other hand, started and finished more or less outside the stables. However, to get to the start of the first section of roads and tracks, you had to go in a horse box and work your way back across country via the steeplechase course.

I liked the cross-country course because it reflected the character of the countryside and looked completely different from a British course. It was also designed to give spectators a better chance of seeing more fences from one place rather than having to walk round the whole course and see only one fence at a time. Walking didn't appear to be a very popular pastime with Americans – even the State Department protection team had to take it in turns when I walked the course, and when I walked it for the third time I think they felt that British eccentricity had gone too far. I also walked it at the same time of day that I was due to compete, in order to see where the shadows would be, and it was quite warm by my standards.

Arthur went pretty well and jumped a good clear round, by which I mean that I had no really anxious moments, but I didn't enjoy the ride very much. It was so tiring avoiding being shot over his head every time he landed, because he tended to overjump and land at a very steep angle. We finished the second day in about fourth place, but he disgraced himself in the showjumping, knocking down two fences to finish eighth. I had already thought that I ought to sell him and that performance decided me, mostly because I didn't get on with him and felt that somebody else might appreciate him more.

That was, in some ways surprisingly, the only occasion on which I competed in the USA, but not the only occasion on which I rode there. Over the next fifteen years I managed to visit the states of Colorado, New Mexico, Texas, Missouri, Tennessee and Virginia and enjoyed completely different equestrian experiences in each.

Colorado

Denver is in the foothills of the Rockies, but the hills get steep very quickly. I had been lent a house on a property just outside the city for the duration of a short official visit in June 1982. The generous owners were both riders and had their own horses. They took me on a short mounted tour, which opened up the view of the Rockies, making the skyline of Denver pale into insignificance. At one stage of the planning of the visit, I thought that was as close as I was going to get to the mountains, but we managed to persuade the organisers to let us head for the hills.

They took us trail riding, on a comparatively short trail, I must admit, but it was enough for most of my inexperienced party. We met up with the group who had produced the horses up in the hills. The horses were mostly of the quarter horse type with Western saddlery, which for those used to the English style of saddle can be difficult to come to terms with. As luck would have it, I had ridden in one before, when the Canadian Cutting Horse Association brought a group over to Britain to give demonstrations at some of the big shows. During the period of the Royal Windsor Horse Show they were stabled in the Mews at Windsor and they arranged for The Queen to watch them exercising in the riding school one morning. I happened to be there as well and, after they had shown us their considerable skills, we were offered a ride. Cutting horses have extremely quick reactions in order to prevent the steer or cow they have separated from the herd from rejoining it. The rider wanders into the herd to locate the animal he wants. He then has to communicate to the horse which animal that is by very quietly using body weight and neck reining to encourage the beast to the outside of the herd. When he has reached a point where there is a gap between the cow and the herd, he drops the reins on the horse's neck to indicate that it is now up to the horse to keep this animal from returning to the fold.

That is when the fun begins. What happens next is entirely dependent on the horse's strength and speed of reaction as it has a nose-to-nose confrontation with an animal that wants to go past it. The rider just has to sit there. Everybody knows that that big pommel on a Western saddle is for tying the rope to after you have roped a calf, but it is also for hanging on to when your horse is trying to outwit a cow. It is also very important for greenhorns like me to stop us flapping about when the horse's sensitivity and speed of response send us rocking to and fro, completely out of rhythm with the horse, which then proceeds in a series of leaps and bounds from which there seems to be no escape.

Fortunately I was a bit less ambitious, but I could not sit still enough to avoid the occasional abrupt start or stop. I did learn, though, that your stirrups needed to be long enough so that you could only just reach them. First you sat deeper and stiller in the saddle and second you didn't bruise your kneecaps on the solid front of the saddle. Luckily for the horse, there were no cows immediately available for me to practise on.

These were working horses, impressive in every way but not everyone's idea of the ideal hack – a polo pony, possibly. The Cutting Horse Association gave my father a three-year-old filly, Max Charge, with the idea of seeing if she would play polo; but the result was not a complete success. The inbred ability of these horses is like that of a sheepdog – they need something to 'cut out' or follow. This filly decided that she was obviously meant to follow the ball, which was fine in theory but had unexpected repercussions on the field of play. For instance, when the ball was in a mêlée (stationary under a lot of horses with the players unable to reach it), the filly would barge her way in until she stood over the ball, where nobody could get at it. She thought that was the object of the exercise, especially as the referee had to blow his whistle for the foul of obstruction.

Her other and more alarming habit was revealed when her rider hit a backhand, which meant that they were galloping one way and he would hit the ball back the way he had come. Hitting the ball with a reverse swing meant that his centre of gravity went forward, not a good place to be if his pony stopped and turned round very quickly, which is exactly what this one tended to do. It was decided that, in spite of her undoubted talents, Max Charge was not cut out to be a polo pony.

That chance ride at Windsor certainly helped me to enjoy the trail riding in the Rockies. We 'limeys' were given the choice of English or Western saddles but, quite honestly, if you were a real beginner, and three members of my team were, the Western saddle made you feel much more secure. Trail riding is exactly as it sounds and the trails we were following were single-track. As the terrain was quite steep it meant that the trails tacked across the side of the slopes, which inevitably made our progress slow. The slopes were not heavily wooded and we were treated to some impressive views, yet the rest of the time we seemed to be in splendid isolation. The ride was a great success and there were no dramas.

New Mexico

From Denver we went to Sante Fé, in order to see the work of the Save the Children Federation, USA. They had a number of projects with the Indian populations still living on reservations. New Mexico is one of the south-western states of America, bounded in the north by Colorado, in the east by Oklahoma and Texas, in the south by Texas and the Republic of Mexico, and in the west by Arizona. The borders are high plateaus cut by deep canyons, but the central mountains are surrounded by comparatively level areas. Sante Fé is on the level area about 7,000 feet above sea level and the highest mountain, Wheeler Peak, rises to 13,600 feet.

We stayed at what is known as a 'dude ranch' consisting of individual cottages around facilities such as swimming pool, tennis courts and the stables. One of the attractions on offer was a ride out into the hills in the evening to a real open air barbecue supper or, if you preferred the dawn, breakfast. We all decided to go for the evening option. This place was geared for greenhorns and had a selection of very quiet cow ponies, but there were also some horses for more advanced riders, so we set off in two groups. I went with a guide, and two of the State Department team who could ride, on an extended route to the barbecue site.

As we cantered through the sage brush I contemplated what it must have been like for those people who travelled across this country, looking for a new life. Unless you were on the top of a rise, you could see very little and the vegetation was thick enough to make progress in a straight line impossible. By this time I was feeling quite at home on my Western saddle, but as we crossed a track not far from the other group a voice floated up the valley from one of the greenhorns apparently enquiring of me, 'You do this for *fun*?' Obviously this enjoyment of riding horses was not shared by everybody.

I arrived at the picnic site slightly before the main party and watched with interest as they dismounted. For some, this was only a slight improvement on the unaccustomed position they had just abandoned, and the barbecue was enjoyed from the standing rather than the sitting position. It was just as well they were not required to ride home afterwards. I rather suspect that most of the greenhorns put their venture down to experience and have never been anywhere near a horse again.

Texas

The next stop was Houston, where there were lots of interesting places to see such as the Texas Heart Institute and the National Aeronautics and Space Administration (NASA), but which was otherwise just a big city. Most people think that the wealth of a nation comes from the cities and businesses. It is very easy to forget that, without a strong agricultural base, it would have been difficult to create or maintain the prosperity that many now take for granted. Farming needs to be practised as efficiently and cost-effectively as any other business, but it needs to be more obviously in balance with its environment. The state of a country's agriculture is often a pointer to the state of the nation. When I visit a country I find it vital to be able either to drive out of the urban areas or, better still, visit a farm. It is a bonus if you can fit in a ride as well, but I do not go abroad to ride; I do plenty of that at home.

On this occasion I managed to do both, first by visiting a farm where they were attempting to upgrade their herd of Saler cattle from central France through the use of embryo transfers. This was a very new technique then and was regarded as pioneering work. It allowed more than one calf to be produced each year by the best cows, by transferring eggs that had been fertilised in them to host mothers, thereby allowing the better cows to conceive again. The knowledge gained from this type of work has proved to be of vital importance to the breeding of endangered species. I learned a lot, but I did wonder if it wasn't an awful lot of work which had to be done in very hygienic conditions and these are not what cattle sheds are famous for. It would be interesting to know if they decided to continue with the practice.

Later that day I went to a ranch of a more traditional type; it was also successfully employing modern farming techniques, including the use of motorbikes to help work the cattle, but it still needed horses for the good management of the livestock. If these horses are to pull their weight, they need to have specialist training, and many of the rodeo competitions developed from the teaching of skills such as barrel racing, where the horses race around a triangle of barrels. Some of the best of these horses came from this ranch and we were treated to a demonstration of their abilities of explosive power and agility. I'm afraid that after my earlier experience with the Canadian cutting horse I turned down the invitation to try my luck round the barrels, but readily accepted the offer to ride out into the paddocks.

This was not the 'home-on-the-range' type of ranch, but reminded me more of parts of the Australian Outback and even East Africa – dusty grassland with scattered trees providing necessary shade. The horses we were riding were working animals in their working tack, and by now I was getting accustomed to the saddles. These animals were not just kept for recreation or sport but were actually the most convenient form of transport. Unlike their non-working cousins, they are 'out' more than they are 'in', and they are an integral part of the workforce, thoroughly earning their keep. For most of us, these days, horses are an additional expense, very few contributing to their owner's finances, although of course their value is in the enjoyment or entertainment they give. Fortunately, there are still plenty of people who are prepared to pay for the privilege of having these attractive creatures around.

New Orleans

January is not the best month to visit New Orleans, especially in a year in which it experienced one of the severest frosts on record. This had unfortunate results. The hotel in which I was due to stay was brand spanking new; I would have been one of its first guests. Not very surprisingly, buildings in New Orleans are not designed to cope with temperatures below freezing, which are almost unknown there. The result was a nasty case of broken water pipes, the water from which caused extensive damage to the new interior decoration. This happened about two weeks before my visit.

My host, Mr Colman – who owned the aforementioned hotel and was Britain's Honorary Consul – then demonstrated that the traditional Southern hospitality is alive and well in New Orleans by making room for my party in his own home. The house shared a quiet secluded avenue just off the river with other gracious traditional homes of an earlier period. It was not a big house but there was room in great comfort for my small party.

The visit was to help boost fund-raising for the British Olympic Association (BOA) so that we could send a full team to the 1984 Games in Los Angeles. For tax purposes it made good sense to raise as much as we could from Britons and friends living in the USA, because donations to charity, art and sport over there are tax-deductible. In the UK the BOA was paying nearly a third of the funds it managed to accumulate to the Treasury as tax. Why New Orleans? Because my host was an enthusiastic friend of Britain; I do hope he still is.

The visit had several highlights for me. New Orleans is the cradle of traditional jazz music and I didn't want to go there without hearing the real thing. On the first night we were invited 'across the road' to another private house to meet some of the neighbours. During the evening we were treated to a private performance by some of the great names of jazz music, all of whom appeared to be well into their eighties. They were a pleasure to listen to and a delight to talk to and I felt very privileged that they had wanted to come and play for us. The old town, with its French colonial-style buildings and narrow, crowded streets, was completely un-American as well as very French. After the fund-raising reception we retired to have dinner in one of the best restaurants in town. It was an excellent meal, but the memorable bit was yet to come.

Across the road was the Preservation Hall Jazz Club where, to the horror of the State Department security team, I accepted the invitation to 'drop in'. The Preservation Hall is just that – a plain wooden hall. The people who go to listen are, on the whole, very knowledgeable and casually dressed; we were neither. I was wearing a long, bright orange taffeta dress, diamond necklace and earrings, and the men were wearing dinner suits. Nobody already in the hall batted an eyelid at our not very surreptitious arrival, mostly because they were engrossed in the music but also because in New Orleans this sort of behaviour is apparently not unusual. It was standing room only by the time we got there, so we did not stay too long, but I'm very glad I rose above my initial serious misgivings brought on by my unsuitable attire.

The night was yet young, so we went next door to Paddy's Bar where the entertainment was provided by two pianists, each playing one piano, who played requests as well as their own programme. Here you could sit at tables and be served with drinks. Once again our somewhat incongruously dressed party hardly raised an eyebrow amongst the predominantly jean-clad throng, even when we eventually left through the fire-exit door opening into the street next to our table.

Believe it or not, there was another highlight of this trip: our host had arranged for us to visit a plantation belonging to some friends of his who were also the proud owners of some Tennessee Walking Horses. These horses developed in much the same way as the pasos of South America as a smooth, sensible, handy-sized, convenient form of transport for the plantation owners to get around their extensive properties with the minimum of effort. They were so named because of their very exaggerated walk in which their front feet come up much higher than normal. Another feature of this breed is that they 'pace' at the trot, which is when both legs on the same side move together. This results in an unusual rolling gait which is surprisingly comfortable.

The horses we were to ride were refugees who had been rescued from the show ring. The showing horses have this high-stepping walk – very unnatural and completely useless. To 'help' produce this extravagant walk movement, some trainers use artificial aids. This can mean having the horses shod with extra-heavy shoes during training, so that when lightweight shoes are put on for the competition the horses will feel light-footed and throw their front feet even higher to catch the judges' eye. Another even more questionable method is to rub a blistering agent on the coronet band around the top of the hoof and then clip a small chain around the fetlock so that it rests on the blistered part, rubbing it when the horse moves. Not surprisingly, this makes them very sensitive; it also leaves scar tissue that you can feel. The horse that I rode had that sort of scar tissue and had been very neurotic when his present owners had found him.

He was nearly black, about 15hh, but in spite of his past experiences he was indeed a comfortable and confidential hack – that is, he was entirely trustworthy. There were no Western saddles here, just the old-fashioned straight-fronted English hunting saddle, but you still had to ride with very long stirrups. Apart from steering, there was not a lot for me to do except to start off the trotting, then drop my reins and relax so that the horse could accelerate into his pacing rhythm: left, right, left, right. It was smooth and quick and, although we didn't go very far, the horses could have kept up that pace for a few miles. Historically, great pride was taken in the horses and their breeding, and the bloodlines live on today.

The place where we rode used to be an isolated plantation some way out of New Orleans. Now it seems to be in the suburbs and is surrounded by oil storage tanks. Behind the tanks and all round the plantation was the forest, dripping with green moss. What a mysterious, hot and steamy place this must have been, and what a contrast to Colorado and New Mexico.

Later that day we visited one of the oldest and most gracious of the surviving plantation houses, now preserved as a living museum that can be used for entertaining small numbers of people in both great style and peaceful surroundings. All the outhouses are intact, including stables and slave quarters spread out around spacious grounds. The drive out was over an hour's journey alongside the winding Mississippi, which was hidden for much of the way by the high levees along the river's banks. The river was the main highway through the

A meet of the Piedmont Foxhounds in October 1988. From left to right: Dinah Nicholson (my trainer's wife), myself, Nicky Henderson (another National Hunt trainer), Randy Waterman MFH and Diana Henderson (Nicky's wife). The Blue Ridge Mountains of Virginia are off to the right!

centre of the United States and it was fundamental to New Orleans' growth; it still plays an important commercial role today. Gracious is not a word I use very much, but it seems to come to mind so easily when thinking or talking about New Orleans. There is a real sense of history and enjoyment of life there.

Florida

Some years later I managed to get even closer to the hanging moss, this time outside Tampa, Florida. I was there to watch the final of the Volvo World Cup jumping competition, which fortunately didn't take all day so I was free to do other things too. The World Cup was run in conjunction with Tampa's usual and varied show. I went down to the showground earlyish one morning to have a ride. I did not know until I got there that my ride was to be a Dutch-bred Grade A showjumper belonging to a pupil of George Morris, one of the best showjumping trainers anywhere in the world. What I also did not realise was that George himself was going to be there as well. To make matters worse it was going to be very public as there were already plenty of people about exercising their horses.

I did my own thing to begin with, just walking, trotting and cantering; getting to know the horse and trying to get him more level in my hand, because he took hold of one side of the bit more than the other, which made him crooked through his body. I thought that was all I would be doing, but George had other ideas, and I ended up jumping bigger fences than I had jumped in a very long time. At the end of an hour I wished I had had a lesson from him before. I don't think I did the horse too much harm either. Later that day I did the rounds of the show, which included classes for Arab horses, four-in-hand driving and barrel racing.

The next morning, thanks to an old friend, we drove out to a property north of Tampa, a cattle ranch carved out of the forest and swamp. There we went for a real ride – out across the grassland from the homestead, round the polo ground, past some cross-country fences, into the forest and back via the paddocks. There were animals everywhere, but not quite as many horses as cattle. The stable barn was immaculate, the horses beautifully turned out, the grounds neat and tidy, and all the gates appeared to work. Running a cattle enterprise in that climate is a constant battle with diseases and infections which can only be won with a very well managed immunisation and pest-control programme. That is also true of almost any livestock breeding, but a lot more difficult in a tropical climate like that of Florida. We rode reasonably early for it not to be too hot and sticky, but it was already hot enough for me.

Virginia

More recently I was invited to Middleburg, Virginia, to watch some timber racing and to experience an American foxhunt. Timber racing means just what it says: horses are raced over fixed wooden fences and are usually ridden by amateur jockeys. The nearest British equivalent would be the old-fashioned point-to-point where point A is the start and point B the finish. You had to find your own way between the two, jumping whatever obstacles you felt capable of negotiating, not just the modern version which is usually two circuits of plain birch fences. The timber fences were made of four thick round rails starting at ground level and continuing at intervals to a height of between 3 feet 6 inches and 4 feet. They were not plumb vertical, so they didn't look too bad, but I gather that down in Maryland the fences *are* vertical, made of thinner poles and are up to 5 feet high. I don't think I have any ambitions to try those.

A good timber-racing horse is one that looks after itself; it must also want to jump and gallop. I have put those in my order of preference. The ability to jump and to look after itself does not always follow. If a horse does neither of the first two, the third is irrelevant. Arthur of Troy would have been an ideal type and I would not have minded taking my chances on a horse like him. We were treated to one moderate race, during which one of the horses learnt the hard way just how solid the fences were and broke a pole in the process. Rather surprisingly, horse and rider survived. We were also treated to a copybook 4-mile race between three of the best horses and riders in training. They were never further than six lengths apart during the race and the closely fought finish went right to the line.

The next morning we five English visitors were invited to join the local hunt. We were mounted on horses most generously lent by local enthusiasts and I was honoured to be offered one of the most successful timber racers of recent years, but who was nearing retirement. He knew how to look after himself and, apart from my nearly wrestling him to the ground over a small stone wall, we got on extremely well. I was warned that he might be feeling his feet because it was early in the season for him and the ground was still hard.

It was the most lovely early October morning with the leaves already turning, but we were about a week too soon for the full display of the 'fall' colours that lure the 'leaf freaks' in their thousands from Washington and further afield. From the house where we were staying there was a glorious view. In between there seemed to be nothing but deciduous trees. This was a bit of an illusion because there were plenty of fields of grass and maize, as we were to discover when we attempted to follow the hounds hunting one of several foxes that we actually saw that morning. The fields were, by American standards, quite small and often divided by walls, sometimes by rails. There was a growing number of wire fences with specially built jumping places which looked like chicken coops.

The soil is light and sandy and easily undermined by burrowing rodents, so that you had to be very watchful of where you were going.

We were kept busy and jumped every sort of thing, but I did have to say that I thought my horse had done enough and was indeed feeling a little sore. To my amazement I was put on another horse, this time a young one at the beginning of his career. He was a bit more enthusiastic but jumped beautifully and was quick on his feet. We continued for only half an hour, but I really enjoyed the contrast of experience and youth. The owners of those horses were extremely generous because there is always a risk involved in lending anything to anybody. It was a rare privilege to go out hunting under such ideal conditions with very few people who were such good company, and riding very good horses in lovely countryside. It was also an opportunity to see some more of the diverse landscape that is the United States of America, and not just the airports and cities that are too often the only means visitors have of judging this multi-faceted country.

I know that without the high profile my competitive riding career had achieved I would not have been given the chances to see as much of the countries that I visited as I would have done if my hobby had been, say, tennis or music. It still seems to be true, as I was invited to Qatar only in order to ride the Emir's camel. Nowadays I get asked to ride in races and that is another part of the story.

CHAPTER 10

Starting to Race:

'Ninety-nine per cent out of control!'

WHAT, you might well ask, has the City got to do with horses? The link is the City Livery Companies, institutions peculiar to the City of London, survivals from the medieval trade and craft guilds that were once common in Europe. The Worshipful Company of Weavers, for example, can trace their origins back to 1135 and the Companies pertaining to the horse were not far behind. These included the Worshipful Companies of Saddlers, Loriners (makers of bits and metalwork) and Farriers (who shoe and care for horses).

At the height of their influence the guilds controlled their members by the exercise of powers conferred by charter or ordinances: to regulate apprenticeship and conditions of employment, to examine workmanship and destroy defective goods, and to enforce rules by fines and penalties. The ultimate sanction was that only those free of the City of London could ply their trade, and the freedom of the city was obtainable only through membership of a guild.

After the middle of the fifteenth century the practice grew for testators to appoint companies as trustees; for instance, John Colet appointed the Mercers to administer a trust for St Paul's School (founded 1509). The City and Guilds of London Institute was founded by the Corporation of London and the Livery Companies in 1880 to promote technical education and industrial research. Over the years many Companies have rather lost touch with their trade and craft, although many still have connections with their schools. They came to be viewed from outside the City as nothing more than glorified luncheon clubs. This may still be true of some whose crafts really have died out, but many more seem to have rediscovered the value of their historical links.

I knew a little bit about them from when my father introduced me to the Worshipful Company of Fishmongers by right of patrimony. They are one of the Great Twelve, very wealthy and charitable. When you are sworn in, you make a promise based on their medieval powers of the said ordinances to pay any penalties or fines that the company requires. The occasion is a daunting one because of the tradition and having to read the medieval English declaration.

Coming in at Worcester after
riding my first steeplechase winner.

After my limited competitive success the Worshipful Company of Saddlers thought to ask me to become an Honorary Freeman of the Company. At that time there were no lady Liverymen. The Saddlers still maintain strong links with the craft, although the number of experienced saddlers is a fraction of what it was at the turn of the century, largely as a result of the demise of the working horse. Since the end of the Second World War, the increase in the number of horses required for sport and recreation has reversed the trend. New people were coming into the trade with neither a family background nor a formal apprenticeship to teach them the knowledge and the skills needed to make safe equipment. The Company rose to the challenge and instigated closer links with the trade which was by now centred on Walsall, supporting apprentices and competitions and donating prizes of saddles at the major shows for the more important competitions. They also kept close links with the Army and with their craftsmen.

It was the Worshipful Company of Loriners who alerted the standards authorities to the danger of cheap imports of bits and buckles from the Far East. These were made of nickel and broke very easily. Some of the bits literally shattered in the horses' mouths when they were bitten on.

The Worshipful Company of Farriers is also one of the oldest Companies. They were the original horse doctors. The Company has the responsibility for the Registration of Farriers Act 1975, for which it had lobbied to protect horses from the rogue and untrained farriers that the horse-riding boom had encouraged. The Company is now responsible for the training of all farriers and is trying to encourage them to qualify for higher degrees of training. It has one very pressing problem: it is not a wealthy Company and, since a rather abrupt change of government funding in 1991, has now found itself with the task of raising enough money to pay for the apprentices' training as well as running the registration scheme.

The Farriers' motto is 'No foot, no horse', and no modern technology or veterinary science has been able to change the situation. Horses' feet still cause the greatest number of lame animals, although it is often as a result of ignorance or wilful neglect on behalf of their owners. Lameness in the foot can be described as unnecessary suffering which a well-trained farrier can treat. The Worshipful Company of Farriers takes its responsibility to the welfare of the horse very seriously.

The Company is responsible for something else too – getting me on to a racehorse in a race. It boasts a number of working farriers in its Livery and saw fit to ask me not only to join the Livery, but also to join the Court and therefore be in line to become Master of the Company, the first lady Liveryman and Master. When this duly happened in September 1984, they very kindly decided to recognise the occasion with a special appeal on behalf of the Riding for the Disabled Association. One of the suggested fund-raising activities was a sponsored celebrity flat race at Epsom over the Derby course. Although I had never had any ambitions to ride in a race, I offered to take part on the grounds that it seemed unlikely to happen. Eighty-three rides later (forty-five on the flat and thirty-eight over fences, my total at the time of writing) I think I am glad I was so casual about the possibility and let things take their course from then on.

As my year as Master progressed it became obvious that my rather rash promise was going to have to be fulfilled. This meant that I would have to do some serious training, riding racehorses with short stirrups. Neither my arms nor my legs were fit enough for this sort of exercise, so it was suggested that my local National Hunt racing trainer, David Nicholson, who trained at Condicote near Stow-on-the-Wold, might be able to help me. I had already met 'the Duke', as he was known, and I also knew of his reputation as a teacher of apprentices who later became successful jockeys, as well as of many aspiring amateur riders. I needed somebody who was prepared to tell me what I was doing wrong and David did.

The first thing to do was to raise my centre of gravity by shortening the length of my stirrups so that my weight, when standing, was over the withers, the highest point of the horse's body. This had two effects: one was to allow me to hold a horse between hand and leg, using my legs as a brace for my arms to pull against the bit; the second was to remove my weight from the horse's back, therefore giving it greater freedom of movement.

Before I did any of this, I had to learn how to get on. This is not normally a problem when your stirrup leathers are long enough for you to reach from the ground, or you are athletic enough to vault on unaided, but it is impossible with short stirrups. Instead you are given a leg up. You raise your left leg behind you which the person who is helping you then grabs and, on an agreed signal, you hop and he or she lifts and you rise rapidly into the air to descend gently on to the saddle – well, that's the theory. In practice there is endless scope for getting it wrong. Trainers, lads and jockeys seem to have a built-in understanding of when to hop and lift; I needed a clear countdown to take-off and even now can be seen hopping down the road with the head lad desperately trying to get me off the ground.

Physically, short stirrups have the same effect as a week's skiing: your thighs ache. Nowadays I can go skiing and never get stiff. But more difficult for me was adjusting to a changed centre of gravity, because I felt very precarious sitting right on top of the animal and very vulnerable to any hiccup or lateral movement. The first few horses I rode made me feel as weak as water and it was a toss-up which bit of me went limp first, my fingers or my forearms.

I also had to learn about a professional sport. Horse racing has been described as the most nearly universal of the great spectator sports of modern times and as one of the oldest diversions of man. Certainly in my travels I have visited very few countries where the racing of horses hasn't featured somewhere in their history. When Caesar invaded Britain in 55 BC, he was greeted by skilled charioteers who had no doubt honed their skills in hot competition. But the rise of racing on the turf really belongs to the period of the Stuart dynasty when James I, who had patronised the sport in Scotland, sponsored meetings at Croydon and Enfield. He was also involved in the beginnings of racing at Epsom and Newmarket, although it was Charles II who was the most enthusiastic and knowledgeable supporter, sometimes riding his own horses to victory.

It wasn't until about 1750 that a body was formed to exercise control over racing and breeding in England. Known as the Jockey Club, its purpose was to regulate races and promote the sport, but its most important function with regard to racing was, and still is, its law- and rule-making powers. I needed to know the rules because the Jockey Club quite rightly expected amateur jockeys to abide by the same regulations as the professionals. We were going to ride at an official race meeting with public betting. We would be riding at published weights and on declared horses. The Jockey Club's prestige can be attested to by its imitation worldwide: for example, in such aspects as the weight-for-age scale, the official handicapper and the code of discipline and punishment for offences both on and off the course. The more I became involved with the International Equestrian Federation, the more I became interested in how racing managed itself, but for the moment, as a mere amateur jockey, I was keen to avoid any official encounters with the Stewards.

As the day of reckoning approached I was allowed to work the horse I was going to ride in the race, Against The Grain, and I was relieved to discover that his manners were a lot better than those of the other horses I had been riding. This was good news because I was – and still am – more worried about getting down to the start than about any other part of the proceedings. We also went to walk the course at Epsom, because it was just as important to know where you were going in a flat race as in a three-day event. British flat racecourses are seldom 'flat' and Epsom definitely isn't. If you watch the Derby on television or even if you are at Epsom itself, you are probably not aware of how much of a hill there is after the start or how much of a right-hand bend there is before you go left-handed down the hill into Tattenham Corner. After walking the course I was not too bothered by the hill or the corner; I was far more concerned about whether my legs and my lungs would stand the strain of trying to kick all the way up the straight.

The day of the race dawned and there was a very good turn-out for that time of year – St George's Day, 1985. The facilities for lady jockeys at Epsom were non-existent, so we used the Royal Box. The first real worry is whether you have everything you need, and this is quite different from what you need to

Leading in after work at Condicote.

On Canon Class at Condicote.

go eventing. I was lucky to have David Nicholson's wife, Dinah, whose own riding career had included race riding, to be my 'jockey's valet'. These people are vital to the professional jockeys as they rush from one racecourse to another and from one horse to another during a meeting. The valets help keep track of all their tack as jockeys usually use their own saddles, and little things like stock pins, elastic bands for the cuffs of the colours and whips can, with all the activity, easily get mislaid unless someone watches over them.

The correct attire is lightweight white breeches, which I didn't have – only a pair of stretchy white nylon ones of which the trainer did not approve. But for just one race it didn't seem worth getting a special pair. I did need lightweight racing boots, which he had managed to 'borrow' for me – they turned out to have been made for the good NH jockey Graham McCourt and either didn't fit him or he is still wondering what on earth happened to them. They fitted me perfectly and I have used them ever since. (I'm not sure whether it was good or bad news to be identified on *A Question of Sport* as John Reid, the flat race jockey, and to have legs like Graham McCourt as well!) Gloves, stock and stock pins I had, the elastic bands were produced by Dinah, the whip had to be the approved length and width, and the crash helmet had to be the approved Jockey Club standard, which I had been using ever since I started riding out.

Wearing a crash helmet had been obligatory at all racehorse training establishments for some time, although before that I used to wear one only for schooling over cross-country fences and at competitions, I quickly got accustomed to them and now never ride anything without one. Apart from being a sensible precaution to prevent a potentially fatal or disabling accident, wearing a helmet gives a sense of security which in turn gives the rider greater confidence to be more positive, especially with the more difficult horses. But it won't stop you getting hurt if you underestimate the inherent risk of climbing aboard an unpredictable animal with a mind of its own.

At Epsom there were so many things to remember that the immediate risk seemed lost in detail. The atmosphere before the race was fairly relaxed, based on the 'ignorance-is-bliss' theory. In the weighing room everybody had to be officially passed, with their saddle, weighing what it said on the racecard you were going to weigh. It was a hive of unusual last-minute activity for those not used to the strict requirements of a professional sport. There was a photo-call for the jockeys before being transported to the paddock in a mini-bus. Waiting and watching the horses going round was a mixture of relief – that the horse was there – and of wondering what on earth *you* were doing there.

The 'Jockeys get mounted' call turns the peaceful well-ordered scene into one of frantic activity, or so it seemed then, with the horses being turned in and their rugs taken off; last-minute adjustments were made to the tack and then you

The photo made famous by A Question of Sport. I was riding Salmon Run in the colours of Mrs Jenny Mould in atrocious conditions at Cheltenham in April 1986.

were 'thrown up'. This was the other bit I was dreading. No, I was not ill: this was legging-up time, made much worse because the horse will not stand still and an untidy landing in the saddle tends to crack the thin veneer of competence you have been carefully nurturing. Fortunately I got it right and I felt much better once I was actually on the animal. Parading down past the stands and back, for the benefit of the punters, seemed fraught with potential disaster, but there were no nasty moments on the way to the start.

The starting stalls were next on the agenda and obviously worried some people a lot more than others. I had been put through 'the Duke's' rather Heath Robinson version, which bore very little relation to the real thing; the racecourse stalls are padded, for a start. It gets quite noisy just before the 'off' and the crash of the gates opening is very intimidating and almost impossible to recreate at home. I'm sure that the advice I was given was right, which was to sit quietly on the horse in the stalls with a finger hooked round a neck strap or under the saddle and not to try to anticipate their opening – well, it worked most of the time.

The mood changes when you are called forward to be loaded into the stalls. Everyone becomes more businesslike and concentrates the mind on all the things they have been told about how to ride the race: how to come out of the stalls – forwards seemed to be the best answer; where to be in the field at the first bend – galloping on your horse in the same direction as everybody else seemed sensible; where to be at Tattenham Corner – going round it and not straight on; and, of course, what to do in the last furlong when you weren't where you were supposed to be, which was cruising into the lead – not getting so tired trying to ride a finish that you fell off before pulling up.

I don't know how everybody else's plans went, but my race bore no relation to the instructions that I had been given. With hindsight I may have relied too much on the horse who had, after all, had a lot more experience than me, even if his most recent outings had been over hurdles. Lack of recent stalls practice may not have helped either as we were both a little too relaxed when the gates opened. I can only describe the first two furlongs as a cavalry charge and the third as a shoving match to get a place on the rails before the corner. I have always been allergic to crowds and it was now that I knew for certain why it was that I had never had any ambitions to ride in a race – there were too many other people who all apparently wanted to be in the same place as me. Against The Grain and I opted for remaining upright. We came down the hill very safely and I let him turn a little wide into the straight on the basis that we then had a free passage to overtake the stragglers as we stormed up the straight. That was after I

With Ginny Leng (then Virginia Holgate) after the first race I ever rode in at Epsom, April 1985.
I finished fourth on Against The Grain.

managed to persuade him I needed his finishing burst now and not after the other circuit I suspect he was expecting. As it was we finished strongly to be fourth, but if they had gone another furlong we would have won!

I did remember that the getting-off had to be done very deliberately and a firm grip on the stirrup leather would prevent an ignominious descent to the turf when I discovered – too late – that my legs refused to hold me up. I had been told, and remembered, and was grateful. The other thing not to forget is to weigh in to prove that you weigh the same as you did when you weighed out just before the race.

It had been a tremendous experience; the speed and the effort of staying on take you by surprise. I thoroughly enjoyed the whole thing, especially as it was

Riding out with my children Zara and Peter from David Nicholson's stables at Condicote.

for a good cause, but I was not 'hooked' in the sense of being determined to repeat the experience. It had, though, opened up a new line of equestrian activity that I had never been involved with before. If I was surprised by the fact that I had ended up riding in a flat race, what happened subsequently surprised me even more. More immediately I had failed to take into account the great British betting public; when I was about my official business, some of them were moved to tell me exactly how much money they had lost by backing me.

I honestly thought that that would be the sum total of my racing experience, but I was keen to continue to 'ride out' for 'the Duke' whenever I could. The more I did, the less of a liability I was, and the more useful I became to the whole yard. 'First lot' rides out at seven in the morning and is usually back by half-past eight, so there is time to ride out and then get on with a day's work. I was interested in the horses' work patterns and found a good variety on offer: walking out; trotting on the relatively quiet country roads, which is very good for strengthening human leg muscles as well as the horses'; cantering days; and work mornings for those about to run.

Thanks to being welcomed at Condicote, during September I was offered another chance to ride in an amateur race, this time at Goodwood and then at sunny Redcar on the north-east coast. As this was a proper amateur race and not a 'one-off' celebrity race, I had to get an Amateur Jockey's Licence from the Jockey Club and a Medical Record book, which was even more important and had to be shown on your arrival at the course or you weren't allowed to ride. The Medical Record book contained all information pertaining to any treatment you might have had at the course, or as a result of a fall, and gave the Jockey Club doctors control over, for instance, cases of concussion. Over the years my book remained clean; I did myself more damage at horse trials than I ever did at a racecourse.

At Redcar I rode Lulav, who had been my introduction to the racehorse at Condicote and who had consistently ignored me, but only once had I failed to stop him at the end of the shavings galloping track. He always pulled hard but only flattered to deceive, because if you let the reins go he seldom went any faster. Unfortunately this was also true at Redcar and we finished down the field.

Another outing was at Goodwood's autumn meeting, riding the Nicholsons' home-bred filly Little Sloop, and little she certainly was. She was also only a three-year-old, which meant that she carried a relatively light weight – lighter

Setting off from Condicote with 'the Duke', as David Nicholson is known.

Being pursued by Zara on Snoopy at Condicote.

than me and the saddle as it turned out. There is something about hearing how much overweight your horse is carrying being announced over the public address that makes you want to avoid it happening again. Since then I have eaten less! The next year I was to discover how little I needed to eat to remain healthy in order to ride a lightly weighted horse in the Diamond Stakes at Ascot. As it happened, I managed to get down to the right weight, but the horse wasn't feeling too good.

That was a horse trained by Gavin Pritchard-Gordon, a long-time friend of David's, at Newmarket where I went to make his acquaintance and to ride out two horses so that I could get the feel of them before riding them in a race. The year 1986 was the first time I rode at Ascot in the main race of the year for lady jockeys. Its atmosphere was quite different from that of the other amateur races, which were normally at the smaller tracks where everything was more relaxed. At Ascot we were also riding better horses.

After Ascot I went back to Redcar to ride Gulfland, the other horse, trained by Gavin Pritchard-Gordon, that I had ridden at Newmarket. He was a rather special horse, previously owned by Lord Cadogan. He had been diagnosed as having chipped the bone in his knee and would therefore need a lot of rest and might never be fit to race again. Lord Cadogan didn't want to sell the horse, so gave him to his trainer, Gavin, as his hack, to lead the young horses and for the apprentices to ride, but not to do any serious racing. Amateur races were not serious to a horse of Gulfland's breeding, so Gavin and the joint owner, Sir John Mowbray, very generously offered me the ride.

Gulfland was a real gentleman, but he also knew about racing and needed to be kidded along a bit. My instructions were not to hurry him in the early stages and definitely not to hit the front before the final furlong marker. I nearly ruined everything when my sitting still in the stalls resulted in his bouncing out of them so quickly that he was in the lead. Fortunately we were rapidly overtaken by something rather over-enthusiastic and after 2 furlongs we were nearer last than first. A mile and a half is quite a long way, and as we rounded the bottom bend better than most we found ourselves among some horses that had already run their race. The straight at Redcar is over 5 furlongs, so there was still a long way to go.

Gulfland immediately took a more serious interest in the race, although I thought that the leader was so far in front that we could never catch him. But

My first winner on the flat – Gulfland winning at Redcar on 5 August 1986.

first we had to go outside one horse, then back on to the rails to go inside the next, and then we were really galloping. We swept past the horse in second place as if it were cantering, and to my absolute amazement as we reached the final furlong marker we caught and overtook the long-time leader. I didn't dare stop kicking until we were well past the post. That was another cardinal rule – that you should never look round, for the movement can unbalance the horse and lose your momentum, and races have been lost because of it.

Walking the course at York.

First emotion? Relief. For the horse, for the owners, for the trainer, for the travelling head lad who drove the horse box from Newmarket and for the 'lad' who looked after Gulfland, and right at the end for the punters who had put their money on him. I still had to weigh in before the result became official, then, if there were no objection and no Stewards' Inquiry, the prize-giving would happen at once. As soon as that is finished it is time for the next race, and so it goes on. I have been lucky enough to ride Gulfland three times since that special 'first', once again at Redcar and twice at Hamilton, where he was second on both occasions. In between he had been very successfully ridden by his 'lad', Abigail, from which it could be deduced that he goes better for the ladies!

I was beginning to discover that horse racing was a lot more time-efficient than eventing. Riding out with a trainer early in the morning was one advantage; the other was that you knew precisely what time your race would be. You needed only to add the time for walking the course, if that was necessary, and to wash and change afterwards, so that your total time at the course could be as little as just over an hour.

I was given the opportunity to have several more rides that year on different horses. I was getting braver now and would take on rides that I had not had the chance to sit on before the race. But it was mostly 'the Duke's' homework that made sure the rides I was being offered were within my capabilities, and it is to his and his fellow trainers' great credit that I have no bad memories of any of the horses that I have ridden.

I have some very amusing memories and there is one in particular that always makes me smile. Do you remember the Hamlet Cigar advertisements? A few months after my first race, I rode a charming little horse called French Union in a flat race at Chepstow. Trained by David Nicholson, he had been bought to go National Hunt racing, but David thought that a run on the flat would do him good before he ran over hurdles. I was allowed to ride him because I had been riding him a lot at Condicote. We knew he had raced in Ireland before he came over, but nobody knew if he had run from stalls. He had been perfectly good in 'the Duke's' version, so we weren't too worried. He became very excited when he got out on the track and was bouncing around down at the start. The starter thought it safer to load us into the stalls last and I did my best to remain icy-calm and sat even stiller than usual.

In the stalls French Union was marching on the spot and I grabbed a handful of mane expecting a violent bound when the gates opened. The stalls crashed open and the field leapt forward, watched by an apparently astonished French Union who remained exactly where he was – inside the stalls. That was when the vision of the Hamlet Cigar advertisement sprang into my mind and I started to laugh. I did pull myself together enough to get us under way and, having given ten of them about a twelve-length start, we were only six lengths adrift and a fast-finishing fifth at the finish.

I have caused some apprehension to Clerks of the Course from Hamilton in Scotland to Folkestone in the south of England, from Devon and Exeter in the west to Huntingdon in the east, regarding the state of their lady jockeys' changing rooms. There was a considerable discrepancy in the standards of those facilities. The Clerks are responsible to the Jockey Club for the condition of the individual racecourse and some had not had to cope with many lady jockeys. Suffice to say that if I have achieved nothing else in my racing career, I have got the ladies some new loos!

By the end of the flat racing season in 1986 I had had eight rides, one win and several placings. I was beginning to feel more at home on a racecourse than at a horse trial, although I was still taking young horses to events. I had to keep separate bags for the different sports, but the helmet went everywhere. It also went to America when I rode in an invitation flat race just south of Nashville, Tennessee, in October 1987. The meeting, organised by George Sloan, was to try to revitalise jump racing in the States, and he enlisted the help of some of his friends in Britain, one of whom was David.

The course was one of the most attractive I have ever seen, set in a natural amphitheatre surrounded by deciduous woods which were a riot of colour in October. The course was only a mile round, left-handed and rural in the sense that much of the track was marked by small privet-type hedges with only sections of rails round the corners. The jumping track went round the outside of the flat course and was extended at the corners. The fences themselves were alive; they looked like privet hedges growing on top of little banks to a height of about 4 feet. The hedges were quite soft, which made them more like hurdles to jump.

The object of the meeting was to attract good jumping horses and George Sloan had managed to persuade some British owners and trainers to bring their horses as part of the 'Sport of Kings' Challenge that would include two races in America and two in Britain. The flat race was a sweetener and the field included some of America's best amateur riders. Thanks to the generosity of Abbreviation's owner, Peter Hopkins, and his trainer, Josh Gifford, I had a very nice ride, but he missed having hurdles to jump. We finished an honourable third. It was quite a rough race and the consistency of the soil was very fine grit, which seemed to get everywhere and particularly in my mouth. The atmosphere was tremendous, however, and it was a very good two days, even the official part which included a smart dinner in one of Nashville's old mansions to the accompaniment of real country music.

Staying with George had been even more fun, with a mounted tour of his property which had included jumping all his hunt jumps. Dinah and I thoroughly enjoyed our ride, but I'm not sure that 'the Duke' did. I don't think he had jumped a fence since he stopped race riding.

On the basis of the fun we had had the first time, we – the Nicholsons and I – agreed to go in 1988 as well. Because of my diary I couldn't go out until the day of the race, but help was at hand in the form of one of the 'Sport of Kings' sponsors, British Airways. For the first time since a quick trip during her proving trials, I got a flight on Concorde. I left Heathrow on the Friday morning flight to New York, where I was picked up by a private jet to fly on to Nashville, arriving at the course in time for the

Racing in Tennessee. I'm on the right about to take the lead 100 yards from the winning post.

race at two o'clock in the afternoon. Time-wise, it was like riding in the seven o'clock race at an evening meeting at Warwick.

I was to ride a horse I had ridden at Newmarket the year before, trained by Barry Hills and called Wood Chisel. He had since been sold to America and was now trained by George Sloan. A year older, he had obviously reacted well to the change of air, he looked a picture and felt a different animal. After my previous experience on the course, I was in a better position coming into the very short straight and, when I had given him a kick, he outsprinted his nearest rival and won by a couple of lengths. That was enormously satisfying for George and me.

The day after the race we went up to Virginia, leaving poor George in agony with gall stones which fortunately were quickly diagnosed and flushed out. Sadly, he had to miss our day's hunting which followed. To complete this high-speed weekend, I then flew back from Washington in Concorde and was home on Sunday night.

I continued to ride out through the winter of 1986–87 on David's jumpers and then one morning I was asked to ride Bagdad Gold, an ex-hurdler who was ridden by everybody and who acted as lead horse for the young horses, especially when they started jumping. He was a very quick, careful jumper who had never wanted to negotiate anything bigger than a hurdle but who was quite prepared to jump the logs that David kept for teaching his youngsters. I was allowed to ride Baggy on these occasions, which was good for me because he liked to go more quickly than I would have done. This gave me the feel of racing over a fence, but it was slow by their standards. I was to discover how slow when I graduated to leading the schooling over hurdles, also riding Baggy. There are only three hurdles to negotiate, but using a horse that knows what it's doing and is enthusiastic ensures that the pace is realistic. I thoroughly enjoyed it.

To my great relief I seemed to be doing the right thing, but I was still surprised to be asked to ride David's great old horse, What A Buck, who had made himself indispensable in his retirement as the lead horse for the galloping and over the schooling fences. I rode him over the hurdles first and was completely out of control, but subsequently discovered that he thought hurdles were beneath his dignity. Over the fences I was still out of control, but the old horse was so positive that as long as I kept a tight rein he would jump from anywhere. I found it very exciting stuff. There were only two fences in a line but there were three different sizes. They were beautifully built, small replicas of the regular steeplechase fences that would have to be jumped in a race.

Then, in February 1987, David said that he had found a horse for me to ride. Cnoc-na-Cuille, owned by Tommy Keogh, was with Josh Gifford, had been hunted by his wife Althea and was an ideal ride for an amateur. I was surprised because I didn't think that I had ever given the impression that I wanted to ride in a steeplechase, but I was flattered that these two experienced ex-jockeys and successful trainers thought that I could. The goal seemed to be the Grand Military at Sandown, which is a race confined to members past and present of Her Majesty's Services, or those with honorary positions such as colonel-in-chief of a regiment.

On the basis that the horse could come on a month's trial, it was not hard to persuade me to agree to try him. So Cnoc-na-Cuille was brought to Condicote. He was a bright bay with black points, not very big and rather narrow, not quite my idea of a strapping steeplechaser from whose back the fences would look smaller. He was not a perfect gentleman on the gallops, being prone to bouts of serious over-enthusiasm, and he was guilty of trying to turn and set off too early at the schooling fences. Never mind; Cnoc knew about jumping – he was quick and accurate, although stiff in his back which dissuaded him from 'standing off'. He liked to take the extra stride to get closer to the fence. We seemed to get on quite well and I felt fairly confident with him.

Before the decision was made as to whether I was ready for a race, David took us to jump full-size fences at racing pace at a real racecourse. This exercise had to be carefully arranged with the agreement of the chosen racecourse, because there would need to be an ambulance and doctor in attendance as well as course staff to man the crossings on the course to prevent people wandering on to the track at the critical moment. And what course had David arranged for this crucial and, to me, worrying trial? None other than his local track and home of the National Hunt Festival in March each year, Cheltenham.

The term 'a hollow laugh' is not just a literary expression, it is a very good descriptive phrase; I know because the laugh with which I greeted this piece of information appeared to come from the bottom of a bucket. There didn't seem to be anything to say and if I was serious about riding at Sandown I was going to have to do it. I reminded myself that I was the only one who was concerned – Richard Dunwoody, the stable's jockey, who was going to be riding one of David's promising young horses, wasn't worried and Cnoc certainly wasn't worried; all I had to do was hang on.

This turned out to be very true. We were to jump the three fences across the middle of the course and then join the main track to jump the two fences at the far end of the straight. I had never been renowned as a quick starter, tending to set off rather steadily while I let the horse and myself get our eyes in. There was never any danger of that happening on this occasion because Cnoc was much keener than I was. When we set off, he seemed to go from stationary to flat out in a few strides, and any attempt by me to moderate this headlong rush was completely ignored. But he knew what he was doing and he proved that I should learn to sit still and let him get on with it. After we had jumped the first three fences I made another futile attempt to slow down and became aware of Richard's grinning face beside me. He seemed perfectly happy, so I let Cnoc do his own thing. I was beginning to understand that, riding in an event, you expect to be between 50 and 75 per cent in control, but riding in a race you need to be 99 per cent *out* of control.

When we pulled up in front of the stands, I felt exhilarated and brave enough to ride in a race on the basis that, if I could survive what I had just survived, a race couldn't be too much worse. What was more important was that David seemed to think it was a satisfactory trial, and the possibility of riding at Kempton on 28 February became a firm objective.

I kept having to remind myself of that feeling of confidence after schooling at Cheltenham, and to persuade myself that it couldn't be much worse than riding in a cross-country race; at least all the fences were the same and were more inviting than sets of solid wooden rails. Fortunately there were only four of us in the race and the other three were professional jockeys riding horses that had better form than Cnoc. This was Cnoc's first run for some time.

Curiously, in flat racing, amateurs can race only against amateurs, and it was not until recently that men and women took part in the same race. In NH racing you can get a Conditional B Licence which allows you to ride against the professionals. I was fortunate to get one because I was relatively inexperienced. I had no point-to-point background, but I had had fifteen rides on the flat and I was given credit for my eventing experience. There are two main advantages to being able to ride against the professionals: they are safer and the horse doesn't have to carry so much weight, because in the amateur races the minimum weight is 12 stone, whereas in handicaps Cnoc might get only 10 stone to carry.

So there I was, on a cold day in late February, walking the course at Kempton Park where the King George VI Steeplechase is run on Boxing Day. The fences looked big but well-built and inviting. The course is flat and triangular, and we were to race one and two-thirds circuits. Walking the course made me feel better, but I would like to have been able to come back, change and then go

Cnoc-na-Cuille at Kempton – my first ride over fences on a National Hunt course.

out and race straight away. As it was there was at least an hour to wait, and this was when I was grateful for all the training in controlling nerves that my life had seemed to consist of.

Getting changed was a careful ritual and once again, with Dinah's help, I hadn't forgotten anything. An important piece of equipment was the body protector, which was to become compulsory not only for NH jockeys but also for riders in UK horse trials. In spite of some early scepticism and feelings of discomfort – I felt I looked like the Incredible Hulk – everybody has come to appreciate their value.

When you are the only lady, the changing room can get a bit lonely, and the time hangs heavily until they give you the call 'Jockeys out'. On the way out of the weighing room I was introduced to one of the other jockeys, Richard Rowe, who had ridden Cnoc in some of his previous races, and he made some cheerful and encouraging comments about him. The professional NH jockeys are a pragmatic, good-humoured and polite bunch of people – most of the time. NH racing is a risky business, which they all know, and they face and respect those risks every day. They are normally generous to the conditional jockeys like me, but you are beholden to make sure you observe the rules and above all keep a straight line.

Goodness knows what they thought that day. The parade ring looked very empty and it was a relief to get on and out on to the course, even if I was worried about being run away with on the way to the start. We made it safely but I felt so exhausted when I got there that I was seriously worried whether I was going to last the race. My arms felt like limp asparagus and I appeared to have difficulty breathing. Too late: we were under orders and then away. My orders were to follow the others, something I was very keen to do. Unfortunately, Cnoc seemed to be overcome with enthusiasm for his first race-course appearance in eighteen months and set a fearsome pace down the back straight. If I hadn't been so worried about him running out of breath and about wasting my energy trying to steady him, I would have enjoyed that first circuit. We were bowling along in front and he was jumping beautifully. When we turned to go out on the second circuit, I thought I detected a lessening of the initial enthusiasm, so while the others started to race, we continued to bowl along at the back where he still jumped beautifully. I almost began to enjoy myself, except that I did want to complete the course in one piece. We finished a distant but completely satisfied fourth, and if I had never ridden over fences again I would still have been thrilled with that experience.

The distance of that race was only 2 miles and 5 furlongs; the Grand Military at Sandown was over 3 miles, but that would not worry Cnoc. Sandown is a very different course from Kempton and you actually start downhill to the first fence. It is then flat alongside the railway line, but starts to climb from the bottom corner all the way to the finishing line and past the stands. The Grand Military meeting is a popular traditional fixture which attracts supporters of owners, riders and regiments who may go to only this one race meeting in the year. For many of the amateur jockeys it is their major race of the year and possibly of their career. Because of this there is a very special atmosphere.

Needless to say, there weren't any other ladies riding, so I had the Porta-kabin round the back of the weighing room to myself. I must admit I was considerably more nervous before this race than before my first, mostly because of the number of other runners, and they were all amateurs except one who, by the standards of the rest of the riders, was virtually a professional. He had also won the race several times for the same owner. There was another reason for feeling more nervous and that was the presence not only of my grandmother, who was a regular attender and winning owner, but also of my mother, who very seldom went to an NH meeting and even less frequently watched me ride – a decision I sympathised with then and even more so now my daughter is competing!

Strangely enough, I don't remember much about the race except that Cnoc wasn't showing much enthusiasm at the end of the first circuit but managed to overtake one or two before the finish. In the words of the trainer, we had gone out and looked after each other. In spite of that rather unsatisfactory performance, I was keen to try again and to do a better job of riding a proper race.

I tried to get it right at Liverpool, Ludlow and Chepstow and finished the season with a run at Towcester. I nearly got it right at Towcester, where I let Cnoc bowl along in front, hoping that he would settle there, but he wasn't allowed to by a horse ridden by Richard Dunwoody who kept coming alongside and off we would go again. We stayed together and some way in front of the rest right to the second last fence where Cnoc, who was feeling tired, didn't get very high and hit the fence harder than I expected. I went up his neck and thought that I had saved myself until his head went down and I slipped off over his shoulder. I shouldn't have done and I blamed the fact that, with my reins 'bridged', I had not managed to slip them as I would normally have done.* I would therefore not have been pulled over his head. If my lower leg had been in a better position, it might have helped me stay on. It was a shame, because the winner broke the course record largely as a result of Cnoc's front-running.

That was the end of the NH season and Cnoc came back to Gatcombe for a holiday. The flat racing season was in full swing and I managed to get one or two rides. There are ups and downs in any sport and horses are certainly no different and in some ways worse. In my limited racing career I had some successful rides, but I had a lot more that were unsuccessful and some major disappointments.

The Diamond Stakes at Ascot in 1987 was a success, thanks to trainer Michael Stoute from Newmarket and his owner, Mrs P. L. Yong from Singapore, giving me the ride on her three-year-old colt, Ten No Trumps. I went and rode him out at Newmarket with Stoute's string which was an experience in itself.

---

* With bridged reins, instead of holding just one rein in each hand, you cross the trailing end of the rein over the neck of the horse just in front of the saddle to the opposite hand, thereby creating a 'bridge'. This gives you something to lean on, but it limits your ability to lengthen your reins in a hurry, as I had done coming out of the Trout Hatchery at Burghley on Doublet.

Ten No Trumps winning the Dresden Diamond Stakes at Ascot on 25 July 1987.

The lads at Newmarket are not of the same standard of tidiness that would be expected at Condicote and I was amused to see a lad of advanced years casually knocking out the contents of his pipe on his heel as he rode out on a skittish-looking two-year-old.

Ten No Trumps was a kind horse who had missed much of his early career because of an injury. He was a relaxed individual, which was to prove vital on the day of the race. We had no problems getting down to the start in spite of being overtaken by somebody who couldn't slow down. Because of the number of the draw, I was one of the first to be loaded into the stalls. This isn't a problem unless one of the later ones refuses to go in – which is what happened, and Ten No Trumps and I stood patiently waiting for the recalcitrant horse to join us. I thought all this standing about might prove a major disadvantage, but when we finally came under the starter's orders and the gates opened, we were the first out. My orders required me to tuck in behind something, which was going to be difficult because we came out so quickly from our inside draw.

My only winner under National Hunt rules. Cnoc-na-Cuille winning at Worcester on 3 September 1987.

Fortunately, another horse pulled itself to the front, but it wasn't going to be able to keep up that gallop for long, so I would have to be careful not to get trapped behind it when it ran out of puff.

As we came to the corner into the home straight, the horse in front started to slow down quite quickly and I made the decision to pull out from behind it then, while I had room to do so. At that stage there was another horse with me and we turned into the straight more or less together. The other instruction I had received was that Ten No Trumps would certainly stay the distance and therefore I was not to wait to be challenged. So I set sail three furlongs from the post and hoped nobody would catch me. It was then I became aware of the noise from the stands. One thing that had surprised me about horse races was the amount of noise, especially at the end when the sound of galloping feet is joined by vocal encouragement of all kinds and the slapping of whips. If you happen to be in front, you can hear other horses coming up behind you. Thanks to the noise from the stands, I couldn't hear anything else and kept kicking, hoping that I wouldn't have to work any harder. Ten No Trumps won by six lengths.

It is always nice to ride a good horse and it's much easier too. It's even nicer to win, especially when your family are there; in this case both my parents and my grandmother.

The next and possibly most satisfying success of my racing career came at a Worcester NH meeting with Cnoc. Cnoc had returned to Condicote at the beginning of August, having enjoyed himself climbing our hills. He was fit and strong but not galloping fit and he would need some fast work to sharpen him up. He was probably· one gallop short when he went to Worcester for his first run of the season, which was run on firm ground and was a fast-run race. That's my opinion, but if you ask 'the Duke' he will tell you that Cnoc was short of work when he returned from Gatcombe!

When we went back to Worcester a few weeks later, he really was fit to

Being led into the winners' enclosure with the Condicote team after Cnoc's win at Worcester, 1987.

run. The other advantage was that I now knew the track and was probably more relaxed both before and during the race. Worcester is a flat course beside the river, which you have to worry about only if your horse gets loose or your steering doesn't work. In a 3-mile steeplechase you do nearly two complete left-handed circuits, starting at the top end of the back straight with the stables on your right. This, combined with the fact that the second fence is an open ditch, can cause some interesting problems. With a small field it's not so bad, except that if the leader shows any signs of reluctance or attraction to the stables, the others can also lose enthusiasm very quickly.

There was a small field for this race and it was Cnoc's jumping over the first few fences that got us off to a good start. At the end of the first circuit he was 'in touch' but a long way from being in front. As they started to race in earnest down the back straight, other horses were making mistakes and Cnoc was gaining ground because of his jumping. As we turned into the straight we were on the heels of the leaders, and once we had jumped the open ditch I knew I had to get serious. By now – if we stood up – there were only two of us with a chance of winning and the other horse was (I later discovered) the odds-on favourite. The cheering was not for me! We jumped the last fence together, but Cnoc jumped it better and got back into his stride more quickly. The distance from the last fence to the finishing post at Worcester is only a furlong, for which I was heartily grateful. Cnoc got his head in front and I tried not to interfere with him too much, but there comes a point when you feel you have to look as if you are doing something. Fortunately Cnoc was not slowing down and when we finally reached the winning post we had half a length to spare over the second horse.

That was a real thrill. I've probably ridden better races since, but nothing quite compares with that final commitment of being 'upsides going to the last' and the excitement of a horse going as fast as it can to beat another horse. It was tremendous to see the pleasure on the faces of the Condicote team and to be congratulated by the other jockeys as well as by Brendan Powell who rode the second.

My victory was definitely not popular with everybody. As I went to leave with David after the end of racing, I could hear somebody grumbling that 'it was a fix!'. This complaint came from a large, apparently somewhat inebriated gentleman who was being encouraged away from us towards his car. My trainer and my policeman got in the car, but I'm afraid I got out and went over to this man. I went to inform him that I was not the person to complain to if he thought the result was fixed, because I had certainly been trying *my* hardest. I had even asked Brendan if he was sure he had been trying his hardest, just to reassure myself, but then *I* didn't know he was riding the odds-on favourite. While I stood my ground, the irate punter explained his wrath by bewailing the fact that he had been on a 'six-timer' and I had beaten his sixth choice. I told him I sympathised with his disappointment, but he still had no business taking it out on me – we parted quite good friends. I returned to the car where David and my policeman were waiting – poised and watchful, they assured me.

I was to have many more enjoyable rides on Cnoc but never another win. At the Grand Military in 1988 he was going much better when a slightly awkward jump made me lose my stirrup. It wouldn't have caused me much concern on an event horse with a jumping saddle and full-size stirrups; however, on a racing saddle with small, lightweight stirrups and one leg much shorter than the other, when you are approaching the next fence at racing pace, getting your foot back into the stirrup becomes impossible – well, it was for me, so I decided to pull up. That wasn't easy to achieve either, but I'm sure it was the right thing to do.

Towards the end of the season I rode Cnoc at Towcester, where he did not feel right, and I pulled him up at the end of the first circuit. When he got back to Condicote, the vet listened to his heart and took some blood to test. The results were fine and the horse himself seemed bright and fresh. It was decided to run him once more at Warwick. He was a bit naughty in the race, dropping himself out and not trying very hard until he saw the horses in front of him slowing down or falling. Then you could see his ears prick and feel his stride quicken. We were a long way behind the leader but overtook the horse lying fourth in the straight and finished faster than anything else in third place.

Cnoc had his ears pricked when he crossed the line and seemed rather pleased with himself. I was delighted that he had finished so full of running. We pulled up and walked back in front of the stands towards the unsaddling enclosure, chatting to the other jockeys. Cnoc's lad was leading him when I felt him falter and start to wobble. Instinctively, because I had seen it happen to other horses, I knew at once that he was dying. David, who had just come up, realised too and told me to get off, but I was already half-way to the ground. The travelling head lad took in what was happening and went to help the lad. Cnoc collapsed very quickly towards the racecourse while they were trying to take off his saddle and weight cloth. When they succeeded, I was sent off to weigh in as if nothing had happened. There was nothing more I could have done and I think I was grateful to be sent away with a purpose; if I hadn't weighed in, Cnoc would not have been credited for his well-deserved third place.

I felt bad about leaving everybody, but I knew from experience there was no point in going back because of the added interest my presence would have encouraged from the press and public. As it was, having Dinah with me was a great help for both of us. We both knew the pain of loosing a good companion and we both understood the feeling of loneliness that would be felt by the staff going home in an empty horse box. Before I set off for home I went round to the horse box to find Cnoc's 'lad', who was a girl. I wouldn't be able to help her, but I hoped she would know that we all cared and that her misery could be shared. I had been looking forward to having Cnoc at home because he was such a nice individual and seemed to enjoy his time at Gatcombe where he behaved so well. He would jump any of the cross-country-type fences in the park and yet he wouldn't go anywhere near a showjumping pole, even if it was lying on the ground. Anybody could ride him at Condicote and he would be missed by many.

His death did make me wonder whether we had asked too much of him. With me riding him that seemed pretty unlikely, because I was incapable of giving him a hard race. I hadn't got the energy, never mind the inclination. No – he had been happy during his last race and had gone no faster than he wanted to; I'm afraid it was just one of those things that could have happened any time and might have even happened on the training gallops. I was extremely grateful that I had General Joy to look forward to.

In the 1988–90 seasons I was lucky enough to be riding two horses. Save and Prosper showed an interest in extending their sports sponsorship from rugby to NH racing. This move had quite a lot to do with my nanny's brother-in-law, who had recently joined the company. I was then asked whether, if they bought a horse for me to ride, I would ride in their colours. As I had ridden on the flat for all sorts of people, including a garage, I didn't see anything wrong with riding for a company in NH racing. They were taking more of a risk than I was, because if they were keen on winning races I was not the best amateur jockey around, never mind professional. However, when I wasn't available, the horse would be ridden by Richard Dunwoody, and you couldn't get a better jockey than him.

Save and Prosper subsequently agreed to a package that included owning a horse and sponsoring six races around the country in which they hoped I would be able to ride. This was how my second NH ride came about and General Joy came straight from the stables of 'Mouse' Morris in Ireland in March 1988. He was a bright chestnut, tall, slender and carried his head very high, but he was a gentleman about everything he did. To me, he jumped very flat, but that made him very smooth. His only major drawback that I noticed was that he had such a long galloping action that when he needed to shorten his stride in order not to hit a fence, it took him a comparatively long time after landing to get back up to speed.

Our introduction race was at Chepstow – an undulating, left-handed course – and he was going well turning into the very long straight. I had been warned about the first fence in the straight, which seemed to cause a disproportionate amount of trouble on the second circuit for no apparent reason. It nearly tripped us up – he jumped the fence perfectly well but then almost fell over. It is as a

General Joy at Stratford-upon-Avon.

Following pages: Winning The Queen Mother Cup at York on 11 June 1988
with Insular, owned and trained by Ian Balding and bred by Her Majesty The Queen.

precaution against this kind of happening that you bridge your reins and my bridge saved me from being shot up his neck, as well as my lower leg being in a better position to stop any rapid forward movement. We lost some ground and although the General set off in pursuit we were now too far adrift to catch the first two but finished a highly satisfactory third. Everybody was pleased with that run and despite the fact that the General had to carry a lot of weight in some of his owners' races, he never ran a bad race and I always enjoyed riding him.

In the summer of 1988, on one of his trips to Ireland, David found a horse called Canon Class, trained by Edna Bolger. Dinah rode him and thought he would be an excellent ride for somebody like me. He was sired by a stallion called The Parson, who was a son of my mother's good stallion Aureole, and out of a mare by Pall Mall, who had run in The Queen's colours. My mother's interest in bloodlines must have encouraged her and she very generously helped me to buy Canon Class.

He was very like Cnoc, being a bright bay with black points, but physically there was more of Canon. He was more of a thinker than either the General or my subsequent horse Bobby Kelly, but apart from his habit of rushing off with his head in the air when you started cantering, he didn't pull and was a sensible ride. If I said he was the best jumper of the steeplechasers I rode, it would be because he was more careful and 'classical' – the shape of his jump was rounder. He was not necessarily quicker. By the start of the season he was ready to run.

Our first race was at Stratford – a flat, left-handed course – and he set off in front with his ears pricked. He lasted about a circuit at the head of affairs until the professionals started to race in earnest. We remained in touch until he sensibly avoided being the meat in the sandwich at the last open ditch and so lost a lot of ground. After that, I had a lovely ride at the back with Canon measuring and jumping his fences like an old hunter.

I was looking forward to our next outing, which was to be at Windsor – a flat, figure-of-eight course that needs careful walking. Down at the start, one of the jockeys was warning the rest of us not to follow him because his ride was such an unreliable jumper. I tried to avoid him and to get Canon to settle in behind by not jumping off in front. As we approached the first fence there were two horses in front of me; the first one fell, the next one landed and sidestepped the horse on the ground. Canon jumped the fence beautifully and landed as the fallen horse got up in our path. It is one thing to side-step a horse on the ground, but it is much more difficult to avoid the bulk of a stationary animal and Canon hit the backside of the loose horse with his shoulder. The

Dinah, me, David Nicholson (my trainer), Zara, Barry Wilkinson the policeman, Jeremy Willis,
travelling head lad, Clifford Baker, head lad, in the paddock at Stratford-upon-Avon.

shock of the collision shot me out of the saddle, and when I came down Canon was not in the same place. There was a moment, as I was falling through the air, when I was aware that my right foot seemed to have gone through the stirrup and I was not looking forward to what might happen next. What happened was that I was lucky, landing on my backside, and the horse disappeared into the distance.

Our next outing nearly ended in disaster too when we narrowly avoided slipping up on the turn at Leicester – a flattish, right-handed course. The jockey on my inside doesn't know how lucky he was, because there was a split second when I thought of grabbing the closest upright object. We survived, but the experience made Canon lose interest and once again we hunted round at the back. This and his subsequent runs were not encouraging. There was nothing obviously wrong with him, but he wasn't prepared to exert himself. Then David discovered a clue. After he saddles a horse for a race and has done the girths up, he likes to pull the front legs forward, one at a time, to make sure that the girths aren't pinching the horse's tummy. He was doing this at Ludlow when Canon crouched back on his hind legs as if in pain. He ran with Jamie Osborne riding, but didn't try any harder. So I took him home for a hill-climbing holiday in Gloucestershire.

Working on the theory that his collision at Windsor may have caused muscle damage down his right side, I took him into our covered riding school to warm him up doing some circles. I discovered that he could not bend to the right at all. I spent the next few weeks working on him so that he could turn equally well in both directions, mostly at the walk. Just so that he wouldn't get bored, I jumped him over show jumps and the logs in the park. He went out with the children's ponies, herded sheep and cantered up our banks. He went back to Condicote a much happier horse.

In November 1988 I came back from two days in Canada on a Saturday morning and went more or less straight to Ascot – a right-handed course on a slope – to ride General Joy in a race that was a class above our normal level. He was going flat out from the start but never gave me an anxious moment and finished better than anything else to be a very good fourth.

I couldn't ride him in his next race, which was sponsored by his owners, so Richard took the ride. Richard told me afterwards that he had been going really well and he felt that he had only to ask him and he could have gone on to win. Instead he felt him falter jumping the third last fence, after which he took three or four more strides and then collapsed on the inside of the course. Fortunately, Richard escaped injury, because with a horse falling at that speed on the flat it is difficult to avoid getting crushed. The horse would have felt nothing; he had probably died in the air over the fence. For the second time in a year I had lost a good companion and the stable had lost a popular member of the team.

I would then have seriously questioned whether the 'ups' of having anything to do with horses really compensated for the 'downs' if it hadn't been for the attitude at Condicote. I had always been impressed by the standard of stable management, the quality of the staff and the care and attention that was lavished on their charges. The horses lived an interesting and positively cosseted existence, and those that did not show ambitions to be racehorses were not kept. An unenthusiastic horse is not a successful one – in any stable. Working with horses of all sorts is a constant stream of disappointments, but if you are doing your best for them – as the people at Condicote did for their horses – then, after a disaster, you must carry on doing your best for the other horses in your care.

Horses teach you lots of things, but especially that life is not fair. In life you cannot have fun without disappointments and responsibility. You can share the responsibility of looking after one of God's creatures, but you must be prepared to accept it too. There is not a ready explanation for every personal setback and you can't sue God. I had decided long ago that if I couldn't take the disappointments along with the pleasure that horses had given me, then I might as well take up watching paint dry or resign from the human race, because life is full of disappointments. And there *was* Canon, even if at that stage he wasn't running that well.

After Canon's Gatcombe experience, we managed one run before the end of the 1988–89 season at Wetherby, a flat, left-handed course with stiff fences that needed careful jumping. He seemed more enthusiastic and was jumping really well. The bottom corner of the course had already caused more than one slip-up and one fall, and we went round rather carefully. It was a small field and I thought I was going to get left as they sprinted up the straight, but not this time.

Bobby Kelly, Huntingdon: 'standing off'. This was on 9 February 1989.

In the paddock at Sandown before the Grand Military.

Canon found that he was feeling no pain and set off in serious pursuit, only to have to avoid a falling horse that took us right across the course. It was a shame, but it didn't stop him overtaking all the other runners except the winner, who was just too far in front. It was the best race he had run for me and was a great encouragement for the 1989–90 season that would start in August.

Life at Condicote went on and Save and Prosper wanted to buy another horse. Bobby Kelly turned up in January, a pale chestnut, also tall, but with more substance. He had an eye with a white rim that gave him a rather wild appearance. He was not an easy ride and I was always struggling to hold him. One morning we were supposed to be cantering round the grass gallop and I was just going faster and faster. As I went past the head lad, whose horse would have followed me, he told me to go into the plough. I turned Bobby into the ploughed field where, if anything, he went even quicker until I managed to pull him up at the top of the hill. After that I schooled him only over the fences, when he struck me as a more powerful jumper than the other horses I had ridden.

Our first run was at Huntingdon – a flat, right-handed course – and the only information I had was that he took a nice hold on the way to the start: I only just managed to stop when I got to the start. If I thought I hadn't had much

Bobby Kelly's first race. With Peter Scudamore, the champion National Hunt jockey, at Huntingdon.

control before, Bobby had only one way of going and the jockey was the passenger. It was an exciting ride because he 'stood off' his fences further than any horse I had ever sat on.

Save and Prosper were generous enough to lease Bobby to me so that I could have a ride in the Grand Military in 1989. He gave me a very good ride but was a little short of speed over the last quarter of a mile. If we had jumped the last two fences more quickly and if the going had been softer, we would have caught the first two by the post. As it was we finished faster than anything else up the hill at Sandown to be third, my best result in the Grand Military Gold Cup.

I discovered after a few more rides that Bobby's 'stand-offs' were partly my fault because I rode him with a tighter rein and more contact with the bit in his mouth than he had been used to. This he seemed to regard as an incitement to go faster and take off earlier. I learnt the hard way at Towcester when we were approaching the first open ditch with about four horses in a line. There was a horse on my inside on my right and as Bobby had a tendency to jump to the right I pulled the left rein to keep him straight. We were still a full stride away from the fence but he translated my effort to straighten him as the message to take off. He came down very steeply through the birch and I let go on the basis that he couldn't possibly stand up. I did wonder where the rest of the field was, but hanging on in those conditions can be much more painful. It's never much fun watching the backsides of horses galloping away from you when you are sitting on the ground, but it is even worse when you realise that your horse never actually fell. When I learnt to ride him on a loose rein, he became much more relaxed.

Bobby and I had an unspectacular but consistent record. In hindsight our greatest claim to fame was a run at Newbury. Like the race at Ascot, this was a step up in class for us and again we seemed to be going flat out all the way. We probably should have finished closer to the winner, but I knew that I could not keep kicking right up the long straight at Newbury. Bobby made ground all the way because of his stamina and when we landed over the last fence we were not far behind the horse lying second. I was guilty of getting excited in an effort to catch it, which we jolly nearly did, and both of us were gaining on the leader. Bobby was going the best of the three at the post and we were beaten only a length and a half into third place. The horse that won was a hitherto unremarkable animal called Norton's Coin. I admit that when I saw him in the paddock before the 1990 Cheltenham Gold Cup I was guilty of inquiring what on earth he was doing there, on the basis that if Bobby and I could run him so close at

Newbury, it couldn't be good enough form to justify his running in the Gold Cup. I was rather impressed to be proved wrong!

Our last race was the Midlands Grand National, which was run at Uttoxeter – a flat, tight, left-handed course – over 4 miles. This meant going round the course four times with the accompanying danger of losing count of the circuits. We didn't, but the going was too dry and quick for Bobby to make use of his stamina.

Bobby developed some heat in a front joint so David decided to finish his season early, and when the heat had gone he went out in the field. Because I was unable to ride in the Grand Military I lent Canon to the previous year's winning jockey, but unfortunately a loose horse carried them past the third fence, which was very disappointing for everyone. I then rode Canon at Wincanton – a flat-tish, right-handed course – in a three-horse race over 2 miles and 5 furlongs. I had a great ride and was leading coming to the second last. It was the only fence we didn't meet right and we must have lost three lengths. Canon did his best to catch up and jumped the last fence just behind. All the way to the post he was gaining on the other two to finish a neck and half a length third to an odds-on favourite. It was the best race of the day. That was probably Canon's best race with me – two runs later he pulled up lame and ten days later he was at home for a long rest.

And Bobby? While David was away on holiday he was brought in from the field because he seemed to be lame in a hind leg. There was no sign of external damage on him, so the staff didn't think he could have been kicked. Five days later David returned from holiday to find a horse that was obviously in pain and so thin that he described him as 'a toast rack'. The vet was unable to diagnose anything specific and they regretfully decided to put him out of his misery. The post-mortem showed that he had broken his hip.

I felt really sorry for Save and Prosper who had not only been so generous, but whose staff had begun to enjoy going racing. After losing two horses in eighteen months, they couldn't be blamed for not wanting to try again.

Do you think somebody was trying to tell me something? It looked like the end of my NH career. As I had been two years older when I started race riding than the great jockey Jonjo O'Neill had been when he retired, I felt that perhaps I should take the hint and stop while I was ahead. I shall never forget the fear of anticipation, the excitement of the race itself and the thrill of being in a real horse race when you knew you were giving the horse a good enough chance to be truly competitive.

There was another aspect of NH racing that made it special and that was

Riding at Condicote with Peter and Zara.

the people in it. A great deal of the enjoyment that I gained from racing has been the result of the way that the professionals have treated me – and I don't just mean the occasional 'Are you all right, Madam?' as you recover from some minor hiccup. They were always helpful and ready with advice to any newcomer. NH jump jockeys are an exceptional group of pragmatic and resilient professional sportsmen and sportswomen; the lads and lasses that 'do' the horses are dedicated professionals; the owners are pragmatic and resilient as well, and even the

punters and spectators are cheerful in the face of adversity from the weather and luck. It is a tough sport, a risk sport and not for the faint-hearted, animal or human. It is not a cruel sport – as I've said before, you cannot force a horse to do something it doesn't want to – but it does demand commitment from everyone, including the Clerks of Courses, Racecourse Executives and Stewards of the Jockey Club. My limited experience of National Hunt Racing has given me as much satisfaction as anything I have ever done.

CHAPTER 11

Rules and Regulations:

'Could you have a sport without them?'

S INCE 1976 I had been involved with the beginnings of a new British three-day event in Windsor Great Park, and since 1981 we have run an advanced one-day event at Gatcombe. The complexities of running a one- or three-day event require precise planning, especially when you consider that all the work is done by unpaid volunteers in their free time.

Windsor became a three-day event after having been a two-day event for several years. The theory was that if you could run a horse trial for two days, you could run one for three days. This is only partially true; for although we enjoyed having many of the same people on the organising committee, there had to be a new site and a greater support structure for riders and officials who would need to be on site throughout the four days of the event. In the end it took us several years and three moves of site to get the whole thing in the right place. The cross-country course was easier to place – the track and the site of the fences, being dictated by the terrain, have hardly changed – but the steeplechase course has been moved to four different places in an effort to find the best ground on which to gallop.

What causes most trouble to the organisers? For the competitors the cater-ing; for the horses the ground conditions; and for the public the loos. For the horses the long-term solution has been good repair work with harrows and heavy rollers and digging out the areas in front of and behind the fences, filling them with hard core, covering them with topsoil and reseeding them with grass. This means that, whatever the weather, we can ensure safe conditions to jump. The solution for the public has been more loos in more places, though the answer for the riders is much more difficult!

The agenda for the committee meeting is long, starting with accounts; and continuing with arrangements for dressage – arenas, judges and stewards; roads and tracks – marking flags and stewards; steeplechase – fence judges and time-keepers; cross country – fence building, fence judges, communications, time-keepers, scorers, Pony Club score collectors, ten-minute-halt box, vets, doctors

Presenting awards to the best Riding for the Disabled
pony at the Horse of the Year Show.

and ambulances; stabling – security fence, isolation box and steward; public address; horse examination – vets, judges, stewards and purpose-built 'trot-up' ground; trade stands – cost of space, number of pitches; press, publicity and advertising – quantity, cost, catering for journalists; membership – facilities, catering, Land Rover tours of the course, priority parking; hospitality units – dependent on state of the economy; arena attractions – from side saddle to Services tug o'war; catering tentage and site plan – fitting everything in, especially the loos. Thanks to the enthusiasm and professionalism of our volunteers, the Windsor three-day event has become a friendly, popular and respected competition.

At Gatcombe the situation is rather different. I'm not involved in any of the organising; Mark runs it and designs the course. I picked up the jobs that had either been forgotten or weren't going to be done by anybody else. With the help of some willing friends, this developed into the menial tasks division – painting posts, hammering posts into rock-hard ground; running string from post to post around the course and along the roads to try to prevent people from parking and blocking the relatively narrow Gloucestershire roads; putting up signs; putting down sand on the landing side of fences to alleviate the jarring to the horses when the ground is hard; visiting all the fence judges on the day of the competition and trying to get round the trade stands.

At Windsor I see the event from the front, at Gatcombe I see it from the back, so I should – in theory – have a balanced view of organising a horse trial.

It is important to understand what is involved in putting on a competition if you are to contribute anything to the sport for the future. Competitors are often guilty of taking the organisation for granted and do not seem to understand just how many volunteers are needed in order that they may take part in their chosen sport. Since being involved with the Royal Yachting Association (RYA) and the British Olympic Association (BOA), I have confirmed my suspicion that this phenomenon is not confined to equestrian sport – it is a common problem. And since I became involved with the International Equestrian Federation (Fédération Equestre Internationale or FEI) and the International Olympic Committee (IOC), it has become obvious to me that it is a world-wide problem as well. The sports world is fortunate that there are so many people who are prepared to give up their time to administer, organise, officiate, judge, coach, train and baggage-carry. This last job usually falls to parents.

As a competitor I have experienced one aspect of sport, as a parent I'm beginning to experience another, but there is a third. I can't really explain why I was invited to become President of the various sports bodies that I have presided over – you would have to ask them. Perhaps my record as a competitor and possibly the professional neutrality that being a member of the Royal Family demands might have had a bearing on their choice. Perhaps one of my advantages was that I was a very average competitor and enjoyed watching most sports, but then watching anything done well is interesting.

Since becoming President of the RYA in 1987, I have heard and seen the arguments that come before the body that represents not just the Olympic classes, but all water users, both inland and coastal, powered by sail and motor. The rowers look after themselves, the jet-skiers are on the agenda and everybody tries to talk to the fishermen. I have always loved sailing since my father had a 52-foot ketch called *Bloodhound* for about ten years and the RYA has given me the opportunity not only to meet club administrators but sailing members as well, some of whom have been brave enough to let me sail with them. The individuality of clubs, the variety of classes and the huge growth in popularity of waterborne sports make the Council meetings of the RYA long but never boring.

I do have to smile when they talk (complain would be a more accurate description) about decisions of the International Yacht Racing Union (IYRU), which is their international federation, because I have been President of the FEI since December 1986 and I have no doubt that the national equestrian federations complain about our decisions in exactly the same way. Sometimes I try to explain that there might be a good reason for the IYRU's proposals, but on the whole I keep quiet and make a mental note to try to render the FEI's decisions more understandable. There is a danger with all such bodies that nobody wants to take what they know will be an unpopular decision, however important it may be for the sport. But if you want to have any credibility as a rule-making body, you have to be prepared to do so. Equally you have to resist the popular clamour for a knee-jerk reaction to every unusual infringement of the rules that may prove impossible to police. Although the national federations run their sports nationally, there is no question (and I have often asked myself the question) that there is a necessity for an international body to co-ordinate and rationalise the different attitudes and understandings of different countries.

Such a body can have other roles, and the FEI has been involved in supporting research into the stress suffered by horses when in transit by road, by sea or by air. Horses have successfully travelled long distances in every sort of transport. The modern sporting horse travels more often and faster, which would suggest that it might well be under more stress and that there might be something that could be done to prevent physical manifestations such as breathing problems and muscle cramps.

The FEI also runs the Medication Control Programme to prevent the abuse of horses through maladministration of genuine medication and pain-killing drugs that would allow them to compete when they might not otherwise be fit to do so. There are very few drugs that can improve a horse's natural performance, but there are plenty that can make it forget that something hurts. All sports are faced with the problem of greatly enhanced detection capabilities of laboratories which can detect minute quantities of forbidden substances. Nobody yet knows how much or how little of a substance does affect the performance of an athlete, equine or human. The FEI believes that the situation with horses is more diffi-cult because, unlike humans, they have no choice in the treatment or administration of a substance. Long-term effects are equally unknown, but short-term remedies that cause long-term damage may well mean shortening the lives of horses, not just their career. Humans can have the risk explained to them and can therefore be considered to be responsible for their action and its consequences.

The BOA – of which I became President in 1983 – is quite different from the FEI or the RYA in that it exists to get our qualified athletes to the Olympic Games. It negotiates with the organisers on behalf of all the Olympic disciplines and undertakes to raise enough money to clothe and feed the competitors as well as getting them there and back. In the past this has meant a major fund-raising appeal every four years which just about covered those costs. Thanks to the efforts of our director of fund raising, our last campaigns have encouraged more support for the periods between the Games so that we can help potential Olympic competitors receive better preparation technically, medically and nutri-tionally. Some of the 'positive' results of blood tests occurred as a result of ignorance of the content of medicines and herbs. My work for the BOA and my visits to the accommodation, competition and training sites at the Olympics have introduced me to the problems faced by other sports and their competitors. I found a very high degree of similarity in their requirements and in their attitudes. This knowledge has helped me most when trying to make some con-tribution to the IOC.

I was 'elected' on to the IOC in 1988 as the replacement for Britain's long-serving and valued member, Lord Luke, who, with our second member, Mary Glen Haig, had been an incorruptible supporter of standards. I haven't yet found out how this body actually works but I suspect that it has very little to do with

Talking to British competitors in Seoul, as President of the British Olympic Association,
with Mark Phillips, David Broome and Graham Fletcher.

the members. All the important decisions are taken by the executive board and the work is done in the smaller committees. I am a member of the Eligibility Committee, or at least I thought I was, but I never receive any notification of any meeting until it is too late for me to do anything about it. I can't believe I'm any busier than the other members, so how do they get anyone to attend? Perhaps I've got my priorities wrong and I should cancel everything else and go, but I'm afraid I do believe in fulfilling long-standing engagements, such as to visit a group of disabled riders or to open a new occupational therapy facility in a hospital. That doesn't mean that I don't regard the Olympic Games as a worthy ultimate ambition for many athletes – I do. I will qualify that slightly by saying that it is true of those sports which consider the Olympics to be their major championship, though it is patently not true, for example, of football and tennis.

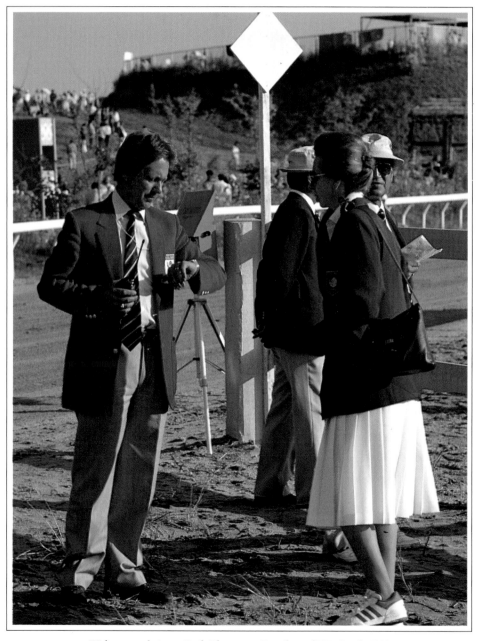

With course designer Hugh Thomas as President of FEI, Seoul, 1988.

The Olympics are still much more important for the athletes than for the IOC. The national Olympic committees, the international federations and the national federations matter more to the athletes than the IOC. Having said that, I must acknowledge the assistance given to the Olympic disciplines by the IOC through the Olympic Solidarity Fund with money from the Games that allows federations to run judges' and coaches' courses in the less developed countries.

No matter how irksome rules and organisers appear to be, there could be no genuine competition without them. First, rules: could you have a sport without them? Have you ever had that problem of going to visit friends when they suggest, for instance, a card game but with the proviso that you play house rules? If you don't know them, it puts you at an immediate disadvantage; and if you do know them, you get them confused with the rules that you play elsewhere. It doesn't make for a very relaxed game.

What are rules for? To create an artificial fairness in order that people, no matter where they live, know what they have to do, what standards they have to achieve and what training they might need to do for any sporting activity. Having the same start and finish must be relatively obvious, but numbers of players in a team and the number of points in a game or games in a set are equally fundamental to 'fair' competition. The participants are the ones who dictate what and how many rules a sport will have because of the way they behave when they are competing. If being competitive means pushing the interpretation of the rules to each letter rather than abiding by their true meaning, then you can expect more and more of them.

Why volunteer to organise a competition? Personally, I felt that I should put something back into a sport which had given me so much. There are others who may never have had the opportunity to compete, but who enjoy the sport and want to give others the chance to do so. Perhaps they are watchers rather than doers and are happy to add up the scores and watch the clock. From an organiser's point of view, even if there were no formal rules there would need to be some structure to enable any competition to be run. But many organisers must wonder at the strait-jacket conditions that are often now imposed on them when they are only trying to help.

If a sport is popular enough and attracts spectators, it causes the organisers a different problem – can they cater well enough for the paying customers to make them want to come again? Most organisers don't run events to make money, but they certainly don't want to lose it, so there is a difficult balance to be struck between the altruistic support of the sport and the need to cover costs by attracting people who are prepared to pay to watch. If a competition becomes very popular with spectators, it may well become popular with commercial sponsors who can see an opportunity to advertise.

Organising a relatively low-standard local competition can be easier and more cost-effective, because of the numbers of paying competitors, than a top-level event which requires a higher standard of everything but has fewer contributing participants. The battle for sponsors then needs some control by the national sports body to encourage the spread of funds to all levels of competition. For a sport to be healthy there needs to be a broad, solid base – the analogy of a pyramid – from where the talented will be able to progress up through clearly defined and controlled standards to the highest level of competition.

It is at the highest level of sport that commercial sponsorship can become a double-edged sword. The organisers are put under pressure to ensure that the best and most popular competitors appear rather than accepting those who are qualified to come. The organisers feel that they need sponsors to be able to put on a good show that will attract spectators. They feel they owe it to the sponsors to get those competitors that spectators want to see. What this can mean is that the best and the most popular are not necessarily the same people. Everybody wants to see the winners and some of them will become popular in their own right and not just because of their results. But, if you are not careful, that same group of competitors will continue to be asked to the highest-level events in spite of the fact that they are no longer the best. That doesn't really matter in itself, but it does matter if their presence is preventing the new young talent from experiencing the best competition and therefore stifling natural regeneration. National bodies need to be able, if not to control the funding, certainly to gain some financial advantage which they can redistribute for the general good of the sport.

It is the international federations who have to try to do the same for aspiring international competitors who may not get the same opportunities that their predecessors had before the influence of sponsors. I see their role as establishing 'best practice' rules that enable participants from all over the world to compete on equal terms. But almost more important is their role in co-ordinating the training of judges and officials, which will mean organising and supporting international courses to establish standards. The closer that the national bodies can follow those standards, the easier it will be for organisers and competitors.

The international federations have to rely on the national bodies to put forward workable solutions, because they carry out most of their decisions.

Some countries, like Great Britain, which have been involved in establishing many of the original rule books and have had many years of practice, have had their regulations accepted almost *in toto*. The danger is that the more successful federations try to maintain the *status quo* by establishing rules that favour their greater choice of qualified competitors. The international federations must – politely – guard against that happening, because it actively discourages participation from smaller federations.

The most difficult area for sports, as it is for the individual clubs, is in accommodating the wide variety in standards. But somehow when the prizes are nominal there seems to be less of a problem. Big prizes, monetary or in kind, add to the competitiveness of participants and make for an unusually keen awareness of the rules which can be conspicuous by its absence when more humble rewards are available. The extra publicity that tends to accompany international events has made the adherence to qualifying standards paramount and flexibility much more difficult. This is particularly true of the sports that involve an element of risk. This is a shame in many ways, because international competition used to be a method of encouraging wider participation from countries that had limited competitive opportunities but enjoyed taking part, no matter where they finished. As standards have improved generally and the numbers of participants and costs have increased, it has become almost impossible to continue to be so generous.

The adherence to qualifying standards in the sports that have paid professional practitioners is also vital. Having been involved with the 'professional sport' of racing, I know there is a difference in the attitude of the participants and the administrators which seems to come from familiarity with their subject. There is a difference between jockeys who go out to ride every day to earn their living and those who are not racing regularly. They can both be 'professional' in their behaviour and their application, but the amateur is likely to derive more enjoyment from his or her less frequent rides.

One complaint made by modern competitors in different sports is that too many of their administrators are part-timers and that it isn't good enough when there is so much money involved and there are so many competitions going on. They should be careful; for whose benefit are these part-timers giving up their time? If the competitors want professional administrators, they must be prepared to pay for them. If there is a fully professional element of a sport, like boxing, badminton, cycling and so on, there is an income that can be deducted from earnings in order to employ professional administrators.

Racing has a mixture of full-time officials, like the Clerks of Courses and the Stipendiary Stewards who advise the Stewards of the Jockey Club, who are the people who make the decisions but who, though appointed, are not paid. Then there is a commercial company that manages the paperwork, register of names, owners, entries, etc. The Jockey Club also employs a security officer and has a testing laboratory for dope-testing of horses. There is a very clearly defined procedure for disciplinary matters and a timescale for their implementation – something I would love to be able to adapt for other equestrian disciplines.

If, on the other hand, there are few or none who are earning any appreciable amount from their sport, then unless the participants are prepared to pay much larger entry fees, they should be grateful that anybody is willing to give up time to allow them to pursue their chosen form of activity.

Today there are many more opportunities for ex-competitors to earn a living after finishing their competitive career than there were twenty years ago. This is good news for them and for the future of many sports. Some may have made an early career decision to take advantage of any God-given talent they may have and enjoy teaching others. Some may decide to cash in on a successful competitive career. That's fine, and I hope they remember their coaches and the hundreds of volunteers who made their competitive careers possible.

Coaches and trainers are a particularly important part of the equation. They are the people who teach the techniques, set the standards, interpret the rules and establish the respect and understanding of these rules. With the increase in the numbers of participants in all sports, there is an understanding by most national associations that more support and training is required by the coaches. In the past there has been great reliance on enthusiastic parents and friends, and there still is, but there are now good coaching courses, some compulsory, with national qualifications for those who want to help. This is another aspect that I would like to improve at an international level.

Any improvements that administrators, officials or competitors might want to make will cost money. I believe that the sports concerned should be prepared to stand the expense from their own income, but if they can persuade a sponsor of the importance of their case, there is no reason not to accept commercial funding. The more popular sports are often regarded as being part of the entertainments business and the participants as performers. This is a fair analogy, but there are relatively few sports that justify such a description. There are many more which exist by the enthusiasm and for the enjoyment of their participants.

All sports – whatever your definition of sport – will need to rely on enthusiastic amateurs to function and grow. The interface between them, the administrators and the better competitors will always be an exercise in good communications that will be subject to intermittent breakdowns. The advantage of professional administrators is their continuity and their knowledge of the rules; the disadvantage is that it is easy for them to become isolated from the 'coalface' and the elected officers or sometimes to be too close to one or the other.

I don't know that the UK is different from everywhere else, but the growth of sports here seems to stem from groups of individuals, private clubs and finally a national sports association. In many countries it happens the other way round. Some might say that their results would indicate that to be the better way round, and for those who think that winning is all there is, they may be right. I would accept that, in the past, there haven't been the same support and facilities available for our best athletes as in many other countries and that it is important to create an environment in which they can flourish. That is changing. At international level the success of a country's athletes reflects positively on everybody, but don't let us ever forget that these athletes are first and foremost individuals who have channelled personal talent, motivation and determination into their ambitions. They themselves have been encouraged, taught, judged, organised and administered by equally enthusiastic individuals.

From left to right:
David Nicholson, me, Robert Bellamy, returning from
the gallops at Condicote.

CHAPTER 12
~

Conclusions:

'Sport is about interaction'

WHEN I first considered putting my thoughts on paper, I was inspired by the persistent perception of horses as a rich man's playthings and that they had no other role or, if they did, it was too small to alter the image. This is not an autobiography, for my sporting career certainly doesn't warrant one. It would be insulting to the many more talented and successful individuals who have put pen to paper to encourage others. However, throughout the rest of my life I will have cause to thank the experience that I gained from my association with horses and competitions. I have no idea what I would have done if horses hadn't been so available.

It certainly helps to have a regular income if you wish to be involved with horses, and the better off you are, the easier it is. But more than anything you need commitment. There are many horse breeds and traditions that survive thanks to benefactors, who are people committed to some aspect of the world of the horse but who do not expect anything in return for their generosity. Commercial sponsors, quite reasonably, need to see some return for their outlay through publicity or entertaining their customers, and therefore it is the competitive equestrian activities that attract their support.

In the sporting disciplines there are plenty of examples of riders from families who could never have afforded their own horse who have become successful entirely because of

With Peter and Zara at Gatcombe.

Peter riding at Gatcombe.

Zara and Peter riding at Gatcombe.

their own determination and talent. Alison Oliver was one of them. There are hundreds more who will never be 'successful' and yet will continue to pour all their meagre resources into the pleasure and satisfaction they gain from taking part. If winning were all-important, there would be many fewer riders.

Horses are no respecters of reputation or ego and certainly not of wealth, making them a challenge to everybody, whether looking after them or riding them. The aspect of challenge strikes me as undervalued. The challenge element is important and is different for each individual. Horses are a constant challenge because they have a brain – or at least, that's what the scientists say, so it must be true! They are capable of making their own decisions and are physically strong enough to carry them out. There is a risk in working in close proximity to a large animal like a horse, or just getting on one, and for many that will be sufficient challenge; but those who want more risk can ask the horse to do specific actions such as jumping, galloping or avoiding onrushing bulls. The variety of risk levels is as infinite as the number of horses.

Humans are naturally competitive creatures as a result of their centuries of struggling to survive, but as their societies developed and became more secure they also needed codes of conduct to control anti-social behaviour. Status was still acquired by establishing bravery or competence and there were very clear requirements to be fulfilled before being accepted as a member of that society. Games were used to practise war-like skills. Children played games that imitated their elders. Owners held competitions to show off their hunting dogs, their falcons and their horses. Life was a challenge that demanded physical fitness as well as a brain.

Life has become a lot less physically challenging for those in the Western world because of better basic hygiene and health care, safer water, more sophisticated medicine, and greater availability of food and education. Apart from academic exams there are few opportunities in young people's lives when they can establish their credentials in the eyes of their peers, unless they take up a sport or hobby; but too often they end up leading or being part of a band of trouble-makers who think they are being different or, worse still, use cars, motorbikes and the public road to get their kicks. Being 'tribal' is not being different; it is merely fitting into some anthropologist's treatise.

There must be some way in which a modern and supposedly more tolerant society can still challenge members of the next generation enough for them to establish their own personality without that feeling of failure if they don't enjoy the same success as others. Failure is a strong word, but if you have tried your best when failing to reach a certain standard that is not failure. Failure is not trying at all. I would have to say that I am a strong supporter of the 'It is not the winning but the taking part' school of thought, partly because I seemed to learn more from my 'failures' than I did from my occasional successes, but also because it encourages participation.

Each individual has their own 'perceived level of risk' which dictates what risks you are prepared to take in your life. Some children are physically more adventurous than others, but it can apply to mental challenges too. It is important for young people's self-respect that they should have the opportunity to find out where their level of risk is, under relatively controlled circumstances. The interesting thing is that if standards of safety are increased and the level of risk in any given occupation reduced, then the participants take more risks than they did before. This is true, for instance, of rock climbing or ocean sailing, motor racing or parachuting, to name some of the more obvious examples. In these sports the huge improvements in safety equipment and clothing have made them appear much 'safer' and they have therefore attracted people who previously would have thought that they were too dangerous. They also attract people who are less well prepared for the essential dangers that are inherent in risk sports. The participants and their trainers need to be aware of the balance that is necessary between the challenge, safety and risk.

There are other attractions and uses for horses. It is tempting to write the species off as a luxury because they are no longer considered as working animals – an opinion that is not shared by many police forces and some brewery companies, coal merchants, foresters and farmers. That denies centuries of experience and knowledge. Man has cosseted and abused the horse, but the two have developed together. There is no reason that this should change simply because horses are not an essential part of the economy any more. They still have benefits to offer the human race.

The value of horses to the community is not just as a form of recreation. I have written about the Riding for the Disabled Association and the benefits of riding as a therapy, but I have not mentioned the animals' contribution to the rehabilitation of young offenders. At one such institution there is a successful Suffolk Punch stud where most of the horses' needs are catered for by volunteer inmates. They learn quite early on that you cannot push around a horse of that size and a frightened one can cause a lot of damage. The horses work too, towing the Danline 'Towsweep', a specially adapted road-sweeper.

I can't describe horses as pollution-free transport (one man's recyclable waste is another man's pollution), but they do offer a genuine alternative form of land use. To live a reasonable existence horses need grass, which is exactly what our present over-production of food requires, instead of acres of arable land. Their care is also labour-intensive and creates numerous related occupations in rural areas. They are environmentally friendly, producing good-quality organic fertiliser or bio-gas. In countries like the USA and Sweden draught horses are used in the forests because they are considered cost-effective, doing much less environmental damage than the mechanical alternatives.

There is still potential for the horse to be used as a working animal, especially when you consider what improvements modern technology could bring about to horse-drawn equipment. They would become even more attractive if they shared the same agricultural status as their EEC cousins. *History with a Future*, the report of an investigation commissioned by the Shire Horse Society, compiled and edited by Keith Chivers, comments on the anomalies – especially concerning taxation – that exist throughout member states and highlights the positive contribution that draught horses could make in appropriate types of work.

There have been attempts to persuade our government to change its attitude which have so far failed, not so much because a good case cannot be made, but because of the weakness of the horse lobby. The only powerful horse lobby in the past has been the Jockey Club, which may explain why the

Treasury is not as sympathetic as it might be. But the Club is not representative of the average horse owner. The trouble is that there are too many societies fighting their own corners, from the highly organised breed and sporting societies to the individual owners who don't want to be organised by anybody. The lack of an effective lobby could have other repercussions.

Horses kept on the cheap are not only less likely to be healthy or happy but they also create conditions which are an eyesore. Keeping animals is an extra responsibility and the cost of doing so needs to make people stop and think. Yet it would be a shame to stifle the real advantages of having horses, with controls applied by people who have no understanding of or interest in them or their potential for good. I hope the equestrian enthusiasts in this country understand that externally applied controls are a real danger unless they act together to police the irresponsible horse owners.

Sport is about interaction. It was my 'sport' that broadened my horizons. Riding has been good for me. Perhaps my parents felt the same way as a well-known sports personality, who told me recently how grateful he was that his daughter was spending all her time with ponies when she could have been out looking for excitement in other ways! His other comment was that her riding and competitions involved the whole of the family, whether they liked ponies or not.

Competition opened up new experiences for me, but most of all it was about meeting people. Sports are a shared social activity in which people from all walks of life share a common purpose and common problems. In your own sport you learn from talking to other competitors and watching how they perform. I find that there are common experiences in all sports which have allowed me to talk easily with participants of apparently unrelated disciplines about such things as training schedules and warm-up preparations, both mental and physical.

The competition itself is about people because your day can be ruined by the other competitors performing better than you. It helps your future performances to understand how others respond to the pressures of competition. Team sports – I played lacrosse at school – are about people relating to each other under pressure, sharing their talents and commitment for a common cause, and where the less-gifted individuals can more than make up in effort for what they might lack in technique.

The emotions created by the desire to do well should be positive ones; this is not always easy when the spectators and supporters who aren't doing the work get more emotional than the players. The players need to keep their emotions under control or they will not perform at their best. Being combative is often considered a requirement for performing well in a sport, but only when it can be harnessed and used at the right time and in the right place. The sooner you learn to control those emotions, the better it will be for you as an individual in your sport and in your relationships with other people. Almost by accident, it will help your working life as well.

Sport can change people's lives for the better, even in the less developed countries, but it is still a diversion from the priorities of and a relaxation from the rigours of life. Sport reflects life and should help participants to learn tolerance towards each other and to understand the need for rules and discipline. Above all, when an individual decides to take up a sport, it should be for fun. I shall enjoy watching and trying to help my children in their chosen sports, although parents have to be prepared to be the last people their children will listen to or turn to for advice. I hope I shall be able to enjoy riding for many more years to come. Without doubt there are many more things horses can teach me about themselves and about myself. The process of learning never stops and if you can keep an open mind you are never too old to learn. My late, much-loved mother-in-law was quite right: horses are 'character-building'.

Potential jockey!

Appendix 1

Horse Trials

THE Princess Royal's riding records in horse trials and on the racecourse have kindly been provided by the British Equestrian Federation and by her trainer, David Nicholson.

Principal Competitions

1971 5th Badminton on **Doublet** (Mark Phillips' first win, on Great Ovation)
      1st Burghley European Championships on **Doublet** (competing as an individual)
1972 retired steeplechase Burghley on **Columbus** (too strong for her; subsequently ridden by Mark Phillips)
1973 8th Badminton on **Goodwill** (Lucinda Prior-Palmer's first win on Be Fair)
      defended title at Kiev European Championships on **Goodwill** but retired after crashing fall at notorious second fence
1974 4th Badminton on **Goodwill** with only dressage penalties, withdrew **Doublet** from speed and endurance on second day, having led in the dressage (Mark Phillips' third win, on Columbus)
      12th Burghley World Championships on **Goodwill** (competing as an individual; Bruce Davidson's first World Championship title, on Irish Cap, USA)
1975 competed Badminton on **Goodwill** but event abandoned due to weather after dressage
      2nd Luhmühlen European Championships on **Goodwill** and member of British Silver Medal team
1976 completed Montreal Olympic Games on **Goodwill**, despite heavy fall on cross country, one of only two British competitors to finish (the other was Richard Meade, 4th on Jacob Jones; USA won team and individual Gold Medals – Tad Coffin on Bally Cor)
1978 completed Badminton on **Goodwill** (Jane Holderness-Roddam's second win, on Warrior)
      7th Luhmühlen International Three-day Event on **Goodwill** (only other British competitor was Clarissa Strachan, second on Merry Sovereign)
      retired Burghley cross country with **Goodwill** (Lorna Clarke's second win, with Greco)
1979 6th Badminton on **Goodwill** (Lucinda Prior-Palmer's fourth win, on Killaire)

Her Royal Highness's wins and placings at horse trials with:

DOUBLET

1969	Burgess Hill Novice	4th
	Osberton Novice	1st
	Eridge Novice	3rd
	Wylye Intermediate	2nd
	Chatsworth Novice Championship	6th
1970	Crookham Advanced	8th
1971	Rushall Open Intermediate	4th
	Badminton Three-day Event	5th
	Burghley Three-day Event	1st
1972	Crookham Advanced	8th
1973	Forest Mere Open Intermediate	3rd
	Lockerbie Open Intermediate	2nd
1974	Downlands Advanced	2nd

GOODWILL

1972	Everingham Novice	6th
	Lockerbie Novice	5th
	Eglington Open Intermediate	4th
	Knowlton Intermediate	1st
	Tweseldown Intermediate	4th
	Chatsworth Intermediate	2nd
	Ermington Open Intermediate	2nd
1973	Rushall Open Intermediate	6th
	Badminton Three-day Event	8th
1974	Badminton Three-day Event	4th
	Annick Open Intermediate	3rd
	Burghley World Championships	12th
1975	Tidworth Midland Bank Section	6th
	Cirencester Open Intermediate	2nd
	European Three-day Event Luhmühlen CCIO	2nd
1977	Brigstock Advanced	4th
1978	Luhmühlen Three-day Event CCI	7th
	Annick Advanced	3rd
1979	Badminton Three-day Event CCI	6th

OTHER HORSES RIDDEN BY HER ROYAL HIGHNESS IN BRITISH HORSE SOCIETY HORSE TRIALS:

Black Ice, Collingwood, Columbus, Flame Gun, Inchiquin, Maggie Jo, Mantilla, Mardi Gras, Mission Lake, Purple Star, Royal Ocean, Stevie B, Tod. Candlewick, Charlie Brown, Arthur of Troy.

Appendix 2

Racing

Flat Rides

YEAR	DATE	COURSE	HORSE	PLACE
1985	23.4	Epsom	Against The Grain	4th
	14.9	Goodwood	Little Sloop	
	26.9	Redcar	Lulav	
	21.10	Chepstow	French Union	
1986	21.3	Doncaster	Little Sloop	
	10.5	Thirsk	Solar Cloud	
	7.6	Warwick	Snake River	2nd
	19.7	Newmarket	Coral Harbour	
	26.7	Ascot	Cresta Auction	
	2.8	Newmarket	Well Wisher	
	5.8	Redcar	Gulfland	1st
	9.9	Folkestone	Well Wisher	
	4.10	Haydock	Innishmore Island	3rd
	20.10	Chepstow	Cronks Quality	
	3.11	Folkestone	Glowing Promise	3rd
1987	27.3	Doncaster	Final Alma	
	27.7	Ascot	Ten No Trumps	1st
	1.8	Newmarket	Wood Chisel	2nd
	3.8	Redcar	Gulfland	3rd
	23.10	Nashville	Abbreviation	3rd
1988	7.6	Hamilton	Gulfland	2nd
	10.6	York	Insular	1st
	2.7	Jersey	Kuwait Sun	2nd
	25.7	Ascot	Marasid	4th
	30.7	Newmarket	Vayrua	1st
	2.8	Redcar	Lord Justice	2nd
	3.8	Pontefract	Red Twilight	3rd
	6.8	Newmarket	O.I. Oyston	
	14.10	Nashville	Wood Chisel	1st
1989	14.6	Hamilton	Gulfland	2nd
	17.6	York	Nicholas Mark	3rd
	22.7	Ascot	Rejim	6th
	8.8	Beverley	Tender Type	2nd

YEAR	DATE	COURSE	HORSE	PLACE
1990	13.6	Kempton	Parking Bay	5th
	6.10	York	Mill Pond	6th
	29.6	Doncaster	Prayer Wheel	4th
	8.8	Pontefract	Aardvark	2nd
	11.8	Newmarket	Sau Paulo	9th
1991	20.5	Hamilton Park	Shadowland	2nd
	24.6	Windsor	Akimbo	2nd
	15.7	Beverley	Croft Valley	1st

National Hunt Rides

YEAR	DATE	COURSE	HORSE	PLACE
1985/86	23.3	Newbury	Well Wisher	4th
	17.4	Cheltenham	Well Wisher	
	17.4	Cheltenham	Salmon Run	
	26.4	Sandown	Well Wisher	
1986/87	20.2	Kempton	Cnoc-Na-Cuille	4th
	13.3	Sandown	Cnoc-Na-Cuille	
	6.4	Liverpool	Cnoc-Na-Cuille	
	16.4	Ludlow	Cnoc-Na-Cuille	
	4.5	Towcester	Cnoc-Na-Cuille	3rd
	22.5	Towcester	Cnoc-Na-Cuille	
1987/88	17.8	Worcester	Cnoc-Na-Cuille	2nd
	3.9	Worcester	Cnoc-Na-Cuille	1st
	19.9	Warwick	Cnoc-Na-Cuille	4th
	11.3	Sandown	Cnoc-Na-Cuille	
	4.4	Hereford	Cnoc-Na-Cuille	4th
	5.4	Chepstow	General Joy	3rd
	30.4	Worcester	General Joy	
	2.5	Towcester	Cnoc-Na-Cuille	
	13.5	Stratford	General Joy	
	21.5	Warwick	Cnoc-Na-Cuille	3rd
1988/89	10.9	Worcester	General Joy	4th
	22.10	Stratford	Canon Class	
	29.10	Worcester	General Joy	3rd
	12.11	Windsor	Canon Class	
	19.11	Ascot	General Joy	4th

YEAR	DATE	COURSE	HORSE	PLACE
1988/89	1.12	Warwick	Canon Class	
	6.12	Leicester	Canon Class	
	14.12	Haydock	Canon Class	3rd
	10.1	Leicester	Canon Class	
	9.2	Huntingdon	Bobby Kelly	
	10.3	Sandown	Bobby Kelly	3rd
	27.3	Towcester	Bobby Kelly	
	1.4	Newbury	Bobby Kelly	3rd
	18.4	Devon and Exeter	Bobby Kelly	
	22.4	Uttoxeter	Bobby Kelly	
	3.5	Wetherby	Canon Class	2nd
	13.5	Warwick	Canon Class	
1989	23.9	Worcester	Canon Class	3rd
	4.11	Worcester	Bobby Kelly	P/U
1990	23.3	Newbury	Canon Class	4th
	30.3	Wincanton	Canon Class	3rd
	16.4	Wincanton	Canon Class	11th
	28.4	Worcester	Canon Class	11th

Index